D0205403

A Joyous Revolt

Recent Titles in the
Women Writers of Color Series
Joanne M. Braxton, Series Editor

Lucille Clifton: Her Life and Letters
Mary Jane Lupton

June Jordan: Her Life and Letters
Valerie F. Kinloch

Zora Neale Hurston: A Biography of the Spirit
Deborah G. Plant

Border Crossings and Beyond: The Life and Works of Sandra Cisneros
Carmen Haydée Rivera

Nikki Giovanni: A Literary Biography
Virginia C. Fowler

Tracks on a Page: Louise Erdrich, Her Life and Works
Frances Washburn

WOMEN WRITERS OF COLOR

A Joyous Revolt

Toni Cade Bambara, Writer and Activist

Linda Janet Holmes

Joanne M. Braxton, Series Editor

 PRAEGER

AN IMPRINT OF ABC-CLIO, LLC
Santa Barbara, California • Denver, Colorado • Oxford, England

Library of Congress Cataloging-in-Publication Data

Holmes, Linda Janet, 1949–
    A Joyous Revolt : Toni Cade Bambara, Writer and Activist / Linda Holmes.
        pages cm. — (Women Writers of Color)
    Includes index.
    ISBN 978-0-275-98711-4 (hardback) — ISBN 978-0-313-05077-0 (ebook)
1. Bambara, Toni Cade. 2. African American women authors—Biography.
3. Authors, American—20th century—Biography. I. Title.
    PS3572.A473Z66 2014
    813'.54—dc23
    [B]   2013045222

ISBN: 978-0-275-98711-4
EISBN: 978-0-313-05077-0

18 17 16 15 14   2 3 4 5

This book is also available on the World Wide Web as an eBook.
Visit www.abc-clio.com for details.

Praeger
An Imprint of ABC-CLIO, LLC

ABC-CLIO, LLC
130 Cremona Drive, P.O. Box 1911
Santa Barbara, California 93116-1911

This book is printed on acid-free paper ∞

Manufactured in the United States of America

To cultural workers worldwide.

If we were to present all the things that happened out there—the hardships, the pain, the struggles that we went through, no one would try to change the world. When we got on stage, we knew—Toni knew and I knew—we had to put a good face on: and that was a face of survival, a face of commitment. We thought if they knew what we were going through, they would decide to simply write a book.

—Sonia Sanchez, May 25, 2012

Contents

Series Foreword *by Joanne M. Braxton*   xi

Acknowledgments   xiii

Introduction   xvii

One   At Home in Harlem   1

Two   A Zone of Her Own   19

Three   Bridges to Bambara   35

Four   Cultural Worker on Southern Ground   57

Five   From Atlanta to Vietnam   77

Six   Making Dreams Work   97

Seven   In the Sun, Resplendent   121

Eight   Moving the Global Movement   143

Nine   New Life in Film   167

Ten   The Struggle Continues   185

Appendix   A Call to Action   205

Selected Bibliography   209

Index   215

Series Foreword

The Women Writers of Color Series offers enjoyable reading for an enlightened multi-ethnic audience that includes scholars and critics, poets and writers, librarians, and young adults who read both critically and for entertainment; each volume is published with a user-friendly bibliography so that the readers can pursue original reading by these women of color authors and find prior critical writings more easily.

Among women of color writers in the United States, women of African descent have been preeminent, setting high standards and opening doors for other minority writers from underrepresented groups. Beginning in the eighteenth century, the tradition of black women writers in the United States has been one long struggle, or perhaps a series of interrelated struggles for freedom, literacy, justice, and self-expression. Graced with few treasures other than what they could carry, Africans new to the Americas brought with them a rich cultural heritage that included a vibrant oral tradition. Having endured the dreaded Middle Passage to the New World, the first Africans in America still had to survive its harsh climate and the cruel conditions they would encounter as enslaved men and women without legal rights.

Contemporary women writers of color, including those women writers who are not of African descent, have looked back to these foremothers as heroes and miracle makers. Because of such women, the Women Writers of Color Series exists. It exists for everyone of any race who can read or hear these words and appreciate them, for every little girl of any race whoever wrote a poem and hid it, and for every woman writer of color whose work we will never know. This series is not only for the scholar and the critic, but also for the daughters of those mothers whose creativity and intelligence were suppressed or denied—daughters who went on to become poets, essayists, novelists, and activists who inspired others in the creation of artistic models with the vision for a sustainable future.

Toni Cade Bambara was one such daughter, a consummate novelist, short story writer, teacher, and activist whose creative spirit and commitment to social justice lives on in the body of her work. Her very choosing of the name Bambara is an act of celebration and reconnection. With a loving eye and a steady hand, she reaches through the jagged dislocations and displacements of the ancestral past to portray our ordinary foremothers and forefathers and to pour a literary libation for their remembrance. Bambara has joined the great cloud of witnesses who went before, and today we remember and give thanks for her stunning literary achievements, which continue to push our artistic and social consciousness to illuminate and inspire.

A seasoned writer as well as a former student of Toni Cade Bambara, with whom she studied during her formative years as a student at Rutgers University, Linda Janet Holmes comes to this biographical project as one who has already made significant contributions to the commemoration of the Toni Cade Bambara legacy. *A Joyous Revolt* presents not only an engaging account of Bambara's life and work, but also a critical consideration of the people and places and the political and historical events that underscore Bambara's aesthetics and her philosophical commitments as a writer and a social activist. We therefore welcome *A Joyous Revolt: Toni Cade Bambara, Writer and Activist.*

Joanne M. Braxton, Series Editor
Director, Middle Passage Project
College of William and Mary

Acknowledgments

Writing this biography on Toni Cade Bambara has been a journey, requiring more than seven years to complete. Without the support and encouragement provided by Karma Smith, Toni Cade Bambara's daughter, this book could never have been written. I am deeply indebted to her for her kindness and will always treasure the fun moments we shared while working on this project.

I also am grateful to the Spelman College Women's Research and Resource Center for the support provided during my research at the Spelman Archives where the Bambara papers are housed. During the weeks that I worked at the Spelman Archives as a researcher-in-residence, Taronda Spencer, archivist and a former Spelman student, provided extraordinary assistance through her first-hand knowledge of the collection, and she fondly remembered Bambara's influence when the author was a writer-in-residence at Spelman. During my several visits to Spelman College, all of the staff at the Spelman Woman's Research and Resource Center were welcoming and helpful. Years ago when I told Beverly Guy-Sheftall, director of the Spelman College Women's Research and Resource Center, that I wanted to write a biography on Bambara, she encouraged me then and throughout the years needed to complete the project. In a special concession, the Spelman Archives also agreed to provide me with access to the Bambara papers before they were fully processed.

Other Bambara family members who contributed to my understanding of Bambara's life story include Walter Cade III, Bambara's only sibling, who generously shared information about his sister's childhood and provided insights about their family that no one else could. In the final stages of the project, Walter agreed to share family photographs and selected letters written by Bambara, critical to the book. Kenneth Morton, Bambara's cousin who knew her when just a baby in a crib and in later years typed her manuscripts, agreed to extensive interviews. Carole Browne, also a cousin, not only provided interviews, but became a friend to me and the project. Having conducted more than 20 interviews as part of my research on the life and work of Bambara, I appreciate all of the family members along with the many friends, colleagues, and cultural workers who agreed to share their memories. Since I can't list every name, please know that each interview provided vital information.

Research and writing on this project also received support from friends. As a result of a coincidental meeting of Natalia Kanem at Spelman College, I was invited to be the first writer-in-residence at her new home in Popenguine, Senegal. That is where I wrote two of the final chapters for this book. My reward at the end of a writing day would be a barefoot walk on the beach at sunset. In Popenguine, I also met writer and scholar Ayi-Kwei-Armah, who shared his wisdom in conversations and in a special workshop. From Senegal, I traveled to the University of Ibadan in Nigeria, where I learned about aspects of Yoruba that influenced Bambara's writing and honored the spirit of Esi Kinney, an ethno-musicologist who was Bambara's friend and taught for many years at the University of Ibadan. Chukwuma Okoye, Katherine Toure, and Ian Brown Peterside provided encouragement and critical support during that leg of the journey. The University of Ibadan, Department of Theater, opened many doors of kindness during my visit.

Bringing this book to the light of day required a much longer journey than initially anticipated. Beth Ptalis, acquisitions editor at Praeger/ABC-CLIO, and Joanne Braxton, editor of the Women Writers of Color Series, provided understanding in agreeing to extensions for submitting the manuscript. I am grateful to my editors who persevered with me to see the completion of this book.

Chantal James also contributed her skills and caring to this project. Without her assistance, I might still be writing and rewriting. James, a Spelman graduate whom I first met a few years ago in an Atlanta bookstore where she worked, impressed me immediately. James became a Bambara comrade who provided research assistance and kept an untiring critical editing eye on the manuscript.

In the long run, Aishah Shahidah Simmons, Khadijah Robertson, Laurie Nsiah-Jefferson, Andrea Benton Rushing, Chadra Pittman Walke, Deborah Wright, Louis Massiah, Niyi Ousandare, Stoel Markes who was a special friend in my kitchen, Remica L. Bingham-Risher, and members of her Muse poetry workshop are among the many who cheered me on in completing the project. The Kentucky check-ins with my former professor, Jan Carew, always reminded me to never tire of writing and activism as did communing with ancestors on the Howard family Royster Road farm. In the final phase of the project, colleagues—Pamela Browne Peterside, Eleanor W. Traylor, and Cheryl A. Wall—agreed to read a couple of manuscript chapters and provided critical feedback. But it is without question that my daughter Ghana Smith and my grandson KeShawn Everett became my lifesavers. Several times when I thought the book would never be completed, my daughter's patient assistance and my grandson's practical jokes saved the day.

While it is impossible to name every person who provided encouragement in the process of writing this book, please know every conversation mattered. Through our tears and laughter, we shared Bambara memories. At several points, the process of writing this book reminded me of the collective energy that was the hallmark of Bambara's workshops. Because so many believed in this project, this book is finally done.

Introduction

I first met Toni Cade Bambara in 1970 when I enrolled in her Black Litera-ture class on the newly opened Livingston College campus at Rutgers Uni-versity. At the time, I remember someone telling me that my new teacher was a published writer, but like many others on campus I knew Bambara as a creative and inspiring teacher. A few years later, I attended one of the several black writers' conferences that my former teacher helped to organize in the mid-1970s. After hearing Bambara—by now a widely recognized writer—speak on a panel about the need to find new avenues for publishing black writers, I found myself in a lengthy conversation with an unnamed man about Bambara's work. At one point in the conversation, he shocked me when he said, "You should write a biography about your friend." I immediately responded: "No way. I would never invade her privacy. She really values her personal space." If that gentleman happens to read this biography, he will know the significance of his inkling.

Toni Cade Bambara now is known as being among an important handful of black women fiction writers whose powerful writing ushered in a new wave of critically acclaimed works. When considering the historical significance and influence of the black women writers who emerged in the 1970s, greater rec-ognition of this chapter in American literature is long overdue. Even during the Harlem Renaissance, the reach of black women writers like Zora Neale Hurston and Nella Larsen did not have the national and international impact of the emancipatory black women writers of the 1970s.

In the 1970s, Bambara along with Toni Morrison, Paule Marshall, and Alice Walker reached a black audience that hungered for women writers who knew and interpreted the realities of the black female experience in ways that were different from the black male fiction writers who dominated the field prior to that time. The women fiction writers who emerged in this era enlarged the lit-erary circle of "sister" black women poets—Nikki Giovanni, June Jordan, and Sonia Sanchez, among others—who also had a significant role in shaping the Black Arts Movement. This new breed of emancipatory black women fiction writers opened doors for the next generation of black women writers who were determined to challenge stereotypic images of black women in literature, broadcast media, music, and film.

Although deeply influenced by the political and social movements of the 1960s, 1970s, and 1980s, Bambara's writing is much more than a marker of time. Bambara envisioned multicultural movements that crossed geographic boundaries including forging alliances among women of color, "the seven sisters." The significance of Bambara's writing also includes its enduring impact on the understanding of African American culture and language—setting a new standard in her ability to dignify authentic black voices in print. And, as an essayist, fiction writer, and editor, Bambara is groundbreaking as she brings to the fore in all of her writing, black female voices, young and old, who are independent, bold, and unwavering in the power within themselves to speak for themselves.

Using her writing as a tool for transformation, Bambara's clarion calls for change within individuals and communities are not in the margins, but are embedded in the soul of her literary masterpieces. Bambara's insatiable curiosity, political zeal, wit, passion, and commitment contributed to both her writing and activist life. As a cultural worker, Bambara found innovative ways to win recognition for other emerging writers and filmmakers, particularly women and cultural workers across the African diaspora, who also aimed to make their creative works political swords.

Bambara often identified herself as a cultural worker.[1] For this writer being a cultural worker meant using the arts—literary works, film, theater, music, dance, and the visual arts—as instruments of self-renewal and transformation. As a cultural worker, Bambara was engaged in the struggles and challenges that everyday people faced in the black community. For the writer, cultural work in the black community included celebrating victories—large and small—offering criticism, and making calls for action that linked the past with the present.[2] Bambara explained: "As a cultural worker who belongs to an oppressed people my job is to make revolution irresistible."[3]

Each of the chapters in *A Joyous Revolt,* organized chronologically, focuses on Bambara's writing and its intersection with social movements in communities worldwide and in places where she lived: Harlem, Jersey City, Queens, Atlanta, and Philadelphia. All of the chapters include excerpts from interviews with activists and friends about organizing activities that involved them. Also included in this first biography about Bambara are reflections from noted intellectuals and writers such as her friend and long-time editor, Toni Morrison, who defines Bambara as one of America's most brilliant writers.

In addition, this biography documents the extent to which Bambara valued and protected her free and independent lifestyle. Images of Bambara as mother, lover, and adventurer, gleamed from interviews, offer some insight into her private life. In *A Joyous Revolt,* never-before-published letters written by Bambara to her mother provide evidence of her optimism and determination to remain upbeat in the face of some of the daunting challenges she faced in her work and writing life. Her personal letters also reveal the extent to which Bambara resisted being defined by others and set her own standards.

Bambara's first published book, *The Black Woman* (1970), is a groundbreaking work that ignited a new political movement within the black community. Edited by Bambara, the book, a literary bombshell, included an array of essays, reflections, and poetry such as her own compelling and pivotal essay that addressed challenges black women faced when confronted with black male chauvinism at home, at work, and within political organizations. Published in paperback in 1970, black women across the age spectrum sensed a new age dawning of women exerting their power in reading *The Black Woman*.

Her next book, published in 1971, is a collection of short stories, *Gorilla, My Love*. In this popular and widely anthologized work, Bambara rolled out authentic characters, mostly women and young girls, who carried messages about the strength of being black and female that are as solid as armor. Bambara's sharply attuned listening ear absorbed the vocabulary and rhythms of street orators including the family members, window sitters, and beauty parlor and barber shop patrons whom she heard when growing up in Harlem, and made them central to her stories. These characters addressed themes of survival through Bambara's writing spirit which included humor and wit in a way that prompted American publications like *Redbook* to publish a number of Bambara's stories and essays in the 1970s.

Bambara's short stories also have been widely anthologized in children's textbooks and integrated into school curriculums, reaching countless American children and youth. In 1971, Bambara edited another collection of short stories, *Tales and Stories for Black Folks,* which includes her writing as well. Generations of young black girls have been surprised to find girls like themselves as heroes of stories in their required textbooks.

When Bambara moved from New York to Atlanta in 1974, one of her goals was to do more writing. In fact, Bambara did more concentrated writing in Atlanta than any place else. *The Sea Birds Are Still Alive,* Bambara's second collection of her short stories, and Bambara's only novel to be completed in her lifetime, *The Salt Eaters,* were both written and published when Bambara was living in Atlanta. Even so, a torrent of writing never deterred Bambara, a tireless community organizer, from pursuing the activism that led her to become a major architect of the Neo-Black Arts Movement in the South.

From Atlanta, Bambara also travelled the world. In 1975, Bambara visited Vietnam with an anti-imperialist feminist delegation as guests of the Vietnamese Women's Union. Not surprisingly, Bambara's collection of short stories, *The Sea Birds Are Still Alive* (1977), includes stories with strong voices championing political movements in urban and rural communities. Bambara is most likely first among the black women emancipatory fiction writers of the 1970s to set one of her short stories, the title story of the book, in Asia.

Bambara's first novel, *The Salt Eaters,* set in the South, won the American Book Award in 1981. Easy access to rural southern roads made it possible for Bambara to tap into the wisdom of root workers, midwives, herbalists, and other healing traditions among black women in Georgia, Alabama, and Louisiana. At certain points, some of the characters in *The Salt Eaters* take timeless journeys and meet up with mud mothers more than a million years old. Other characters in *The Salt Eaters* encounter orishas, leave pots of water hanging in trees for the ancestors, and honor other spiritual traditions emanating from African culture. Bambara believed that in reclaiming body, mind, and spirit, one can cross over to one's true center—one's authentic self.

Bambara's second novel, published posthumously, began as notes in a journal and grew into her epic work of fiction, *Those Bones Are Not My Child*. This novel focuses on the Atlanta murdered and missing children cases that shocked the nation in the early 1980s. Toni Morrison edited this internationally acclaimed novel as well as a collection of essays and short stories, which also was published posthumously as *Deep Sightings and Rescue Missions*.

In 1985, Bambara moved to Philadelphia and dedicated the last 10 years of her life to another lifetime passion—work in films. At the Scribe Video Center, Bambara taught scriptwriting classes and encouraged young filmmakers to pursue their dreams and to challenge the status quo through their cinematic works. Bambara also broke new ground in the narration she provided for *The Bombing of Osage Avenue,* an award-winning documentary produced by Scribe, where she offered a community-informed style of narration that differed from the standard objective voice historically projected by narrators in documentary films. When John Akomfrah and Lina Gopaul produced *Seven Songs for Malcolm X* in London, they invited Bambara to bring the strengths of her story-telling style to that documentary film. In another documentary produced by Scribe, *W.E.B. Du Bois: A Biography in Four Voices,* Bambara as the coordinating writer expanded her creative narration style to include her voice along with three other writers: Amiri Baraka, Wesley Brown, and Thulani Davis.

Since Bambara's untimely death at the age of 56 in 1995, it makes sense that among the first to recognize the significance of Bambara's legacy as a writer and activist have been cultural workers, feminists, women of color, and scholars across the African diaspora and within indigenous communities. Why? Because the stories Bambara wrote reflect their own stories and dreams.

Cherríe L. Moraga, an award-winning playwright, poet, essayist, and activist, is among those in the indigenous community who pay homage to Bambara and her calls to honor memory to have special significance for women of color. In her essay, "From Inside the First World," published in *A Xicana Codex of Changing Consciousness,* Moraga wrote:

Toni Cade Bambara believed that we women of color have not forgotten, not in that cave of memory where the freest part of us resides, the basic elements of our lives: the mother-ground that brings sweet sustenance to the world's children; the mother-ground in which we finally lay down our bones and brains to rest. A woman of color movement is an act of *remembering earth*. Ultimately, our politics remain beholden to it. To her.[4]

Chadra Pittman Walke, an African American woman who previously worked with the African Burial Ground Project in New York and is now involved with a growing movement to remember the spirits of enslaved Africans whose lives were lost in the Middle Passage, also acknowledges Bambara's influence. In her work to combat cultural amnesia, Bambara called for rituals and ceremonies that might lead to reclaiming the authentic self. Today these rituals have become a reality.

In June 2012 at Buckroe Beach in Hampton, Virginia, just a couple of miles away from where Africans were forced onto American soil at Point Comfortin 1619, stands today's Fort Monroe in Hampton. Here Walke organized what has become an annual International Day of Remembrance ritual through her organization, The Sankofa Projects. Years earlier, as a college student, Walke first read Bambara's anthology *The Black Woman,* which had a deep impact in shaping Walke's consciousness as a woman of African descent. Later, Walke became aware of Bambara's talk at the National Black Storytellers Conference at Medgar Evers College where the writer-activist made a plea for rituals of remembrance for the bones of formerly enslaved Africans lying unburied in the depths of the Atlantic Ocean.

Explaining how Bambara inspired her to organize a ceremonial homage of remembrance in Virginia, Walke said:

> When I read her words about those "'African bodies in the briny' deep" which was so powerfully written and poignant, it spoke to my soul. I knew that I had to incorporate this quote into every flyer, article, radio interview and speech I did about remembrance. Today, the words of Toni Cade Bambara, now an ancestor herself, come alive in Hampton, Virginia, Charleston, South Carolina and in many other places throughout the United States and across the globe where remembrances for African ancestors are held. If I could whisper Toni a prayer, I would tell her that we are doing as she suggested "tapping into the Ancestral presence in the water. Toni . . . and that we do in remembrance of them and you my dear sistuh."[5]

And Walke is only one among many who have been inspired by Bambara's call for the creation of rituals of remembrance.

Additional testimonies to Bambara's influence include conferences, recognitions, and awards that celebrate Bambara's legacy. The Women's Research and Resource Center at Spelman College makes recognizing Bambara's legacy an annual tradition through hosting an annual conference for activists and scholars. In 2003, scholar Anne Wicke, who translated Bambara's short stories and novels into French, organized the first international conference on Bambara's writing and film work. In 2010, the New Orleans Afrikan Film and Arts Festival, NOAFEST, inaugurated the Annual Toni Cade Bambara Award for Cultural Leadership. And Bambara is a 2013 inductee into the Georgia Writers Hall of Fame in recognition of Bambara as a writer who addressed social issues and made a singular contribution in bringing long-overdue international attention to southern black literature.

There are still areas of Bambara's writing and work, however, that demand attention. At the end of her life, one of her visions was the creation of a garden of the goddesses, a reflection of her lifetime commitment to fostering the well-being of women and an example of her pan-religiosity, free of ties to any one religion, spiritual text, or scriptures. Initially developed in work that Bambara did as part of Toni Morrison's Princeton University Atelier workshop program, Bambara envisioned a garden that was both celebratory and functional. She wanted to create a place where artists, filmmakers, dancers, actors, musicians, wood carvers, astrologists, dream analysts, union organizers, farm workers, hoodoo specialists, herb gathers, healers, conscientious objectors, environmentalists, and of course gardeners—all characters in Bambara's fiction— might gather to celebrate themselves and to map new blueprints for needed political and social change. Surely, it was a space where time is circular and the present meets the past; where the unimaginable is imagined; where barriers to creating wholeness are penetrated as effortlessly as walking through spider webs. It is my hope that this biography will be a pathway to that garden.

NOTES

1. For definitions of cultural worker, see Peyton McCoy, *Walk into Your Season: The Art of Cultural Work* (Bloomington: iUniverse, Inc., 2013).

2. Kay Bonetti, "An Interview with Toni Cade Bambara," in *Conversations with Toni Cade Bambara,* ed. Thabiti Lewis (Jackson: University Press of Mississippi, 2012), 35.

3. Ibid.

4. Cherríe L. Moraga, *A Xicana Codex of Changing Consciousness: Writings, 2000–2010* (Durham: Duke University Press, 2011), 31–32.

5. Chadra Pittman Walke, Interview by author, July 2013.

ONE

At Home in Harlem

While Grandma Dorothy was teaching me theory, and the bebop musicians I eavesdropped on while hanging around fire escapes and in hallways were teaching me about pitch, structure, and beat, and the performers and audiences at the Apollo and the Harlem Opera House were teaching me about the community's high standards regarding expressive gifts, I was privy to a large repertoire of stories.[1]

More than any other place that Bambara lived, Harlem was this writer's spiritual home base, and the Harlem of her childhood significantly influenced her lifetime of work as an activist, writer, teacher, and filmmaker. During Bambara's childhood, Harlem was home to political and cultural icons such as Paul Robeson, Langston Hughes, Claudia Jones, and John Henrik Clarke, all of whom Bambara met in Harlem as a child. By 1939, three of the nation's largest black organizations—the NAACP, the Urban League, and Marcus Garvey's Universal Negro Improvement Association—all had headquarters in Harlem, as did the Communist Party. Far more strident and bold than a Jim Crow South would permit, Harlem leaders remained vigilant, launching radical demands from the soapbox to the pulpit decades before the Civil Rights Movement peaked in the South. Bambara credits her early growing up years in Harlem for giving birth to the writer and activist she would later become. Although Bambara spent no more than her first 10 years in Harlem, the community's lifeblood left an indelible mark on her, one seen in her early short stories.

Bambara's beginnings in Harlem can be traced to Maggie Cooper Williams, her great-grandmother, who was among the millions of blacks leaving the tyranny of the Jim Crow South in the Great Migration to northern cities. Living in Greenville, South Carolina, Maggie [Williams] then married Alex Austin and gave birth to Bambara's grand mother Annie Austin who married James Henderson. Bambara's mother, Helen Henderson, born September 10, 1911, was an orphan by the age of 10. Henderson was then sent to New York to live with her grandmother, a light-complexioned woman who like many other black women worked in domestic service. Drudgery did not dampen Mrs. Williams' creative spirit, however, as she sparked her granddaughter's artistic interests at an early age by encouraging her to paint landscapes on plates. Nothing is known about Helen Henderson's father, James Henderson, other than that he was born in Pittsburgh, Pennsylvania.[2]

In the care of her grandmother, Bambara's mother was inspired by older women in the family who cherished memories of her mother, Annie Henderson, resisting segregation in Atlanta, Georgia. This often-repeated story was of how her mother, an early race woman known to proudly defend black empowerment, defied the laws of segregation and broke social boundaries in ways that made her a forerunner of Rosa Parks. Decades later, Henderson [Brehon] proudly wrote about her mother's uplifting courage:

> They also retold a story about Annie, one of the old women's daughters. (Those women weren't really old but when you are nine, anyone who doesn't go to school is old.) Annie was visiting in Atlanta after having spent several years in Chicago. The motorman had told Annie that she could not get off 'by the front door' of the trolley. She did not argue the point but stood tall, all five feet, twelve inches of her six feet. She walked back to her seat in the back of the car (where else?). As the trolley car crept along, Annie watched the passing scenery—modest frame houses, all with flower gardens in the front yards. Some houses were freshly painted and some were badly in need of repair and paint. When the Fair Street trolley passed Spelman Seminary (as it was called in those days), Annie walked to the front of the trolley, grabbed the unsuspecting motorman by the back of his neck and the seat of his pants, and put him off the car—front door. She walked hurriedly along Greensferry Avenue, mumbling to her herself (my mother is still known as the Amazon of the Henderson clan).[3]

Growing up in New York City, Bambara's mother attended integrated schools at a time when racism resulted in mandated racial segregation in public places in Georgia and across the South. First attending elementary school at PS 27, black teachers were few. She later recalled that it was a black teacher's racial insults that troubled her most. Years later, she remembered her anger: "One of the Black teachers had a habit of making a Black pupil the butt of his racist quips. This always got a hearty laugh from the class, and he laughed loudest. This was his way of winning the approval of his white colleagues—he thought. I despised him."[4]

The secondary school education Bambara's mother received in New York was remarkably different from the kind of education she might have received in Georgia, particularly as an orphan with little or no financial resources. In New York, Henderson attended Washington Irving High School, where she was among the handful of black students enrolled at the internationally renowned girl's school in lower Manhattan. Attending one of five New York high schools designed by the notable architect Charles B. J. Snyder, Henderson escaped the overcrowded classrooms and the deficient resources that some-times crippled predominantly black inner city schools and schools attended mostly by poor and immigrant children. Instead, Henderson attended a school building wrought with overhanging oak balconies and a huge decorative fire-place in the entry corridor. The school also housed an auditorium ideal for concerts and theater performances. Its large pipe organ and a mural of nude maidens on the decorative walls facing the audience made the auditorium popular for professional artists who could draw community members for their performances. As a high school student, Henderson had access to one of the finest performance stages a public school could offer at the time. Henderson later became an accomplished classical and jazz pianist, who also gave piano lessons to children in the community. In addition to offering piano lessons, Washington Irving also boasted a glee club, orchestra, and special instruction in voice.

More importantly, from its beginnings, Washington Irving High School was recognized for having classrooms where young suffragettes demanded that girls be on equal footing with boys in oratory debates, challenging longstand-ing rules that prohibited girls from participating in such debates a decade be-fore Henderson attended school there.[5] Graduating from a Greenwich Village high school that championed the rights of girls and women, Bambara's mother sparked an independent and assertive spirit in her daughter at an early age. Although Henderson attended a school that encouraged interest in the arts and fostered an independent spirit in young girls, it still suffered from a lack of diversity. Writing about her experiences at Washington Irving High School years later, Henderson, the writer's mother, made it clear that she knew that her high school was not free of the discrimination that plagued the nation, but she had few complaints as she proudly reported that she and her classmates, like other young suffragettes, succeeded in reaching their higher education goals:

> During the high school years at Washington Irving I remember no unpleasant incidents. I also remember no Black teachers. Negro girls were well represented in the executive officers of the General Organization, the Arista, the monitors, and some of the clubs. Black girls were not too welcome in the swimming club. Many of the Black graduates of Washington Irving in the late Twenties and early Thirties entered Lincoln and Harlem School of Nursing, Southern universities, and City College Evening School.[6]

When graduating from high school, in an early reverse migration to the South, Bambara's mother pursued academic work at Clark College in Atlanta. She later studied at Columbia University in New York. After completing her studies, Helen Brent Henderson, 23, married Walter Cade in New York City on June 26, 1933. Some may have wondered whether differences in their experiences and educational backgrounds—Henderson attended college and Walter Cade lacked a high school diploma—might weaken their bond. What they shared was their love for music and a romance with Harlem. Perhaps the two lovers danced at the famous Savoy or listened to music in Harlem clubs as they sealed their relationship.

After marriage, like many black women, the newlywed went searching for work. When entering the workforce, Helen Cade asserted herself, challenging stereotypical roles based on gender. Although she eventually settled into the security of civil service work at the New York City Post Office, Bambara's mother was hired as a truck driver when she cleverly dressed wearing enough layered clothing to obscure her gender, but only worked one night. Even though the post office job paid less, it offered benefits at a time when black women still had few career doors open to them.[7]

Less is known about the life of Bambara's father, Walter Cade, born on August 16, 1911, or his parents, Walter Cade, "son of a runaway,"[8] and Selika Glover Cade. Having grown up in New York City, Walter Cade mastered the oratory often heard in Harlem barbershops, including the dirty dozens, a one-upmanship game where "two or more parties begin cracking on each other slinging insults, casting aspersions."[9] Known to sport a Harlem hip-flashy style of dressing and an overall cool appearance including zoot suits and processed hair, Walter Cade sometimes managed sideline hustles. He also had the ability to hold friends and neighbors captive like a standup comedian.[10] Successfully challenging calls at baseball games at Central Park, where he played on the Ohrbach's Department Store team, Bambara's father also was known to artfully position himself to win word battles on the block by using his polished dirty dozens word play skills.

In the late 1930s, when members of the federally funded Work Projects Administration (WPA) Writers Project recorded the stories of Harlemites, many of the published stories they captured documented the perspectives of professionals.[11] This focus on the educated and professional class tended to overlook the richness of storytelling from ordinary Harlemites like Bambara's father, who lacked extended formal education, but mastered the language that would later become the signature of Bambara's early short stories.

While the Depression Era was leaving many jobless in the 1930s, Walter Cade was ambitious and fortunate enough to find employment. When hat packers advertised themselves in the want ad pages of The New York Times, Walter Cade had the good luck to land a steady job in midtown Manhattan on West 39th Street at the Winchester Hat Factory. It was a step above the butler and custodial jobs that black men were often forced to accept. At a time when hat-wearing was enormously popular and viewed by both men and women as a fundamental component of daytime and nighttime dress, Cade found ways to use his day job at the factory to supply a small sideline hustle of Winchester hats on Harlem streets.

Working in downtown Manhattan, Bambara's father may have witnessed some of the protest marches organized by Adam Clayton Powell Jr., who became the pastor of Harlem's historic Abyssinian Baptist Church in 1937. Some of the earliest protests Powell helped to organize were at the Empire State Building, where actor Ethel Waters—then the first black woman to appear on Broadway—and tap dancer "Bojangles" Robinson joined picket lines in demands for meaningful employment at the 1939 World's Fair.[12] As much as the 1920s was the decade of Harlem's cultural renaissance, the 1930s was a decade of mass political organizing and protest against employers refusing to hire blacks even in the stores of Harlem where blacks most often shopped.

On the day of Bambara's birth, March 25, 1939, a *New York Amsterdam News* editorial headline read, "The Order is to Charge!"[13] Here the focus was on economic empowerment. The editorial urged Harlemites to take their lessons from the French army and "to charge all along the line" in a vigilant fight against discrimination in private industry and government jobs. On the day after Bambara's birth, Lillian Alexander, a Harlem civil rights leader, called for a meeting at the Mimo Club, a popular Harlem dance hall, to organize for anti-discrimination legislation. Alexander declared, "We haven't got the Mississippi chain gang, the sharecroppers' conditions or Judge Lynch, but every once in a while they say in effect in New York State to 'lynch the nigger.'"[14] Years later Bambara reflected on the significance of 1939, the year she was born; she identified it as marked by the World's Fair, the extended mourning over the death of the emancipatory blues singer Ma Rainey, and the breakup of Ma's band.[15]

While Bambara was without question a child of Harlem, she was born in downtown Manhattan in Bellevue Hospital. According to Bambara's birth certificate, her parents, both 27 years old, came home to an apartment at 633 Tinton Avenue in the Bronx, not far from the 145th Street Bridge that connects the Bronx to uptown Manhattan.[16] Walter Cade III, Bambara's only sibling who had been born three years earlier at the Bronx Morrisania Hospital, believes that the Bronx address on the birth certificate is inaccurate and that his sister came home to a Harlem apartment. At birth, Bambara's parents named her Miltona Mirken Cade, a name she detested. Even though their first-born was a son, Bambara's father was so eager for another boy that he chose to name their second child after his white male employer, Milton Mirken. When disappointed by the birth of a daughter, Bambara's parents decided to adapt his employer's name to a female version, Miltona. Long before Bambara had political reasons to reject the idea of blacks naming their offspring after white employers, a reminder of blacks taking on the names of white slave holders after enslavement, she showed early signs of her independent resolve. Bambara told her mother when she was about kindergarten age that she was renaming herself "Toni." While her mother immediately accepted her daughter's decision to name herself, Bambara's official school records continued to record her name as "Miltona."

Following the birth of her daughter, Helen Cade meticulously kept a record book that included photographs, anecdotes, and other keepsakes. At work,

Walter Cade enjoyed some camaraderie with his coworkers, as evidenced by the telegram he received congratulating him as a Dad two days after Bambara was born. A telegram that flaunted his coworkers' undeniable chauvinism read: "Congratulations Walter You Must be in a Whirl Don't Worry Kid You Will Have a Lucky girl. We Wish You All the Luck and Joy, Get Busy Walter and Start a Boy." Not only did "Mirkin Wiggy Irving Jesse and Gang" send a telegram, but they also sent a money gift of $5.50.[17] Along with recording the gift from her husband's coworkers, there also is mention of a brooch with a diamond, a gift from Maggie Williams, Bambara's great-grandmother.[18]

Bambara's brother, Walter, also showed signs of disappointment when his little sister came home from the hospital. Years later in an interview, he remembered with laughter, "My first memory of what it meant to be burdened with a little sister goes back to when she was still in the crib. I made the mistake after spending quite a bit of time crafting one of those little airplanes of trying to fly it, and it landed in my sister's crib. She smashed it."[19] For Walter that marked the beginning of a sibling relationship that was sometimes distant.

Nothing, however, dampened Helen Cade's pride and joy about having a daughter. And Bambara's beauty excited Bambara's mother enough to enter her into the Bernice Food Stores Baby Contest when she was only nine months old. Entering children into baby contests was a popular activity in the Harlem community. When Bambara's mother entered her daughter's picture in the contest, she was testing racial waters: the sponsor was a downtown business on Austen Place, where a black contestant was not likely to be selected as a winner. Nevertheless, before the age of one, Bambara was awarded a $5 cash prize as a winner in the Bernice Food Contest.[20]

Bambara's childhood experiences with her father were less fulfilling than those she shared with her mother and sometimes emotionally difficult. Little can be found about Bambara's relationship with her father during her preschool years. What is known is that a local trip to New York's garment district that her father planned to be memorable turned out to be a disappointment for the young girl. Wearing patent leather Mary Janes and frilly socks, a navy blue swing A-line coat with brass buttons, and a stylish red Milano straw hat with a satin sash tied at the side, Bambara, then about four years old, headed to the garment center with her father.[21] In that moment, her father was no longer the man she knew.

Bambara said years later:

> I am trying to hold my daddy's hand, but he is using his hands to talk. There is a white man way at the end of the aisle of tables wearing big pants and standing astride like he's somebody. My father's voice is not familiar to me, and as we walk to the white man my father gets smaller and smaller. So I let go of his hand and step away from him. He turns to look at me and I pretend to loosen the sash on my hat.[22]

At an early age, Bambara learned the extent to which adults in the black community could assume submissive, humiliating, and even childlike roles in the presence of their white employers. For the young Bambara, it was shocking to see her father's behavior change in the presence of his white employer. In this strange setting, the confident father Bambara knew when walking the streets of Harlem melted into a caricature. Perhaps, her father needed to show subordinate behavior to keep his job. In any case, the visit made a lifelong impression on his daughter.

Later, Bambara provided other examples of how her father's behavior disappointed her, including his failure to support Harlem's mass economic boycott of white store owners in the 1930s. While other family members championed political struggles, her father shrank in stature in Bambara's view when he failed to support the boycott, appearing to be either on the side of assimilation or opportunism.[23]

Eventually Bambara's father left the Winchester Hat Factory for more economically rewarding work as an entry-level employee of the New York transit system, where his job was to open and shut subway doors. After obtaining a GED, Walter Cade benefited from new jobs that opened up when employees left to support the war operation, but membership in all-white unions remained closed. In fact, discrimination blocked entrance and advancement within unions even after World War II. For a black man, even with a union card in hand, equity in pay was not guaranteed.

Before young Bambara reached school age, the Cades experienced some stability and upward mobility, which Bambara's brother attributed partly to their father's good luck. The family moved into the prestigious Dunbar Co-Op Apartments just across the street from their more overcrowded former apartment building when their father apparently hit the numbers, the popular daily Harlem street game of chance, initially operated by underground black bankers in Harlem.[24] Now the Cades had cash in hand for the downpayment for an apartment where neighbors would be among Harlem's emerging middle-class community—entertainers, writers, and new civil servants.[25] Their time in the Dunbar apartments, however, would be short-lived.

Named for poet Paul Laurence Dunbar and financed by John D. Rockefeller, this 511-unit red-brick six-story building was the first major cooperative housing project built for blacks in the nation. It featured sun-filled airy apartments, a laundry room, a well-equipped playground, and on-premise childcare. Among the businesses on the complex were a black-managed co-op pharmacy, doctor and dentist suites, a branch of the black-owned Dunbar Bank, and one of Madam C.J. Walker's popular beauty shops. Completed in 1928 in the heyday of the Harlem Renaissance, the Dunbar apartments became home for many renowned figures including writer Countee Cullen, labor organizer Phillip Randolph, dancer Bill "Bojangles" Robinson, actor Paul Robeson, scholar W.E.B. Du Bois, and Artic explorer Matthew A. Henson. When the Cades moved into the Dunbar apartments, the apartments remained a symbol of progress in the black community.

The Dunbar apartments management focused on maintaining a certain caliber of tenants and established elaborate rules to make certain that class and social standards were considered in the application review. As a result of living in the Dunbar apartments during her early growing up years, Bambara's young peers included members of Harlem's growing black middle class who joined the Cade family for a party celebrating Walter's sixth birthday, which their great-grandmother, Maggie Williams, also attended.

Bambara often mentioned coming from a small family. Kenneth Morton, Bambara's cousin, was one of the members of her extended family who made frequent visits to the Cade's new apartment. When he visited the Cade family, Bambara's mother—who made it a habit not to shield children from adult conversations—would engage Morton in grown-up talk about race achievements in the Harlem community over chiffon pie or strawberry cake that she meticulously prepared from recipe books. Morton treasures memories of walking downhill to the Dunbar apartments from where he lived with his extended family in Harlem's prestigious community, "Sugar Hill." Political luminaries and a host of other black professionals and artists were neighbors and W. C. Handy, musician and composer, lived in the apartment building where Morton's family lived. Running up flights of stairs without landings to the Cades' apartment, the young Morton enjoyed catching the sounds of Debussy, one of Helen Cade's favorite classical composers, flowing into the hallway. When Bambara's mother was giving piano lessons, that's when Morton entertained his young cousin by playfully singing "Little Sir Echo," a 1940s' hit song.[26] Bambara's mother wanted the Cades' to be a musical home that honored diverse cultural traditions.

Similar to Bambara's recollections of her early childhood years, Morton's memories of the Cade household focused almost entirely on Bambara's mother. Morton laughed as he remembered Bambara's mother making particular arrangements in preparing for a dinner party where she wanted to impress Harlem socialites. Morton recalled, "She wanted to lay out her best sparkling silver and make certain that the radio was tuned to a station where classical opera might be heard when her guests walked in the door. She would turn the radio knob searching for the singing of someone like Lily Pond, the famed Metropolitan Opera singer recently arrived from Italy who was the rave at that time."[27] Bambara's interest in classical music, theater, and dance was fostered by her mother at a time when many American stages for classical musical performance discriminated against blacks. The songbooks in the home of Bambara's growing up years ranged from the compositions of Claude Debussy, a favorite of her mother, to songs made popular by jazz pianist and singer Nat King Cole, who both of Bambara's parents appreciated.

When leaving the landmark Harlem apartment complex, the Cades' next move was uptown to an apartment on 151st Street between Amsterdam and Broadway—just blocks away from the Dunbar Apartments—and just one door away from Broadway, a bustling thoroughfare with eight lanes of traffic so wide that there was leftover space to accommodate a middle of the street island for bench sitting. In the evenings, young Bambara could sit on their stoop on 151st Street, large enough for as many as six small children to play street games such as "Lodi," pitch pennies, or simply watch the sun slip into the Hudson River west of Riverside Drive while waiting for her parents to come home.

About the 151st Street apartment building where the Cades lived, Bambara wrote: "There was a family up on the fifth floor, and I used to pass there going to the roof. There were thousands of relatives in this apartment, and if you stepped in or even looked in they always said, 'You want something to eat?' And I would say, 'Yeah.'"[28] In contrast to writer James Baldwin—who was born more than a decade earlier than Bambara and often wrote of the Harlem community as plagued by poverty, crime, and suffering—Bambara continually illuminated the strengths of the Harlem neighborhood. Rather than hearing blues on Harlem's streets, Bambara found jazz.

Unlike many in Harlem who had extensive kinship networks or strong church ties, Bambara and her brother only occasionally dropped into Sunday school at Harlem's St. James Presbyterian Church. As an accomplished pianist and organist, Bambara's mother tapped Harlem churches to make extra money as a freelance church musician. For the most part, Bambara relied on neighbors and other women in the community to create a sense of extended family. Bambara later wrote about these early years in Harlem:

> I talked to people who seemed interested in me. Because we came from a tiny family (my mother was an orphan, and my father was the son of a runaway), I was always looking for grandmothers, because I didn't have any, and everybody else had some. People had grandmothers with them plus grandmothers down South to go to. This seemed extravagant to me; I wanted some. I wanted uncles and cousins, which I didn't have, so I began adopting people in the same way people adopted me. I had relatives, so to speak, that had never met my mother. They were just people in the neighborhood who thought I was interesting, who wanted to talk to me or who recognized that I was available.[29]

Harlem was a lifelong reference point for Bambara when describing positive childhood memories. In one popular short story, "Raymond's Run," Bambara describes the narrator's father in a positive glimpse as having characteristics similar to her own father in the way he enjoys whistling and the games he chooses to play. Bambara writes from the point of view of a young girl named Hazel Elizabeth Deborah Parker who accepts being called Mercury by her friends because she runs so fast, but corrects the adult who organizes the school races for daring to call her by the nickname, "Squeaky."[30]

In "Raymond's Run," Hazel prepares for the May Day Races by practicing her "breathing exercises" when on a stroll down Broadway Avenue.[31] Bambara's brother, Walter, remembers the many times that his father would playfully give them a head start by running backward down Amsterdam to Broadway. Hazel Elizabeth Deborah Parker is similar to young Bambara who was a runner and later won a letter in softball. Bambara writes about the character, who calls herself Miss Quicksilver: "I'm the swiftest thing in the neighborhood. Everybody knows that—except two people who know better, my father and me. He can beat me to Amsterdam Avenue with me having a two fire-hydrant head start and him running with his hands in his pockets and whistling. But that's private information."[32]

Bambara attended P.S. 186 on 145th Street and Broadway and walked and probably sometimes ran down Broadway to get there. The elementary school was an easy six-block walk from their apartment building on 151st Street. The school had been designed by Charles Snyder, who was also the architect of Helen Cade's Washington Irving High, to be airy and filled with sunlight. At the school's entrance was a statue of Minerva, the classical goddess who symbolizes wisdom, medicine, poetry, crafts, and music—all things the young Bambara didn't see according to her later description of her early experiences in public school:

> I was stalking pigeons down Broadway twenty paces ahead of my mother. I had a cap gun in one pocket, a Devil Dog in the other, and under my arm some drawing paper just in case. We kissed goodbye at the corner, and I stomped into P.S. 186 to get an education.
>
> If anyone had asked me why I was there, if that nervous young teacher had been less concerned with getting that aviator cap off my head and more concerned with getting into my head, if anyone had been at all interested in getting a glimpse at what I thought school was all about, and how deep rooted those notions were, and how hard I was going to hang onto the notions for years to come—they would have locked me up from the get go as a menace to law and order. For I thought school was a great hall filled with books and paper and clay and musical instruments and very knowledgeable people who loved children and boxes of muddy colored knitting wool to make sweaters for the English RAF [Royal Air Force]. And I'd figured I'd just march in and snatch some lady to share my Devil Dog with and she'd answer all my why this and how come that questions. And when she ran out of breath, I'd grab hold of someone else who'd teach me how to tell time, and how to cross the Drive without getting killed, and how to keep the dog upstairs from jumping on me. And maybe somebody might be able to explain how come Mister Robinson who lived up the hall and who could sing you right out of your shoes and make the piano rock up and down, how come he had to carry people who couldn't even hum up and down in an elevator a long way from home. My mother had tried, but she wasn't after all a teacher.[33]

Opportunities for quality education, better jobs, and nondiscriminatory housing policies were rallying points for Harlem community organizers. In the late 1930s, activists were outraged that there was only one black school principal in Harlem and that racially biased textbooks and tracking systems steered black students away from college-bound programs.

One group, the Harlem Committee for Better Schools, included parents, churches, and teachers, formed in 1935 and active until the 1950s, who made demands on the education system to hire more black teachers and principals and to increase access to the city's more academically competitive schools.[34] Left-leaning teachers incorporated black culture and achievements into their curriculum through readings, plays, and field trips.

Bambara's mother may have been involved with some of these organized activities, but the protest Bambara recalled was a direct and singular action by her mother, confirming her as the ultimate "race" woman. The author distinctly remembers her mother confronting her teacher at PS 186 in front of the entire class; this event quickly became legendary in the community.

Helen Cade did not tolerate racial insults directed at her children. In this instance, Bambara, then in grade school, requested to use the coffee grounds in her teacher's coffee cup to create the perfect brown shading for making the Chinese, Indian, and African children in her drawing "look cool."[35] While this comment might raise eyebrows anywhere, Bambara's mother found the teacher's response to her daughter about how "ugly and crummy and lousy crayons" were good enough for "poor colored children" demeaning and unacceptable.[36]

The response of Bambara's mother to the teacher's racist quips was so impressive that her young classmates reenacted the classroom drama on their walk home up Broadway. Later, Bambara would repeat this story as well in short stories and in essays about how her mother, impeccably dressed in her suede high heel pumps and eye-catching Persian lamb coat, Harlem style, confronted a racist white teacher. About her mother, Bambara begins:

> She was bad! Now she would stride into the class and lay out the first law: "My children are never wrong, so you cannot be right." All the children would be so delighted because here was a woman come to champion her child, not humiliate, beat, torture, and terrorize everybody and make everybody throw up. The teacher would say, "Can we talk outside?" My mother was not moving. She also had this scary pocketbook. The click on it was like the cocking of a shotgun. Mom allowed how she was a substitute teacher, and she had pull with the Board of Education, she knew everybody, so "your ass is mine." . . . The second law: "You apologize to my daughter and you apologize to the class." The teacher would look at me and finally get my name right (the one my daddy gave me). Then she would turn to the class and try to present some lame story about how the coffee gave her nightmares and she ran amuck and lost her mind.[37]

Bambara's mother's "stand-up" attitude in confronting teachers and other authority figures influenced Bambara at an early age. Bambara's mother had backbone, and she encouraged her children to not allow anyone to dissuade them of their brilliance and artistic talents. Years later Bambara might have been reflecting on just how tough, smart, and creative she considered herself to be in a tone that evokes the spirit of the new generation of black women poets who celebrated themselves in the 1960s' era of emancipatory writing. In the voice of a self-assured adolescent, Bambara wrote:

> The sign said: God Is Omnipotent, Omnipresent, and Omniscient. I vaguely remember the wall—red brick, two stories high, uninterrupted by windows. Perfect for handball. Perhaps the building was a church. But I think though that what kept my Spauldeen in my pocket was the sign. I knew in a flash what I wanted to be when I grew up and right away.

Omnipotent meant a powerful arm for knocking out the way snarling dogs, nasty boys, flashers, do ugly cops and anything else that a powerful glance that could silence a teacher in a rousing sing of 'Old Black Joe.' It meant tough. I wanted to be omnipotent tough.

Omnipresent meant being a fly on the wall and seeing everything going on, and to be an ear grown-ups said some walls had. And it meant taking trips all over. Solid. Riding down 5th Avenue on the double decker bus with the family on Sunday was quasi-omnipresent. I could see right into the trees and imagine myself atop the skyscrapers.

Omniscient was why I tried devouring whole shelves of library books. Why I'd light up when they passed out in class those purple mimeo sheets designed to get students into the encyclopedias, almanacs, etc. . . . I had an indiscriminate appetite for print: salvation bubble gum wrappers, comic books, other people's postcards.

So, When grown-ups got all in my face, as grown-ups are wont to do with little children and with midgets too, asking 'And what do you want to be, etc.?' I would say, 'God,' meaning the Three-O very tough, riding the rails, smart person mentioned on the no-playing-handball wall. Raised eyebrows and chirped teeth soon taught me to say, 'I'll be doctor,' and to keep my real career plans to myself.[38]

It is worth noting that in her early college years, Bambara briefly considered becoming a medical doctor. More importantly this ode to herself reflected Bambara's acceptance of looking inward to find talent, intelligence, and beauty rather than searching for these strengths in external sources, a signature of much of Bambara's later writing.

Perhaps Bambara's mother had an early inkling of her daughter's talent or maybe she feared a lack of stimulating academic experiences in her daughter's public school, for her daughter appeared to be a nonconformist at an early age. Racial bias among the teachers might also have been a factor in Helen Cade's decision to transfer her daughter out of public school and enroll her in The Modern School, a private black-run all-girls school in Harlem. Like the Dunbar Apartments, the school also had name recognition and status among Harlem's black middle class. Recently relocated to 437 West 163rd Street, the school had started with only four students in 1934, but by the time Bambara enrolled there were 200 students at the prestigious independent black school in Harlem. The New York Amsterdam News tracked the school's achievements and reported on the many fundraising activities of the school's founder, a socialite who just years earlier organized the junior league of the NAACP. At fundraisers for The Modern School, Mildred Johnson, director and niece of writer James Weldon Johnson sometimes engaged the poet Countee Cullen or the singer Alberta Hunter to perform.[39] Bambara did not relish her year at The Modern School. She felt socially out of place among children who would talk about "going up to vacation in Martha's Vineyard for the week-end or Sugarbush to ski. They went to Europe and the Met. They were Black people, but they were not my people."[40]

At The Modern School, however, at least one of the teachers recognized Bambara's potential as a writer. Lenore Sellers, Bambara's fifth-grade teacher, found her to be an average student, but she did note that Bambara had an interest in writing:

> Miltona is cooperative, friendly and interested in school activities, generally. She displays much originality in understanding in class, however she is not thorough in the completion of an assignment.
>
> From a social point of view, she has not attained the standard of development expected of a girl on her age level, as she had considerable difficulty adjusting to group activities during recreation period at the beginning of the school term. However, this does not remain a problem as she eventually made a place for herself in the class. Her over all pattern is that of an average Fifth grade pupil, not outstanding from either a scholastic or social point of view, but normally progressive.
>
> Noteworthy is the fact that she is unusually interested in creative writing, including poetry, short stories and plays.[41]

As much as Bambara's mother may have hoped to provide supportive environments for her children during their growing up years, there were insurmountable problems at home that took a toll on the entire family, according to Walter Cade, Bambara's brother, that contrast with Bambara's unpublished writing, which described aspects about her father that she appreciated. Bambara wrote warmly about her father's "back throat cackle" laugh "that featured the teeth as a major attraction, accompanied by tears, followed by his Louis Armstrong handkerchief. Then the belly laugh and sighing that came out like pulled taffy when something funny crept up on him unawares."[42]

Bambara also recalled "non-laughing memories," which hint at problematic behaviors and darker days within the Cade family. Bambara wrote:

> Non-laughing memories of my father are quick, clipped, piecemeal things: whistling when he hit the block, grabbing his baseball bat when a ring came odd in the night, chewing on his White Owl as he hitched up his pants and checked the shine on his shoes, running bases in Central Park amazing everyone with his girth and speed, screwing up his face to call us "nappy headed wombahs," dancing with himself in the kitchenette with his eyes closed and his broke down slippers making shuffly noises over the linoleum, shifting an octave when addressing white people, jumping up at the fights or in the Apollo or at the Palace when some stray gesture insulted his standards of showmanship, threatening us with the hairbrush with his jaws tight, inspecting the ring jar of pig feet for one truly worth a quarter.[43]

At one point Bambara wrote that hearing her father whistle tunes like the one Nat King Cole made famous, "They Say That We're Still Too Young," was a welcoming sign of his approach.[44] Her brother said the same whistles signaled eminent danger.[45]

Years later, Bambara's brother's anger was still palpable as he described his father's philandering and womanizing. As a child he remembered his father taking him and his sister to visit a girlfriend while he was still married to their mother. Walter also remembered his mother's shock and pain when they went to the movies once and inadvertently ran into their father and his girlfriend, wearing his mother's favorite coat.[46]

Then there were real-life nightmares that resulted when their mother refused to be cornered into submission. Bambara's brother explained:

> I remember once my father screaming at my mother. My mother was the kind who didn't back down. We had an apartment where my sister and I shared a bedroom. We had a double-decker bed and I slept on the top and my sister slept on the bottom. My mother and father had a bedroom and there was a bathroom between us and their bedroom. One night we heard them arguing and my mother said, "Sammy and Toni"—I was Sammy and my sister was Toni—"call the police." Now in those days, you only had one phone. The phone was in the living room, which meant I had to pass the bedroom. "Toni and Sammy call the police," my mother kept saying so I got up and my sister got up and we started going toward the living room. Then my father would say, "go back to bed." So we went back to bed, and my mom would say, "Sammy and Toni call the police." So we got up again and my father said, "Go back to bed and stay there." So we went back to bed and stayed there because we knew who the biggest was.[47]

Bambara's brother continued:

> In all the time my mother and father had fights, I never saw the fight. But I heard the fight, and the voices would get louder and louder.[48]

About his mother's resiliency, Walter Cade said:

> It's one thing to be hurt physically and emotionally as my mother was, but it's another thing to feel good about the fact that you stood up—that you didn't cower in the situation. And, I think that was what my mother was all about. My mother was very outgoing, very courageous, a very stand up woman. As a matter of fact she incorporated those things in my character and in my sister's character.[49]

There is no way to document the abuse Bambara's brother describes. Not until the 1960s did long overdue public outrage about domestic violence became a compelling public health and social issue. Even then, cases remained severely underreported. Bambara's nonfiction published writing, however, never mentioned the abuse that her brother so vividly described.

In a short story, however, Bambara does show sensitivity to a young girl, the story's narrator named Peaches who is confused and troubled by her father's abusive behaviors. In "Maggie of the Green Bottles," the central character carries Bambara's great-grandmother's name, "Margaret Cooper Williams," who in real life worked as a domestic servant. In this short story, Bambara noted the pains and disappointments experienced by Maggie who is Peaches' grandmother. Again, Bambara wanted readers to know how much she appreciated independent women who did not conform.[50] Bambara wrote about Peaches' perceptions of this visionary, activist-minded, and mystical woman:

> I am told by those who knew her, whose memories consist of something more substantial than a frantic gray lady who poured coffee onto her saucer, that Margaret Cooper Williams wanted something that she could not have. And it was the sorrow of her life that all her children and theirs were uncooperative—worse squeamish. Too busy taking in laundry, buckling at the knees, putting their faith in Jesus, mute and sullen in their sorrow, too squeamish to work together and take the world by storm, make history, or even to appreciate the calling of Maggie the Ram, or the Aries that came after. Other things they told me too, things I put aside to learn later though I always knew, perhaps, but never quite wanted to, the way you hold your breath and steady yourself to the knowledge secretly, but never let yourself understand. They called her crazy.[51]

Published when Bambara was 28, the story more than any other seems to reveal some of Bambara's deeper feelings about her own family relationships. Maggie, who reads coffee-grounds in the saucer of a 1939 World Fair's coffee cup the year Bambara was born, refers to Peaches' father as "a monster" at one point.[52] In this short story, Bambara wrote:

> Then, right in the middle of some fierce curse or other, my father did this unbelievable thing. He stomped right into Maggie's room—that sanctuary of heaven charts and incense pots and dream books and magic stuffs. Only Jason, hiding from an August storm, had ever been allowed in there, and that was on his knees crawling. But in he stomped all big and like some terrible giant, this man whom Grandma Williams used to say was just the sort of size man put on this earth for the "'spress purpose of clubbin us all to death."[53]

Similar to how Bambara might have felt about her father, Peaches shows compassion toward her father despite his behavior. Bambara wrote, "And I'd feel kind of bad about my father like I do about the wolf man and the phantom of the opera. Monsters, you know, more than anybody else, need your pity cause they need beauty and love so bad."[54]

By the mid-1940s, not only was the Harlem Bambara knew was transforming, but so was her life as her parent's marriage disintegrated. Pushing herself into the edges of herself, Bambara's mother had had little space for her own creativity to fully blossom. Only when the marriage ended did Bambara's mother's beauty, brilliance, and creativity receive deserving attention as she gained weight, began wearing makeup, and became a stylish dresser, Morton remembered.[55] Soon, she would no longer be just the piano teacher behind closed apartment doors or the occasional church musician, but turned to performing on stages across the United States as well as in Brazil and Europe. But first, she had to yet map out a plan for the survival of herself and her children.

First moving into an apartment with one of her friends and later moving to Brooklyn, Helen Cade began to distance herself and her family from her former husband and memories of the troubled marriage. Before the family moved, however, Bambara witnessed new changes in Harlem neighborhoods. At that point the community was becoming more diverse as the flow of immigrants from Puerto Rico and other parts of the Caribbean seeking employment opportunities and better living standards increased. Bambara remembered:

> I was in the 4th grade, living in that part of Harlem strivers called "Washington Heights" and the rest of us called Harlem.
>
> Some new people moved into the building. A large family—babies, children, married couples, two if not three sets of elders. . . .
>
> We thought they were Gypsies. A new kind of Gypsy though, the kind that apparently intended to stay awhile, and so preferred to live in an apartment building rather than in a storefront.[56]

Throughout her life, Bambara would always cherish Harlem as a neighborhood like no other. On the streets of Harlem, Bambara absorbed the voices that became hallmarks of her later writing. At home, Bambara's mother was the family pillar. Both Bambara and her brother credited their mother with shaping who they would become—both creative artists—in their adult years.

It would be nearly two decades later when Bambara would return to Harlem to live and work, but Harlem would always be home.

NOTES

1. Toni Cade Bambara, "Education of a Storyteller," in *Deep Sightings and Rescue Missions*, ed. Toni Cade Bambara (New York: Vintage Books, 1996), 250.

2. Walter Cade III, Interview by author. January 13, 2008.

3. Helen Brehon, "Looking Back," in *The Black Woman* (New York: Washington Square Press, 1970), 288.

4. Ibid., 289.

5. "Girl Orators Barred," *The New York Times*, April 4, 1914.

6. Brehon, "Looking Back," 289.

7. Walter Cade III, Interview by author.

8. Interview with Louis Massiah, "How She Came By Her Name," in *Deep Sightings and Rescue Missions*, 209.

9. Ann Wicke, "Translating the Salt," in *Savoring the Salt: The Legacy of Toni Cade Bambara*, ed. Linda Janet Holmes and Cheryl Wall (Philadelphia: Temple University Press, 2008), 85.

10. Walter Cade III, Interview by author.

11. *WPA Guide to New York City. Federal Writers Project* (New York: The New Press, 1939).

12. Abiola Sinclair, "Remembering Adam Clayton Powell Jr." *The Amsterdam News*, December 26, 1992, 26. Also see Cheryl Lynn Greenberg, *Or Does It Explode? Black Harlem in the Great Depression* (New York: Oxford University Press, 1991), 136.

13. "The Order is to Charge!" *The Amsterdam News*, March 25, 1939, 10.

14. "Harlem Women War on Race Prejudice," *The New York Times*, March 26, 1939, 8.

15. Toni Cade Bambara, "Growing up in a Brownstone." Spelman Archives, Atlanta.

16. Birth Certificate for Toni Cade Bambara, March 25, 1939. Spelman Archives, Atlanta.

17. Winchester Hat Company, telegram to Walter Cade, March 27, 1939, Spelman Archives, Atlanta.

18. Helen Cade Family Record Book, Spelman Archives, Atlanta.

19. Walter Cade III, Interview by author.

20. Bernice's Food Stores Inc., telegram to Helen Cade, January 16, 1940. Spelman Archives, Atlanta.

21. Interview with Louis Massiah, 204.

22. Ibid.

23. Toni Cade Bambara, "Deep Sight and Rescue Missions," in *Deep Sightings and Rescue Missions*, 167.

24. For a discussion of the role of the numbers game in Harlem in the 1930s and 1940s, see Shane White and others, *Playing The Numbers: Gambling in Harlem Between The Wars* (Cambridge: Harvard University, 2010).

25. Walter Cade III, Interview by author.

26. Kenneth Morton, Interview by author, March 28, 2008.

27. Ibid.

28. Interview with Louis Massiah, 207.

29. Ibid., 209.

30. Toni Cade Bambara, "Raymond's Run," in *Gorilla, My Love* (New York: Random House, 1972), 28–29.

31. Ibid., 24.

32. Ibid.

33. Toni Cade, "Something in the Wind," in *The Paper* (City College of New York), April 25, 1968. City College of New York Archives, New York.

34. "Ryan's Removal Asked as Color Discrimination Against Teachers is Charged," *The New York Times*, April 11, 1935.

35. Interview with Louis Massiah, 220–21.

36. Ibid.

37. Ibid. Bambara frequently told this story about her mother. The story is first published in "Thinking About My Mother," *Redbook*, September, 1973, and republished, "Thinking About My Mother," *On Essays: A Reader for Writers*, ed. Paul H. Connolly (New York: Harper & Row, 1981). Bambara also used fictionalized versions of this anecdote in her short stories such as in "Christmas Eve at Johnson's Drugs N Goods," in *The Sea Birds Are Still Alive* (New York: Random House, 1974).

38. Toni Cade Bambara, "Working at It in Four Parts," Spelman Archives, Atlanta.

39. "The Modern School Is 30 Years Old," *The New York Amsterdam News*, September 12, 1964.

40. Interview with Louis Massiah, 213.

41. Bambara School Records, 1949. Courtesy of the Modern School, New York.

42. Toni Cade Bambara, "Working at it in Four Parts," Spelman Archives, Atlanta.

43. Ibid.

44. Ibid.

45. Walter Cade III, Interview by author.

46. Ibid.

47. Ibid.

48. Ibid.

49. Ibid.

50. See Martha M. Vertreace, "Toni Cade Bambara," in *American Women Writing Fiction: Memory, Identity, Family, Space*, ed. Mickey Pearlman (Lexington: The University Press of Kentucky, 1989), 161–62, for discussion of Maggie as an Obeah woman in the voodoo tradition.

51. Toni Cade Bambara, "Maggie of the Green Bottles," in *Gorilla, My Love*, 153.

52. Ibid., 151.

53. Ibid., 155.

54. Ibid., 154.

55. Morton, Interview by author.

56. Toni Cade Bambara, "Puerto Rico," courtesy of Frances Negron-Muntaner is discussed in Negron-Muntaner's essay "Things Toni Taught Me," in *Savoring the Salt: The Legacy of Toni Cade Bambara*, ed. Linda Janet Holmes and Cheryl A. Wall (Philadelphia: Temple University Press, 2008), 216–17.

TWO

A Zone of Her Own

I wanted to say, "You will bear in mind that I am great, brilliant, talented, good-looking, and I am going to college at fifteen. I have the most interesting complexes ever, and despite Freud and Darwin I have made a healthy adjustment as an earthworm."[1]

When Bambara was 10 years old, her mother summoned up the courage and ingenuity to relocate the family to a three-story brownstone at 205 Second Street in Lower Jersey City, ten blocks south and three blocks west of the Holland Tunnel. The move provided Bambara's mother with some geographic distance from her broken marriage, and marked another step in her relentless search for better housing and quality education for her children. Once again, Bambara's mother was stepping out on a limb and daring it to break. This time the Cades did not rely on a favor from the family friend who in the past had squeezed them into an overcrowded Harlem apartment.[2] In moving across the Hudson, the family found welcomed relief in the security and breathing space of a brownstone—at least initially.

In 1949, when the Cades changed their residency to Lower Jersey City, the neighborhood was in transition. Once rich in industrial jobs that had provided upward mobility for generations of immigrants, Jersey City's stockyards, dock work, and factory jobs were now drying up. Increasingly, white families left behind their inner-city three- and four-story brick and brownstone homes for the suburbs. Speculators quickly snapped up and subdivided these buildings into overpriced tenement flats, which they rented to blacks migrating from the rural South and to the small Puerto Rican population and other new immigrants that were beginning to move into the neighborhood.

Even though Lower Jersey City was rapidly changing when the Cades arrived, signs of early continental European cultural influences remained in the funeral parlors, neighborhood candy stores, laundromats, and cleaners that still carried the names of their original Polish and Italian owners. The neighborhood churches that had once served the well-to-do now only whispered of the community's former elegance.

Jersey City was no Harlem. But whenever possible Bambara's mother continued to seek cultural opportunities that linked her children to black culture. The neighborhood that came closest to resembling the entrepreneurial and cultural spirit that Bambara saw in Harlem was nearly two miles away. Beginning in the late 1890s, Jersey City's black neighborhoods were established by the families of Pullman porters and dining car waiters who settled there when the city was a "dead end" stop on the railroad before the 1927 building of the Holland Tunnel.[3] At the same time, Dr. Lena Edwards, who came to Jersey City in the 1920s and later became one of the nation's first certified black obstetricians, began a singular women's campaign to break down racial and gender barriers at Jersey City's nationally recognized Margaret Hague Maternity Hospital. Having previously attended countless home births of Czechoslovakian and Polish immigrants in the Lafayette section of Jersey City where she lived, Dr. Edwards refused to accept the hospital's recommendations that she, as a black woman, should apply only for a residency at Harlem Hospital. After repeated rejections, Dr. Edwards was finally granted a residency at Margaret Hague four years before the Cades moved to Jersey City in 1945.[4]

By the 1940s, Jersey City was not only the state's second largest city, but also home to the state's third largest black population. Jersey City's small but thriving black business community, located primarily on Jackson Avenue near Communipaw Avenue, was home to printing, trucking, grocery, manufacturing, real estate, music, insurance, laundry, and beverage-dispensing establishments along with restaurants. The Jersey City Martin brothers, Fred and Robert, ran a black newspaper—The Herald News—out of Newark, New Jersey.[5] Cordelia Green Johnson, a millionaire who was the founder of the national and statewide beauty-parlor worker organizations—and for decades, their president—later headed the Jersey City chapter of the NAACP.[6] For young Bambara, however, these local achievements could have been occurring in another country. But more than likely, these Jersey City stories of race women, Pullman workers, and alliances of black beauty-parlor workers would have been fodder for champion stories like the Harlem stories she so often touted, if she had known about them.

Also lost to her in Jersey City were the scattered visits from neighbors and extended family that had delighted Bambara in New York. When she lived in Harlem, Bambara had relished conversations where tempers flared over whether to invest in building independent unions such as a black political party or to continue to struggle to humanize a nation with a long history of blatant racism.[7] Even with the Hudson Tubes connecting Jersey City to New York, her cousin Kenneth Morton, who frequently visited the Cades in Harlem, does not remember visiting Bambara's family once they moved to New Jersey.[8]

Because Bambara's later nonfiction writings did not explore the impact of her father's separation on the family, it is difficult to know in what ways she missed her father. Only in her fiction is there a hint of the feelings that the separation from her father might have caused. In the short story "Christmas Eve At Johnson's Drugs N Goods," the young narrator, at work over the Christmas holidays at a drug store, anxiously awaits her father—"figuring it's going to be the last birthday visit cause he fixin to get married and move outta state."[9]

Bambara wrote:

> The overhead lights creating mirages and racing up my heart till I'd realize that wasn't my daddy in the parking lot, just the poster-board Santa Claus. Or that wasn't my daddy in the entrance way, just the Burma Shave man in a frozen stance. Then I'd tried to make out pictures of Daddy getting off the bus at the terminal, or driving a rented car past the Chamber of Commerce building, or sitting jammed-leg in one of them DC point-o-nine brand X planes, coming to see me.
>
> By the time the bus pulled into the lot . . ., I'd decided daddy was already at the house waiting for me, knowing that for a mirage too, since Johnson's is right across from the railroad and bus terminals and the house is a dollar-sixty cab away. And I know he wouldn't feature going to the house on the off chance of running into Mama. Or even if he escaped that fate, having to sit in the parlor with his hat in his lap while Aunt Harriet looks him up and down grunting, too busy with the latest crossword puzzle contest to offer the man some supper. And Uncle Henry talking a blue streak bout how he outfoxed the city council or somethin and nary a cold beer in sight for my daddy.[10]

In this story, the conversations with the narrator's father that follow during his visit include a wide range of feelings—love, respect, misgivings, apologies, and even pain-filled doubts. At the end of the day, her father easily sleeps on the couch to which he is assigned on his visits to the household, but the narrator lies awake in the attempt to sort through a rollercoaster of feelings. Her hope for some peace of mind comes in writing in her journal. At one point, the narrator reflects: "I write for a whole hour in my diary trying to connect with the future me and trying not to hear my daddy snoring."[11]

Now in Jersey City and separated from her father, Bambara held onto the habits that she had developed as a young girl—writing on anything she could find and reading. Although she no longer had her father's *Daily News* strips to scribble on, the young writer could still make use of "those white sturdy squares my mama's stockings came wrapped around" for paper to write on.[12] Bambara's brother remembered his sister as a ferocious reader at an early age, but Geraldine Walker, who lived in the building next to the Cades, separated only by a vacant lot, also knew her new neighbor from playing outside in their neighborhood. Similar to other neighborhood children, Walker knew her new neighbor only as Miltona, not Toni as she preferred to be called.

"Miltona, what kind of name is that?" Walker yelled out to Bambara on their first meeting. "You want to play a game of Old Maid or Monopoly?," Bambara asked, leaning back on the wrought iron railings on the side of the building that led up to the first landing of their brownstone building. As Miltona put aside a book—she often read outdoors—Walker remembered deciding to break away from a street game of War, Kick the Can, or Double Dutch to accept her neighbor's invitation to a board game.[13]

In spite of the welcoming the Cade family eventually received from some of the families in the neighborhood, on their very first day in Jersey City, the Cades encountered troubling police attitudes toward black boys. At 13, Walter had been adept at independently navigating the streets of his old New York neighborhoods, and he had no reason to hesitate in stepping out onto Second Street where the family now lived. His immediate experience in Jersey City, however, was unlike any he ever encountered in New York. Just blocks away from his new home, Walter was stopped by two white police officers who pulled up to him in their police car and taunted him with questions. "Hey Boy, what are you doing here? Are you from Harlem? You must be looking for condoms."[14]

"We were not to take any shit, and we were to report back to her [Walter and Bambara's mother] any stereotypic or racist remark,"[15] Bambara later said. Deferring to whites who disavowed blacks was never an option for her and her brother. When Walter came home and told his mother about the police incident, his mother immediately pulled out the pair of silk stockings she had tucked away and changed into an attractive professional outfit before heading to the Second Precinct on 7th Street and Erie. Once at the precinct, Helen Cade demanded to see all the police officers who worked the shift when her son was inappropriately affronted by the police.[16] Although Walter was unable to single out the guilty officer, his mother's refusal to cower to authority made an impression. Similar to when Helen Cade challenged the authority of her daughter's school teacher when they lived in Harlem, Bambara's mother displayed again her fearless ability to stage a one-woman protest when needed on behalf of her children.

Nevertheless, Helen Cade must have recognized a need for social supports when moving to Jersey City. At Grace Episcopal Van Vorst, an unusual church just a block from her home, three white Episcopalian priests, also new to Lower Jersey City, began developing a progressive activist urban ministry. One of them was Paul Moore, a recent Yale University graduate from an affluent New Jersey family, who would years later be featured in *The New Yorker* magazine as a result of continued civil rights, gay rights, and antiwar involvement as a progressive New York Bishop.[17] In 1950, however, Moore was just beginning to explore his calling to an urban ministry among Jersey City's poor. Moore's wife Jenny later wrote about her Jersey City experience in a 1968 memoir, *The People on Second Street*.[18] Jenny Moore's daughter, Honor Moore, also a writer, confirmed that her mother was referring to Helen Cade when she made pseudonymous mention of the figure "Mrs. Hyde."[19] Rev. Kim Myers, who later became spiritual head of the Episcopalian Diocese of California, remembered the challenges he faced trying to increase diversity at Van Vorst Episcopal Church in 1949. Myers recalled how they wanted to make the church a family parish:

> It was a group of elderly people—all white. . . . There were Negroes in the area, like Railroad Avenue, but none in the church.
>   I remember the sign at the rectory. It said: "Enter Into His Gardens With Praise," but below it was a sign on the fence which said, "Keep Out." I guess that illustrated the nature of the people down there.[20]

As the new priests worked to develop community relationships through an open rectory program that included television-watching nights, basketball games, teen dances, and summer camps, the image of the church changed. Dorothy Day, the radical pacifist and activist who edited *The Christian Worker,* was a friend of the Moores. Day fervently believed that "The greatest challenge of the day is: how to bring about a revolution of the heart, a revolution which has to start with each of us?"[21]

In her memoir, Jenny Moore remembers her husband's excitement when Mrs. Hyde (as she is known in the memoir) volunteered to run a craft program for all age groups, which meant they could cut back on scheduled television-watching nights at the rectory.[22] While in Jersey City, Bambara may have accompanied her mother to craft programs and have known about her mother's integrating the women's guild of the church. When the church celebrated its 100th anniversary, not long after the Cades' arrival in Lower Jersey City, Bambara's mother was an integral part of the inner workings of Grace Episcopal.

Like civil rights leaders who wanted to select individuals who would break down racial barriers, and also project what they perceived as socially accepted images, the Grace Episcopal Church leadership identified Bambara's mother as ideal for the role. As described by Jenny Moore, Helen Cade was "tall, angular, attractive, and astringent but friendly."[23] Other assets that made Helen Cade singularly attractive for breaking down racial barriers was that she had a job in New York and her background included college education, professional experience, and musical training. About a year after Grace Episcopal Church's progressive ministry was established, Bambara's mother was singing in the previously all-white choir.[24] Moore respected Helen Cade's political backbone and intelligence as she reflected, "Prejudice was an occasion for her wry, stiletto humor, and she thought of many ways to trick 'the enemy.' Somehow you knew she had control."[25]

Later, Bambara's short stories expressed the confidence that her mother instilled in her. As a child, Bambara learned from her mother that titles based on age, gender, race, or class did not entitle adults to rank themselves as privileged or superior. In "The Education of a Storyteller," Bambara wrote about a young girl, Miz Gal, wanting to explain Einstein's relativity theory to Miz D, an elder in the community.[26] Depending on circumstances, the hip elder sometimes calls her young friend "Sweetheart, Peaches, You Little Honey, Love, Chile, Sugar Plum, Miz Girl, or Madame."[27] And, the young narrator of the story also had several names of respect for Miz D including "Grandma Dorothy or Miss Dorothy or M' Dear."[28] In this story, Bambara explains that Miz Gal takes her cues from non-authoritarian parents: "I was strictly not allowed by progressive parents to call anybody Ma'am or Sir or to refer to anybody as a Lady or a Gentleman."[29]

While Bambara attended school in Jersey City, civil rights organizations made demands for equality and increasingly challenged the constitutionality of separate-but-equal education. Eventually, the 1954 landmark case, *Brown v. Board of Education*, overturned legal school segregation. As was the case with many public schools in the North, PS 37, where Bambara attended fifth grade, lacked diversity as a result of segregated housing patterns. While the racial and ethnic population of the Second Street neighborhood was beginning to change, the several blocks surrounding PS 37, a different neighborhood from Second Street, remained primarily Polish and Italian. Seven blocks away from the Cades' home, PS 37 was tucked between Victorian brownstones. In a neighborhood that was still largely inhabited by descendants of immigrants, Bambara was often one of the two or three black students in her class.

Walking to school each morning from Second Street, Bambara passed cultural markings that were not her own as she turned left on Eerie, walking past St. Mary's Church and Parochial School on the corner of Eerie and Second across from Grace Episcopal. It is not known whether Bambara was taunted by young white girls or boys when walking to school, but Stella Skipper, a girl two years younger than Bambara who lived across the street from the Cades, walked the same blocks as Bambara and encountered racist pranks. Skipper who sometimes paused to genuflect and make the sign of the cross in front of the looming limestone statue of Mary in the church's front yard remembers being handed a paper bag of dead cats by a young white first grader who wanted to intimidate her.[30]

Once at the elementary school, Frank Conwell, a science teacher who was also known in the community because of his funeral-home business, was one of the two black faculty members at PS 37. The other was Emile Birchett Robinson. Unlike some of the other schools, which honored Negro History Week, there was no formal recognition of Negro History Week at School 37, nor were there assigned readings that reflected African American history.[31] Even though the NAACP widely distributed Negro History kits to school teachers in New Jersey, School 37 did not receive them.[32]

Fearless in rejecting stereotypic roles assigned by teachers, Bambara was schooled by her mother that the singing of songs like "Old Black Joe" to entertain school audiences was not to be contemplated.[33] Moore's book describes the militancy that Helen Cade instilled in her children, a militancy which grew and was expressed throughout Bambara's life. Moore wrote:

> And she trained her two children to be angry. She taught them Negro history at home and urged her ten-year-old daughter to refuse to sing "Swing Low, Sweet

Chariot" and other spirituals at school, because they encouraged a stereotype of the Negro in the servitude she loathed. She taught them both that they ought to expect a lot from life, but that they would have to be tough to get it.[34]

Although School 37 included kindergarten through eighth grade, Bambara did not complete her junior high school years there. In schools outside of Jersey City, Bambara eventually did find mentors who fostered exploration of multicultural literature and opened the door to diversity. Bambara recalled her junior high school years as filled with both anger about distorted truths perpetuated by ill-informed teachers, and the fascination that came from finding new truths that had been omitted in the standard school curriculum. In a reflection published in the City College campus newspaper more than two decades later, Bambara wrote about her junior high school years like a rebellious adolescent who happened to be very well read. There is no way of knowing how much of this reflection is autobiographical or fiction, but it captured the early rebellious spirit that Bambara chose to project about herself:

Junior high was a disaster. The public ones anyway. I did get to go to a few boarding schools, for I had become 'a problem' as they say. At one southern school I learned quite a bit about what makes black people crazy. And I began to look at cowboy and Indian pictures in a new way. At one of the northern schools I did find a group of teachers who were willing to trust me, or perhaps they only indulged me, and taught me only what I asked for—How do I track down Mali and Kush in the library? Why was Howard Fast snatched off the shelves this year? Why do people call A. Philip Randolph the most dangerous man in America? Those teachers were to unleash onto the public school system a veritable monster.[35]

When the Cades moved to Lower Jersey City, Bambara's mother gambled on creating a new life for her children—one that was not intended to stifle the young writer's creativity or independent spirit, but to bring structure and stability to a family life that had been repeatedly disrupted by change and frequent moves. Like many who had initially come to this city on the Hudson River because it symbolized so much expectation in the shadow of Ellis Island, Helen Cade ultimately left this American city of historical promise. She moved on in the continued struggle to provide for her now high-school-aged children and to create an environment that would make them competitive even when they encountered inequities. The changes may have contributed to Bambara's discontent as well as contributed to a sense of cultural isolation.

In the 1950s, the Cades relocated once more—this time to Queens, New York. In moving away from Jersey City, the Cades were leaving behind a brownstone that stood in a mostly white, primarily Italian, Irish, and Polish immigrant community and the Grace Episcopal Van Vorst Church community, where Bambara's mother exemplified the toughness that her daughter would later exhibit in her fights for social justice.

Even after leaving Jersey City, however, Bambara's mother kept in touch with Jenny Moore. Years later, Bambara joined her mother in attending a birthday party for Honor Moore, daughter of Paul Moore and his wife Jenny Moore, who became an activist in peace, civil rights, and anti-poverty movements and later donated her estate to scholarships for writers.[36] Jenny Moore asked Bambara's mother to invite her daughter to meet Honor, a young aspiring writer. At the party of mostly feminists, Honor Moore remembered Bambara giving her a small decorated wooden box that might be used for holding cigarettes or other treasures. Moore remembers that Bambara otherwise did very little intermingling at the social gathering.[37]

An eternal optimist, Bambara later said she made a conscious effort in her writings to focus on aspects of life that fostered "usable truths" and positive movement rather than despair.[38] Perhaps Bambara simply was not interested in tapping into the emotions that memories of her time in Jersey City would evoke. The fact that Bambara was not writing about Jersey City or showing interest in rekindling relationships from that period of her life may be the best evidence that the years in Jersey City were disappointing. In an essay published in 1980, Bambara explained how sentiments guided her writing. Bambara revealed:

> I don't doubt that the horror tales are factual. I don't even doubt that ugly is a truth for somebody . . . somehow. But I'm not convinced that ugly is *the* truth that can save us, redeem us. The old folks teach that. Be triflin' and ugly and they say, "Deep-down, gal, you know that ain't right," appealing to a truth about our deep-down nature. Good enough for me. Besides, I can't get happy writing ugly weird. If I'm not laughing while I work, I conclude that I am not communicating nourishment, since laughter is the most sure-fire healant I know.[39]

Bambara had little reason to revisit her Jersey City memories.

It may have been Father Moore, Helen Cade's friend, who first suggested that she consider enrolling her daughter at the Greer School in Duchess County, New York, a school with strong ties to the Episcopalian Church. The school was established in 1906 by David H. Greer, rector of New York's Bartholomew's Church and later New York Bishop, as Hope Farm for Children in Need.[40] The boarding school targeted children of divorced or separated parents, as well as orphans, at a time when bringing children up outside of the nuclear family was considered a major risk factor for a range of social adjustment problems. Bambara would have met the school's criteria due to her parents' divorce.

How Bambara's mother covered the tuition costs for her daughter is not known. Although Bambara attended the Greer School long after railroad millionaire Edwin Gould established the Gould Foundation which supported the school, the contributions of bankers, brokers, and judges along with volunteer efforts from the women's auxiliaries at St. Bartholomew's Church helped to defray the school's operational costs.[41] Activist singer-actor Harry Belafonte and the Bolshoi Ballet were among several well-known performers, who dedicated shows as fundraisers for the school in later years. Eleanor Roosevelt's family also was among the prominent families who made donations to the school from its beginnings. Eleanor Roosevelt herself provided the commencement address at the Greer School in 1955, three years after Bambara completed her studies there. The fact that governors from New York, New Jersey, and Massachusetts attended the school's 50th anniversary the following year was another indication of the wide range of support that the school enjoyed in the region and nationally.[42]

Located 90 miles away from New York City in the rolling hills of the Hudson River Valley surrounded by horse and cattle farms, the school was known for attracting a stellar academic faculty, who mostly lived on the campus grounds. The faculty made it possible for the school to offer a richly diverse curriculum. Although it was just a two-hour drive away from Harlem, the predominantly white student body and faculty made the Greer School seem worlds apart from Harlem. In addition to the challenging and rigorous academic curriculum that Bambara probably relished at Greer, the school provided each student with a garden plot and offered an array of clubs to choose from including modern dance, dramatics, photography, and an astronomy club. The school was also interested in developing trade skills, such as farming, carpentry, sewing, and domestic skills, promoting both academics and trades.[43]

When Bambara, 13, left the Greer School with certificate in hand, her mother had moved the family to Queens, and Bambara would soon begin her high school education at John Adams High School in Ozone Park. Her mother was part of the growing working-class community that increasingly sought the American dream of better housing and education in Queens, New York. At one time Harlem was a cherished address for jazz musicians who succeeded in breaking the color line. Now, St. Albans, Queens, for example, was rapidly becoming a haven for black music giants, such as Count Basie, Miles Davis, Lena Horne, and Duke Ellington.

As much as ever Bambara as an adolescent longed for Harlem. Her cousin Carole Brown remembered being riveted by stories of her younger cousin and her then boyfriend managing to gain entrance into a popular downtown jazz club when Bambara was underage. Years later, Brown remembered how daring her cousin could be as she recalled, "Toni was 13 and she had a friend— this guy looked like a smooth gangster . . . very well dressed in a beige felt hat and tie. He escorted her to Birdland and we both knew that you had to be at least 18 to get into any New York night club. Toni somehow got away with it by putting her age up to 18."[44] Brown laughed, "At the time, I might have been listening to doo-wop, but she was talking about John Coltrane and Monk. She was a sponge. She carved herself out of her environment. She had a terrific imagination. She was always thinking ahead of everybody else and danced to a different drummer from the first time I met her. There was nobody else like her."[45]

Sylvia Waters, a dancer and choreographer who danced with the Alvin Ailey Company and later directed the famed Alvin Ailey II Company, had similar impressions of Bambara when they met as teenagers. It was at a neighborhood Harlem party, in a small apartment on St. Nicholas and 150th Street, where the lights were down low and the partygoers were all tightly squeezed together.

Waters recalled a stylish Bambara wearing a belted leather coat with her hair piled on top of her head. Waters remembered her first impressions years later:

> Toni was aloof and seemed so grown up. I remember her being in a universe all of her own at that party, kind of looking around at the rest of us like we were just these kids; I was just very well aware that I was not in the same orbit as she was. She was just so sophisticated. I remember we were like little kids compared to her. She must have been 16 or 17, we weren't that far apart in age at all. But she seemed very mature and very sophisticated.[46]

Meanwhile, Bambara was now frustrated by the school experience she was having at the predominantly white high school in Ozone Park. Although they did not know each other when they both attended John Adams High School, Andrea Benton Rushing, by then an established academic, met Bambara many years after graduating from high school. Bambara and Rushing were surprised to learn that they shared harsh memories of John Adams High School. Years later, Rushing recalled the difficulties of attending a high school where the student body was more than 90 percent white. Having spent her early childhood in Harlem before her family moved to New York's Lower East Side and then moved to Queens, Rushing remembered experiencing culture shock at John Adams High School. Rushing explained, "I had gone to school with white people all my life. I knew there was segregation in the United States, but I thought it was all south of the Mason Dixon line." She continued, "I think when you are a smart black person or an intellectual black person, you don't realize that [intelligence] is what some white people think belongs to them. So, you can be an athlete or you can be a singer, but you can't be a brain." Rushing recalled how she had to struggle to be appropriately placed in classes that were academically challenging at John Adams High School because of the assumptions being made about her by teachers and counselors because she was black.[47] Years later Ozone Park was the setting for the popular television situation comedy *All in the Family,* where Archie Bunker, the show's main character, freely tossed narrow-minded racial slurs into his conversation.

Trina Robbins experienced a sense of alienation of a different kind at John Adams High School as someone who was absorbed in the Greenwich Village bohemian life style. Robbins remembered Bambara as a classmate who defied stereotypes, cleverly weaving tales about herself in convincing ways that made her seem exotic and daring. Robbins, who herself would hang out in Washington Square Park with folk singers, remembered being stunned by Bambara. Years later Robbins wrote, "Toni exuded hipness before I even knew what the word meant."[48]

Carole Brown, 15, stepping high with her cousin, Bambara, 16, in the backyard of the Cades' new home in Jamaica, Queens, 1955. Courtesy of Carole Brown.

Robbins also recalled her teenaged friend as a storyteller who held others in thrall of her practical jokes:

Toni must have known we were in awe of her, and she probably got a kick out of it. One day she showed up at school wearing only a single gold hoop earring. "Toni," asked Carole, "Where's your other earring?" Toni answered, "Today is a Muslim holiday, and we're only allowed to wear one piece of jewelry."

Muslim! Who knew of Muslims in Ozone Park, except in myth and legend? Our eyes got really big and we said nothing, out of respect for Toni's religion. Several months later, around Easter, she mentioned going to church on Easter Sunday. "But," I stammered, "You said you were Muslim, and that was why you could only wear one earring, remember?" "Oh that," she said "I made it up. I just couldn't find my earring that morning."[49]

Bambara was achieving a mastery of the art of spinning tales and was clever at rendering them with so much authenticity that listeners did not suspect that the stories that they perceived as pearls of truth were products of her imagination. The storytelling also may have been a way for Bambara to sustain the wall of privacy that she began to build around herself, which was difficult for others to penetrate. Perhaps Bambara wanted to shape an image of herself that would allow classmates to view her differently from other blacks who they knew personally or from absorbing stereotypic media images.

At John Adams High School, Bambara eventually found her niche in the school's bohemian crowd. When Bambara spotted Robbins reading an article about what it meant to be bohemian, a conversation ensued where Bambara indicated that she too was bohemian. Shortly after that Bambara became the only black student on the high school literary journal, *The Clipper,* which Robbins briefly edited.[50]

In her poem, "There'll Come a Day," the spirit of optimism that later dominated Bambara's short stories is apparent. Published in the high school literary journal, this poem of Bambara's reflected the spirit of the folk music that became the protest songs of the times as she wrote:

A new day's awaiting to be discovered by the sun
A new era on earth is just around the corner.
There'll be great times for me,
When hatred shall flee
From every heart and mind.[51]

The closing stanza, however, makes clear that even as a teenager Bambara did not slip into blurry-eyed romanticism, failing to see the challenges that must be faced to achieve social change. In high school, Bambara is conscious of the realities:

The patient will die a thousand deaths
The believers will soon begin to doubt
It will take quite some time,
Some reason and rhyme,
Wit and logic.[52]

In the decades that followed, the paths of the two self-identified high school bohemians, Robbins and Bambara, rarely crossed, but whenever they met, they valued the common ground between them, bound by "reason and rhyme, wit and logic." Robbins later became a writer, noted for her graphic novels and her creative woman-centered comics.

The 1950s was a disturbing time for political progressives unwilling to buy into the Red Scare being promoted by the conservative media and the

Eisenhower administration, but Bambara's Harlem years and the cultural environment created by her mother provided her with the backbone to resist buying into the propaganda of the times. Bambara's fiction and nonfiction are deeply rooted in the belief that some of the most significant education she, or any child for that matter, could possibly receive occurred outside of the public school house and in the community where children could chat with elders in parks or could listen to street orators in places like Speakers Corner in Harlem as she so often did.

Despite disappointments at John Adams High School, Bambara was a high achieving student in academics, arts, and sports. Determined to graduate from high school as early as possible and be free of the stifling environment of John Adams High School, Bambara participated in the high school's January graduation. She did so at 16 with an overall 84.6 high school average. From her first years at the high school, Bambara showed the kind of excellence in scholarship and character that made her eligible for the school's honor society and several recognitions for meritorious service.[53] She achieved in foreign languages, math, and the sciences, which might have contributed to her decision in high school to declare biochemistry as her potential college major.[54]

Bambara's mother also continued to foster the imaginative life of her high school daughter, both by providing isolated spaces for Bambara to pursue her own thoughts and by placing her in the company of artists. She had enrolled her daughter at an early age in dance classes at Katherine Dunham's school of dance where her pioneering artistry was shaking New York's cultural boundaries like a whirlwind.[55] Dunham interconnected African American and African Caribbean styles of dance in her method in a school of dance in New York that supplemented dance classes with courses in humanities, philosophy, languages, aesthetics, drama, and speech.

The Katherine Dunham School may have been the first place where Bambara was introduced to an explicitly vodou-influenced spiritual worldview—and to a spirit world that become a constant force in her life and writing. In addition to being exposed to the philosophy of the Dunham School, at an early age Bambara learned from an array of women including the sanctified church women and activists who spoke on Harlem's Speakers Corner.[56] Bambara's mother wanted her daughter to be exposed to the arts and to the wit and wisdom of black women wherever they lived during Bambara's growing up years. It turned out to be a critical gift.

Other family influences included Kenneth Morton, Bambara's cousin and a widely recognized visual artist and dancer who studied with world-renowned teachers Donald McKayle and Martha Graham. He influenced Bambara in several ways. In later years, Morton supported Bambara's life by meticulously typing manuscripts. When Morton performed at Brooklyn College in a dance where the choreography was based on Jewish folklore, Bambara, a teenager, was there with Brown, her cousin, cheering Morton on. Walter Cade, Bambara's only sibling, would later launch a successful career in the visual arts and become a recognized musician. Reflecting on the number of visual artists, singers, dancers, actors, and other performers in the family, Morton reflected, "I think I can safely say my family was artistic."[57] In fact, Bambara's creativity soon found new avenues of expression at Queens College.

NOTES

1. Toni Cade Bambara, "Sweet Town," in *Gorilla, My Love* (New York: Vintage Books, 1972), 124.

2. Walter Cade III, Interview by author, January 2008.

3. "Railroad Workers Gave Impetus to Jersey City Growth," *The New Jersey Afro-American*, March 27, 1947.

4. Linda Janet Holmes, "The Life of Lena Edwards," *New Jersey Medicine* 85, no. 5 (1985): 431–35.

5. "Railroad Workers Gave Impetus to Jersey City Growth."

6. "Great Woman Leader of Century Rose from Obscurity to Fame," January 26, 1957, 1.

7. Toni Cade Bambara, "Deep Sight and Rescue Missions," in *Deep Sightings and Rescue Missions*, ed. Toni Morrison (New York: Random House, 1996), 169–70.

8. Kenneth Morton, Interview by author, March 2008.

9. Toni Cade Bambara, "Christmas Eve at Johnson's Drugs N Goods," in *The Sea Birds Are Still Alive* (New York: Vintage Books, 1982), 196.

10. Ibid., 188.

11. Ibid., 198.

12. Toni Cade Bambara, "Salvation Is the Issue," in *Black Women Writers (1950–1980)* (New York: Anchor Books, 1984), 42.

13. Geraldine Walker, Interview by author, October 2008.

14. Walter Cade III, Interview by author, December 2007.

15. Interview with Louis Massiah, "How She Came by Her Name," in *Deep Sightings and Rescue Missions*, ed. Toni Morrison (New York: Vintage Books, 1996), 216.

16. Walter Cade III, Interview by author.

17. Jervin Anderson, "Standing Out There on the Issues," *The New Yorker*, April 28, 1996.

18. Jenny Moore, *The People on Second Street* (New York: William, Morrow & Company, Inc., 1968).

19. Honor Moore, Interview by author, May 2008.

20. "Bishop Lived in and Loved Jersey City," *Jersey Journal*, September 15, 1966.

21. Dorothy Day, *Loaves and Fishes* (New York: Harper & Row, Publishers, 1963), 210.

22. Jenny Moore, *The People on Second Street*, 92.

23. Ibid., 91.

24. Ibid., 138.

25. Ibid.

26. Toni Cade Bambara, "The Education of a Storyteller" in *Deep Sightings and Rescue Missions* (New York: Vintage Books, 1996), 247.

27. Ibid.

28. Ibid.

29. Ibid.

30. Stella Skipper, Interview by author, October 2008.

31. Emile Robinson, Interview by author, April 2009.

32. Posters Available for 24th History Week Celebration, *The Afro-American,* January 8, 1949.

33. Massiah Interview, "How She Came By Her Name," 216.

34. Moore, *The People on Second Street,* 92.

35. Toni Cade, "Something in the Wind," *The Paper* (New York: City College of New York, April 25, 1968), 4.

36. "Mrs. Moore Rites Tomorrow Activist Was Wife of Bishop," *The Jersey Journal,* October 4, 1973.

37. Honor Moore, Interview by author.

38. Toni Cade Bambara, "What It Is I Think I'm Doing Anyhow," in *The Writer on Her Work,* ed. Janet Sternburg (New York: W.W. Norton & Company, 1980), 155.

39. Ibid.

40. Peggy Matthewson Sparks, *Hope Farm/Greer School: Memories of Childhood* (Rutland, VT: Parchment Press, 2006).

41. Ibid.

42. Ibid.

43. Ibid.

44. Carole Brown, Interview by author, February 18, 2008.

45. Ibid.

46. Sylvia Waters, Interview by author, January 2009.

47. Andrea Benton Rushing, Interview by author, September 2010.

48. Trina Robbins, "Savoring Toni Cade Bambara," *Bitch Magazine* (Summer 2008): 74.

49. Ibid.

50. Ibid.

51. Toni Cade Bambara, "There'll Come A Day," *The Clipper* (John Adams High School, June 1955), 19.

52. Ibid.

53. High School Records and Diploma for Toni Cade Bambara, Spelman Archives, Atlanta.

54. Ibid.

55. Toni Cade Bambara, Curriculum Vitae, Spelman Archives, Atlanta.

56. Interview with Louis Massiah, 214.

57. Kenneth Morton, Interview by author.

THREE

Bridges to Bambara

I have always, I think, opposed the stereotypic definitions of "masculine" and "feminine," not only because I thought it was a lot of merchandising nonsense, but rather because I always found the either/or implicit in those definitions antithetical to what I was all about—and what revolution for self is all about—the whole person.[1]

Bambara once defined the 1960s as more than a decade. For Bambara, it was a period of time that ranged from 1954 to 1972.[2] Although Bambara didn't provide specific reasons for making those years the benchmarks for the 1960s, it makes historical sense: in 1954, the U.S. Supreme Court issued the *Brown v. Board of Education* ruling which ended the long-standing separate but equal policy as a rational for racial segregation in American public schools, and by the mid-1970s, the most powerful period of the Civil Rights Movement and Black Arts Movement of the 1960s had already peaked.

Bambara came of age as a writer and activist during the same time period. In 1954, Bambara entered Queens College and in the four years until her graduation in 1959 began a journey of self-discovery through the arts—writing, theater, and dance. By 1972, two books that she edited—*The Black Woman* and *Tales and Stories for Black Folks*—had been published, along with the first collection of her own short stories, *Gorilla, My Love*. She was also Toni Cade until 1970, when she entered the new decade by assuming Bambara as her surname just prior to the birth of her daughter. Her new name represented the accumulation of experiences that led her to claim a new sense of herself in the world. In this 20-year period, Bambara emerged as a significant black woman writer.

In 1954, when Bambara began undergraduate studies as a student at Queens College, the school's student population was almost entirely white as was the case in most colleges in the country. The only known black faculty member at Queens College was Deborah Cannon Partridge Wolf, who had joined the school's Department of Education five years earlier. Although she initially planned to pursue a course of study in the sciences with the intention of becoming a medical doctor, Bambara's passion for the arts led her to change her major to English before the end of her freshman year. Later Bambara wrote in an unpublished essay: "In college, writing courses and the theatre club in need of plays lured me away from the H2S generator and jarred-in-formaldehyde frogs."[3]

While an undergraduate student, in addition to writing, Bambara dabbled in multiple art forms and was an avid listener of jazz. As a member of the Dance Club of Queens College, Bambara danced in and choreographed numerous performances.

In theater, Bambara worked both onstage as the lone black actor and behind the scenes as a stage manager and costume designer. In the 1950s when folk singing was emerging as an expression of political protest, Bambara was among the students who played a guitar and sang songs that carried political messages. Her classmates were also impressed by Bambara's encyclopedic knowledge and familiarity with jazz and its masters such as Charlie Parker and John Coltrane.[4] There is no question that while still a teenager at Queens College, Bambara surrendered to the call from the arts.

At Queens College, Bambara's social circle consisted primarily of peers who were part of the left-leaning political set or were artists who generally self-identified as bohemian. There were two cafeterias on campus: a larger one that was preferred by the fraternity and sorority crowds, and the funky, smaller café where Bambara and her friends gathered. Their lengthy conversations around the table ranged from talk about campus theater productions, such as Jean-Paul Sartre's *No Exit*, to decrying biased attacks on intellectuals and artists that persisted throughout the McCarthy era. Art Goldberg—later a writer with *Ramparts*, a groundbreaking political and literary magazine at the time— remembered conversations that included Bambara. Goldberg said, "We learned years later that she was younger than she said she was. We were under the impression she was 18 or 19 and she was actually 16—and she was one of the people this group revolved around."[5] Among peers who may never have known a young black female as a friend, Bambara created a niche for herself as sophisticated, talented, and smart, debunking any stereotypes of the "Negro" that her peers may have harbored previously. Later, Bambara described her Queens College years as a time of cultural isolation and a period of searching for self.[6]

Mary Doyle Curran, a professor in the English Department, was one of the faculty members at Queens College who recognized Bambara's writing skills early on. Curran invited Bambara to social gatherings that included other students at her large one-room apartment in a brownstone on Waverly Place across from Washington Square Park in the Village. Bambara was again the lone black student in this social setting. Another former student of Curran, Bell Gale Chevigny, recalled her memories of Bambara being attractive and friendly in a memorable first conversation.[7]

A descendent of an Irish immigrant family, Curran was the author of the novel, *The Parish and The Hill* (1948)—an important fictional depiction of Irish American life from the point of a view of a young female narrator. Curran may have identified with Bambara's early short stories, where young independent girls are frequently the protagonists within their low-income working-class communities. In Curran's novel, the grandfather, a tradition-bearer, is a master of Gaelic speech and shares some of the characteristics of the elders in some of Bambara's later writings, who honor rituals and look forward and backward in time. The grandfather tells his granddaughter, "There's no way of telling, but perhaps the door between the world of the living and the world of the dead is not shut as tightly as some would have it."[8] If Bambara read this novel as a college student, she may have identified with characters who honored their ancestral roots.

The extent to which Curran encouraged Bambara to submit a portfolio of writings is not known. What is known is that the works written by Bambara— including short stories, a script, and poetry—merited Bambara's receipt of the Queen's College John Golden Award for fiction in 1959.[9] An untitled poem in Bambara's collection of early writings at Queens College expressed some of the themes characteristic of poets who identified as beat poets. Bambara shared with beat poets a weariness of 1950s' mainstream America culture that seemed trapped in illusions and hypocrisy. Bambara wrote:

> What do we do when the calliope dies down
> and the strawberry festival of the blood
> romps wild against the tympanum
> and chokes the roundabout horses?
> What happens when the brass ring tarnishes
> and little kids waiting for the go
> that know neither conch shells or seagulls
> gasp on cotton candy?
> What's to be done when the silent knocker
> hollow and harsh and sticky with molasses
> comes hurdy-gurdying against half a head
> eclipsed in a candy-apple timepiece?
> And what do we do when the moon falls down
> and age scorches already scuffed-grass dreams
> and oceans spit up bloody spume,
> on the half-note stinging in our palms[10]

While there is no clear narrative in this free-verse poem, it does provide evidence that Bambara's acute listening ear, which was later defined as an important asset in her ability to capture black language in her writing, was well developed early on. This award-winning poem from Bambara captures an array of sounds and expresses musicality. There is also the gloom and defiance in this poem expressed through words and phrases like "bloody spume," "tarnishing brash rings," and even "the moon falls down," which reflects the urgent need the writer sees for change in the world.

Short stories submitted by Bambara for the award included an array of titles, including "A Dumb Show," "A Memory of War," "Twosome Blues," and "Sweet Town." There were also excerpts from a novel in progress, "The Star-Fetchers of Soul City."[11] A year earlier, Bambara had received the first Peter Pauper Press Award. As a prize, she had been invited to select 10 books from the "Collectors' Edition" donated by Mr. and Mrs. Peter Beilson of Pauper Press, a publisher that was known for the quality of printing and stellar graphic design.[12] Undoubtedly, these achievements would make Bambara among the first black writers to be recognized as a writer of distinction by Queens College.

In "Sweet Town," first published in 1959, the young adolescent narrator Kit is the first of many of Bambara's confident young girls who are in full voice at an early age to appear in her short stories. Bambara was only 20 when "Sweet Town" was published. In this story, Bambara attributes some of her mother's characteristics to the fictional rendering of Kit's mother. For example, Kit's mother is free-thinking and does not burden her daughter with mundane household chores. In "Sweet Town," Bambara describes how Kit's mother is the source of her daughter's outburst of laughter after reading a note where her mother assigns her with painting a nonexistent fire escape.[13]

"Sweet Town" also reflects Bambara's own interests when she creates a young character with a passion for cinema. Fifteen-year-old Kit even imagines running away to the west coast with her boyfriend B.J., who is "wearing his handsomeness like an article of clothing" in order to land a role in film.[14]

In 1960, the year after Bambara graduated from college, her story "Mississippi Ham Rider" was published in the newly established journal, *The Massachusetts Review*. Nine years later the story was also included in *Black & White in American Culture: An Anthology from the Massachusetts Review*, a volume dedicated to Martin Luther King.[15] Jules Chametzky, coeditor of the anthology, recalled years later that Bambara's Queens College teacher, Mary Curran, originally sent him Bambara's short story for possible publication in the literary journal.[16]

While "Sweet Town" makes no direct reference to the characters' racial identity, "Mississippi Ham Rider" is set in a black town with distinctly black characters and raises questions about equity. In it, a white businessman named Neil McLaulin travels South to lure a black blues singer, Ham Rider, into signing a contract that would require him to move to New York to make records. The writer has as the story's narrator a young black woman, Inez, who constantly writes in her notebooks and has composed liner notes for other blues singers.

Although it is decades later when Bambara pursues full-time work in making documentaries, her interest in film is long standing as frequent references to film in her short stories reveal. Similar to Kitt in "Sweet Town," Inez has film interests.[17] While Kitt in "Sweet Town" wants to be in movies, Inez in "Mississippi Ham Rider" wants to make documentaries. Inez imagines "Ole Ham Rider besieged by well-dressed coffee drinkers wanting his opinion on Miles Davis and Malcolm X" as demanding at least "a few feet of film."[18] Bambara also mentioned "Old Ham Rider" in the context of film when she wrote: "He was impressive, the way a good demolition site can be, the way horror movies from the thirties are now."[19] The author's frequent references to film provides readers with insights of the depth of her passion for cinema from an early age.

As publication of her short stories and poems indicate, Bambara enjoyed unusual success as a young black female writer on a predominantly white campus. Nevertheless, she carried a deep sense of nonfulfillment and alienation. In a retrospective essay 10 years later, the writer reflected on her college years as a time of disappointment. The experience, however, did not damper her determination to be free of boundaries and to live an unconventional life:

> I had dreamed of college for so long that even when it became a reality, it was still a dream that kept me dreaming. Like wanting to feed the rags and old iron horse when I was little. Even when the junk man finally decided to stop and get down and escort me to the wet nose and frothy teeth, even while the muzzle nosed into my hand and the jaws gripped the apple and the eyelids dropped in satisfaction, even when the junk cart was plopping up Amsterdam Avenue, I was still standing there with a hand empty, wet and glistening, dreaming about feeding Mr. Hawkins' ole horse. The dream kept me going through the requireds. And then they told me I had to pick a major. O.K. I wanted to major in ME. I had it all figured out—a year's apprenticeship with a yogi-fakir high priest type, a couple of courses in abnormal psychology, the complete core in anthro and philo, a sabbatical to a brain farm in Big Sur, a research course from Christ to Gurdieff, and for my mentor-counselor: a hypnotist (preferably an Aries or Leo type).[20]

Bambara's early reflections reveal how much her search for self-identity included exploration of various and sometimes unconventional lifestyles.

Once Bambara left Queens College, her peers were not surprised that she continued to frequent jazz clubs and write endlessly in her notebooks. What surprised them was her decision to marry Anthony Batten, an African American who also was a graduate of John Adams High School. Years earlier, Bambara's brother had suggested that they date. When they married, Batten's affinity for media arts was already established; his interests included photography, video, and film production. Batten also later hosted television and radio shows in New York. Married at the age of 20 on July 18, 1959, in a ceremony with all the traditional wedding trappings—a wedding gown, a cake—Bambara briefly stepped outside the downtown beat culture that espoused free love and appeared to be a picture of mainstream American values. But the marriage did not last. Just a year later, Bambara began divorce proceedings, but it would be another five years before the divorce case was heard and granted on the grounds of Batten's adultery.[21]

At the time Bambara graduated from Queens College, a commitment to community work and a need for a job led the young writer to apply for work at the Harlem Welfare Center. Bambara along with other young artists with college degrees were attracted to the salaries at the Harlem Welfare Center. With an undergraduate degree in literature, the young writer found few employment opportunities of interest outside of the job in social work. Bambara briefly worked as a social investigator there. The center's highly bureaucratic system required a major adjustment, but the afternoons of field work in Harlem allowed for some flexibility. It also provided a locale to meet new friends like Berny Horowitz and Paul Morrisey.[22] Morrisey's film work at Andy Warhol's studio was soon to be highly acclaimed. It is not surprising that Bambara would gravitate to conversations with Morrissey, who was beginning early efforts to break free of narrative in his experimental films of the early 1960s.

Later, while working at Metropolitan Hospital, Bambara became an advocate for community-based psychiatric services that recognized people in need of mental health treatment as deserving of services that also respected and recognized their talents. Bambara worked at the Metropolitan Hospital Psychiatric Division as a recreational and occupational therapist and later worked at the Colony House Community Center. Although committed to social work at the time, writing continued to be her passion. Years later, her friend Horowitz recalled no matter where Bambara worked, "She was writing all the time."[23]

Once free from marriage to Batten, Bambara finally saved up enough money to set out for Europe. While it was not unusual for young white students to escape the repressive American 1950s by trekking to Europe on freighters, or to fly there on the Irish airlines that offered economy fares, Bambara was likely a rarity: a young black female writer just out of college who ventured to Europe on a limited budget. While many black male fiction writers lived in Europe for extended periods of time in the 1940s and 1950s—James Baldwin and Ralph Ellison among them—the black women writers who came to the fore in the late 1960s don't appear to have sought a similar experience as a whole.

Horowitz, who met Bambara again later in Italy, recalled her interest in classical theater as well as her study of mime. "She was particularly interested in the works of Goldoni while in Europe," Horowitz remembered.[24] Carlo Goldoni, born in the early 1700s and master of Commedia Dell'arte, continues to be one of Italy's foremost playwrights. It makes sense that Bambara would gravitate toward the works of Goldoni, whose works were marked by humor and free of the religiosity of the period.

At one point while traveling in Rome, Bambara left a message for Chevigny, whom she had met at the home of Mary Curran, indicating that she was in Italy and could they meet. Bambara was living alone in a small room with blood-red wallpaper, which Chevigny recalled evoked "an overwhelming sense of doom."[25] Chevigny also remembered an image of two children praying desperately, which hung over the bed. "We laughed a lot about that," Chevigny said still laughing years later. What impressed Chevigny was that "Toni was well enough equipped to make a cup of tea."[26]

Chevigny recalled, "She offered me a cup of tea without realizing that she had put in salt [in the tea] rather than sugar; I gagged on it."[27] At a book signing nearly a decade later Bambara remembered the humorous moment as she signed her book of short stories to Chevigny: "Sorry 'bout dat salt in de tea."[28] In "The Survivor," published in Bambara's first collection of short stories, *Gorilla, My Love*, Bambara describes a character who adds salt rather than sugar to the coffee—perhaps a snippet of a memory from her time in Rome.

On the evening that Bambara met Chevigny in Italy, Chevigny was in Rome completing her dissertation. Chevigny was struck by Bambara's self-possession and spirit of adventure, traveling alone without a fixed plan. Bambara told her that one of the first things she did when entering a strange city was to visit its university and its zoo. "I thought it was a wonderful way to size up a new city in a foreign country," Chevigny reflected years later.[29] Chevigny also remembered Bambara reading her a story that she was writing about someone who was being forced to take shock treatment. Bambara did not know that one of Chevigny's family members had undergone shock treatment in the 1950s. Like many others at the time, Chevigny's family viewed shock treatment as a taboo subject and rarely discussed it. Chevigny said that being able to critique the medical profession made Bambara seem "a freer thinker than I had imagined anyone being on the subject."[30]

Travel to Europe also provided opportunities for the writer to study European forms of theater. Bambara enrolled at the Comedia dell Arte in Florence, as well as in the corporal mime classes that Etienne Decroux taught. Influenced by Japanese theater, Noh, Cambodian, and Chinese dance and sculpture, Decroux wanted mime to provide transformative experiences for students and used postures and movement in mime as a way to radiate the ethical and the spiritual.[31] Decroux encouraged his actors to use the mask as a prop, in ways resonant with the use of the masquerade in traditional cultures, in order to help the actor experience total possession. Hundreds of students have studied with Decroux including the internationally renowned Marcel Marceau. Corporal mime—which distinguishes itself from white-face mime—is based on capturing "the natural rhythms of all things that move, from trees in the wood to workmen at their labors, and he [Decroux] sought to make gestures as ordered and rigorous as the words of a poem."[32] Students of Decroux viewed him as a visionary who linked the past and present in order to move into the future, creating a "visible portrait of the invisible."[33] The focus of Decroux in linking the past to the present may have influenced Bambara's thinking on the significance of remembrance. It is not surprising that when the writer returned to New York, she enrolled in an Etienne Decroux School of Mime in Manhattan.[34]

But there were challenges when returning to America, beginning with finding a place to live. Just as it did for countless other black Americans who had forayed in Europe, returning home to the United States meant returning home to discrimination in all its systematic and personal guises. Bambara encountered discriminatory housing practices, such as the one that kept her from initially renting the apartment she wanted on Eighth Avenue. Art Goldberg, her Queens College friend, agreed to provide evidence to the civil rights office if the landlord indicated the apartment was available even though he had told Bambara it was rented; that become grounds for complaining about discriminatory practices.[35]

Bambara's commitment to writing was displayed again when she decided to pursue a Master's degree in Modern American Literature at the City College of New York. Having received A's in her last year of undergraduate school, in courses such as the 20th-century novel, the 18th-century novel, American literary texts, U.S. fiction, and U.S. poetry, Bambara had no difficulty being accepted into the program and received graduate credits for some of her undergraduate courses.[36] Upon completion of her studies in 1965, Bambara began teaching in the newly established pre-baccalaureate program at City College headed by Allen B. Ballard, an Associate Dean at City College at the time. That program soon became SEEK, the acronym for Search for Education, Empowerment, and Knowledge, at all branches of City College, the nation's first open admissions college program.

Years later, Ballard recalled how much Edmond Volpe, an American literature scholar who chaired the English Department at City College, respected Bambara. "She held a teaching appointment with the English Department and he told me to hire Toni to teach in the pre-baccalaureate program."[37] Volpe also recommended that Ballard appoint two other graduates from the Master's Program at City College, Barbara Smith and Addison Gayle, who also taught in the new program and remained friends with Bambara.[38]

When Bambara joined the faculty at CCNY, diversity was lacking, but that soon changed. As the SEEK program expanded, Bambara experienced a new sense of herself as a writer in the camaraderie of progressive writers who were activists, new cutting-edge feminists, and leading voices in the Black Arts Movement. Reflecting on the extent of her own transformation, Bambara wrote, "I observed that since becoming a teacher rather than a youth-developer, social worker or recreational therapist in hospitals, people around me, more often than not, were practicing writers. At CCNY, for example, were Addison Gayle, David Henderson, Wilfred Cartey, June Jordan, Audre Lorde, Lennox Raphael, Tom Poole, Larry Neale, John A. Williams and Adrienne Rich to mention a few."[39] Bambara already knew, for example, many of the writers that made their mark on the Lower East Side as part of the Umbra Poets and other emerging young black poets whose works were heard by Bambara and others in downtown bars and coffeehouses. After travel in Europe, Bambara was captured by the strong winds of social and political change coming out of the thundering Black Revolution of the 1960s.

In the new introduction to *Black Fire* (1968), the classic collection of African American writing that remains the key text in capturing the spirit of both the Black Power and Black Arts Movement, the book's coeditor Amiri Baraka wrote about the effect of Malcolm X's murder on the black community of artists. He explained that Malcolm's assassination sent many of the artists included in *Black Fire* "out of Greenwich Village & other similar integrated liberal party 'cool-out' zones up to Harlem & other black communities to take up what we felt now was our 'responsibility' in the Black Liberation Movement."[40]

Years later, Ballard recalled Bambara being a central and influential figure during the rapidly spreading militancy on campus at the time. Ballard said:

> Toni didn't back down for anything. That's just the way she was. She was just a very militant person. We had a lot of militancy on the campus, an approaching kind of storm so to speak. I think Toni fed that a little in the sense that when the students looked for direction they didn't come to me because I was kind of settled and I wanted them in the books all the time. Toni and Barbara [Smith] were different . . . a militant fringe of the faculty who students turned to. I think they looked to them as intellectual mentors.[41]

On campus, the activist scholar viewed the important protests raging there as an impetus for imagining ways to build a radical and holistic curriculum. Bambara's international experience and global perspective informed her thinking about how the curriculum of a new "Harlem University" would be shaped. On the one hand, Bambara suggested "root appreciation courses that tapped community resources as teachers like grandmothers, corner hard heads, restaurant cooks, and authors like Verta Mae Grosvenor who recently wrote *Vibration Cooking*."[42] Bambara also wanted to see classes in comparative studies of revolution using texts by Che Guevara and novels by Dostoevsky and Kipling. She even suggested a course in Ethics through Literature, which would include an examination of early Jewish, Arabic, Persian, Sanskrit, Hindu, Chinese, and Japanese writings, an example of Bambara's global quest. A nutrition course would show students how African staples were introduced to the Americas by enslaved Africans and would tap cooks from soul food restaurants as well as dieticians from southern and urban hospitals as field instructors. There was even a design for workshops on dance, where instructors in religious dance cults and other aspects of Old and New World African dance culture might include Sylvia Fort, Gregory Holder, Katherine Dunham, and Pearl Primus. In these workshops, instructors could develop lessons that demonstrated how one gesture of the body—such as the locked leg with the body pivoting around it—is paralleled in Nigerian, Haitian, and Brazilian dance.[43] Bambara wanted to create an academy that ignites intellectual and creative interconnections in order to generate new solutions to old political and social problems. Her childhood years in Harlem and later years working there as a social worker along with travel to Europe contributed to how Bambara—scholar, writer, dancer, actor—could have a unique vision of a university that would be located in Harlem.

At the same time, Bambara was writing. Bambara's essay on "Black Theater" was one of a few essays by women to appear in *Black Expression,* a groundbreaking collection of essays edited by Addison Gayle. Bambara was well equipped from her own study of theater, including her European travels, to raise thought-provoking and worldly questions in the midst of the Black Arts Movement. Bambara poses questions such as these: "Should the study of so-called Negro drama include African, West Indian and the minstrel past? Should an anthology make a distinction between white and black playwrights? And, what of all Negro casts in white shows? Negro scenes in white plays?"[44]

The writer's short stories were also reaching a growing readership. Her story "Hammer Man" was published in *Negro Digest* in 1966.[45] When Bambara's brother Walter Cade was interviewed in an *Amsterdam News* article about his own recent exhibition of abstract paintings on display in 27 stores along 125th Street, Cade, then working as a New York postman, mentioned his pride in this most recent publication of his sister's work.[46] "Hammer Man" was published at a time when outcries against police brutality were escalating in the aftermath of urban rebellions.

In "Hammer Man," a young female protagonist who owns a stickball and pitches pennies hangs out with boys in the neighborhood so often that Miss Rose, her adult friend in the community, keeps calling her by her brother's name. Known to get into fights with boys, this tough young girl keeps her distance from the young boy, Manny also known as "Hammer Man." The narrator of the story also refers to Manny as "Crazy Manny."[47] Nevertheless, when two white cops assault Manny physically and verbally, this adolescent boldly stands up against the authority figures in defense of Manny.[48] In this story published in the aftermath of the rebellions that swept the black community, Bambara captured community sentiments when the young narrator sees the police attack on Manny as an attack on her. And the young narrator speaks her mind in tune with the militancy of the period: "And crazy or no crazy, Manny was my brother at that moment and the cop was the enemy."[49]

In another early story, "Geraldine Moore the Poet," Bambara describes a different kind of assault. This time a young girl comes home from school and finds herself homeless with furniture and boxes outside of the building where she lived. The trauma makes it difficult for Geraldine to focus in school, until her teacher, Mrs. Scout, affirms the poetry in Geraldine's troubled life.

Geraldine tells her teacher that writing a poem was an impossibility:

I can't write a poem, Mrs. Scott, because nothing lovely's been happening in my life I haven't seen a flower since Mother's Day, and the sun don't even shine on my side of the street. No robins come sing on my window sill.
   Geraldine swallowed hard. She thought about saying that her father doesn't even come to visit any more, but changed her mind. "Just the rain comes," she went on, "and the bills come, and the men to move out our furniture. I'm sorry, but I can't write no pretty poem."[50]

"Geraldine Moore the Poet" is as much a cultural competency lesson for teachers on how to see the strengths and beauty in a challenged student's writing as it is an empowering story for young readers. Bambara's essay, "The Children Who Got Cheated," published in *Redbook* several years later provided multiple examples of how standard American education failed to recognize bias within standard school curriculum.[51]

By the mid-1960s, Bambara's penchant for influencing students and peers to be fearless in challenging the status quo was well established. Along with Bambara's commitment to supporting militant student protests at City College, Bambara remained in contact with former Queens College friends and classmates. Harry Keyishian, who mounted a different kind of challenge of university policies, remembered Bambara's influence as pivotal. In 1967, the State University of New York required faculty to sign loyalty oaths to disavow membership in the Communist Party as a condition of employment. When he was terminated for refusing to sign the loyalty oath, Keyishian's challenge of the policy on constitutional grounds as a First Amendment violation made its way to the United States Supreme Court.[52] In this important freedom of speech case, the Supreme Court ruled in favor of Keyishian. Decades later, Keyishian recalled Bambara's singular influence in his decision to appeal his case in the courts. "Frankly, Toni has to be credited with giving me the courage to stand up and fight," Keyishian said as his eyes watered.[53]

In the midst of teaching and influencing other activists to take political stands, Bambara began collecting work for the anthology that would bring her to the international spotlight: *The Black Woman*. The work emanated from Bambara's determination to collect papers, hold conversations, and reflect on her own experiences in order to fully expose and challenge sexist policies and behaviors within organizations that were part of the civil rights and black power movements at the time.[54]

In 1968, Bambara began collecting materials for what would become *The Black Woman*. Bambara believed addressing patriarchy could be destructive to a number of black organizations whose aggressive campaigns to address racism were necessary; therefore, she decided against publishing some of the information that she collected. But what Bambara did publish exposed in unprecedented ways the sexism that had previously been locked behind closed organizational doors.

Bambara's interest in reaching black women in all economic classes led her to seek that *The Black Woman* be priced by the publisher inexpensively so that all women could easily afford to buy it. For Bambara, it was important that the book not simply be read, but become a tool that sparked discussion groups and led to organizing among black women to address the concerns it voiced. The range of contributors to *The Black Woman* also reflected Bambara's sense that previous publication was not a prerequisite for inclusion in the project. Its featured writers included those who were known and those who were unknown. Now, writers that had not been included in some anthologies edited by black men were a part of a project that created its own black *female* fire. Writers included Audre Lorde, Paule Marshall, and Alice Walker. Contributors to the historic work included Bambara's students and peers from City College, as well as family members like her mother, Helen [Cade] Brehon, now remarried, and cousin, Carole Brown [Lewis]. In the preface, Bambara writes that some of the women in this anthology demand rights as blacks first and others as women first.[55] In a book that included a range of black women writers, Bambara saw the power in connecting cultural nationalist, feminist, and socialist ideologies.

Rather than simply pour political effort into rectifying and enlightening the powerbrokers who perpetuated racism, chauvinism, or imperialism in hegemonic society institutions, Bambara prioritized the work of self-liberation. In her important essay, "On the Issue of Roles" from *The Black Woman*, Bambara makes a call for women to deepen their processes of introspection. She suggests that only by turning attention and energy away from the external forces that aim to victimize black women and focusing on the strengths that lead to self-liberation can transformation occur.[56] This writer would continue to expand on this idea for the rest of her life, producing work whose aim was to create wholeness within self and the community. Bambara's belief in the power to create revolution within one's self also seems to be a search for transcendence.

In 1970, when *The Black Woman* was published, the preface extended a special word of thanks "to my man Gene."[57] On April 1, Bambara and her man Gene became the proud parents of their daughter, Karma. Gene Lewis, six years older than Bambara, was also a graduate of John Adams High School and had known Bambara and her family for several years before they reached their partnership agreement. Lewis, tall and striking, sometimes modeled, and his image occasionally appeared on New York City billboards. Lewis was also an actor and had a small role in the opening scene of the 1970s' film *Cotton Comes To Harlem*. The downtown black arts crowd that Bambara was a part of knew Gene from the years that he managed Pee Wee's, a popular gathering spot for "actors, writers, painters, sports buffs, reporters from TV networks, political screen and stage celebrities, good listeners, simple pimps second story men and the family of regulars," as Ishmael Reed later described the bar.[58] Located on Avenue A between 12th and 13th Street, Reed wrote that the bar also boasted the best jukebox south of Fourteenth Street.[59] At one point, Bambara and friends like Hattie Gossett, Verta Mae Grosvenor and Daisy Voigt were among the regulars who gathered at the popular bar and part of the sisterhood that others referred to as "The Johnson Girls," the title of one of Bambara's most popular short stories.[60]

The same year that Bambara began work on editing her groundbreaking collection of writings that became *The Black Woman*, Bambara received an invitation from Addison Gayle, by then critic and teacher at New York University to join Charles Russell, editor of *Black Onyx Magazine,* and Larry Neal, writer and a primary architect of the Black Arts Movement, as part of a CBS Black Heritage production TV show supported by Columbia University. The show received consultative support from Vincent Harding of the Institute of the Black World.

In the spirit of the cultural movement of the 1960s that emphasized black pride, the CBS stage setting for the show included African décor prints and African sculpture, and closed with African Congo drumming. The conversation focused on the relevance of the writings of Richard Wright, Ralph Ellison, and James Baldwin, all black male writers, in the age of the more militant writing of the 1960s, which was creating a new black consciousness.[61]

Bambara, wearing a fashionably short dress, appeared as a striking symbol of the times with her large afro. Frequently putting her slender hands into motion to accentuate her comments, Bambara showed her own intellectual prowess as she argued that all three of the black male writers being discussed shared an emphasis on dislocation, uprootedness, flight, migration, and movement. She pointed out that these same ideas were embodied in the folk consciousness as expressed in spirituals, that is, always going home, long way from home, looking for a chariot to carry us home.[62] This idea of "ancestral home and returning home"—"flying home" and "crossing over" also becomes an important theme in Bambara's own writing of transcendence and transformation.

In 1970, just before Karma was born, another transforming decision was made: to add Bambara to her surname. For her, the decision was an act of transformation. Years later, Bambara reflected, "The minute I said it I immediately inhabited it, felt very at home in the world. This was my name. It is not so unusual for an artist, a writer, to name themselves; they are forever constructing themselves, are forever inventing themselves. That's the nature of their spiritual practice."[63] At the same time Bambara chose a Hindu name, Karma, for her daughter, evidence of her continued search for spiritual interconnections.

In choosing the name Bambara—a name she said she'd first stumbled upon in her grandmother's scrapbook—Bambara was also connecting with the cosmology of the Bambara people of Mali. The religion of the Bambara people makes central the *nyiam,* spirit, as the connecting force which creates wholeness. The land of the Bambara people lies close to the equator and is often referred to as the bright country where wholeness is tangible: it is a place where time is viewed "as circular, not linear, always returning to that initial 'brightness' which creates the world."[64] The idea of creating wholeness will come to figure as a critical part of Bambara's own cosmology in the years that follow Bambara's decision to become Bambara. At the time Bambara also had a strong interest in the art of the Dogon and included readings on Dogon religious ideas in her black literature classes.[65]

The early 1970s was also the time that Bambara became regarded internationally as a significant writer. After publication of *The Black Woman* in 1970, Bambara edited *Tales and Stories for Black Folks.* Through this book, published in 1971, Bambara wanted to create a tool that encouraged the tradition of storytelling within the black family. Whenever writers employed Black English, Bambara wanted stories to not merely capture the rhythms and pronunciations of black voices, but to become "the written equivalent of the oral expression of Afro-centric behavior and outlook" and "to duplicate on the page

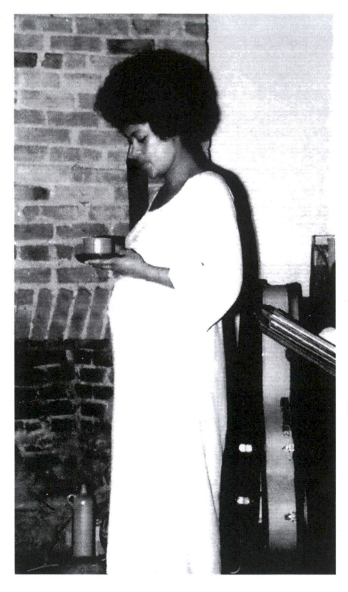

Bambara, pregnant, finds peace in a meditative moment in her
Harlem apartment, 1970. Courtesy of Karma Smith.

what ritual, magic, incantation, and getting happy do to the 'normal' state of
consciousness."[66]

At the beginning of her editing career in the book industry, Cheryl Chisholm,
then an assistant editor at Doubleday, remembered being assigned to work
with black writers already contracted with Doubleday such as Bambara, Alice

Childress, and Romare Bearden. Having recently returned from travel in Europe and a novice in book editing, Chisholm remembered her anxiety when she arranged a series of meetings with prominent black writers who were breaking new literary ground in the late '60s and early '70s. Meeting Bambara for the first time in an East Side Manhattan restaurant that was popular with publishing types, Chisholm vividly recalled the impression Bambara made with her shaved head, giant gold hoop earrings, and her skin tight mini-dress accentuated by spiked heel sandals.

"She did what I now recognize as her typical Toni thing of immediately taking me in and welcoming me as 'hey girl, where you been?' And, we were off and running. As a matter of fact her attitude towards me gave me the self-confidence and the self-possession to simply meet all the other authors without fear."[67]

In the process of editing *Tales for Black Folks*, Chisholm also recalled being blindsided by the structured racism she encountered at the publishing company because it did not occur to Chisholm that she needed to instruct the copy editor on the importance of honoring black language. Chisholm lamented, "It had never crossed my mind that I had to say to the copy editor, 'leave that alone.' This is literature. This is voice. It [the galleys] came back 'corrected' and I was just fit to be tied. Of course that meant they had to redo it. That meant double galleys which is expensive."[68]

In 1972, *Gorilla, My Love* comprised Bambara's short fiction from 1959 up until that point. It was edited by Toni Morrison, who had by then become a strong supporter of her work. At the time of *Gorilla, My Love*'s publication, *The Black Woman* was a bestseller. Morrison's *The Bluest Eye* was published the same year, joining the 1970s' renaissance of a new wave of black woman writers. When Morrison, then an editor at Random House, first read the short stories which became *Gorilla, My Love*, Morrison immediately recognized Bambara's genius.[69]

Years later, Morrison remembered meeting Bambara in her Random House office along with Bambara's then agent Hattie Gossett. Morrison recalled:

> They were interested in selling me *Gorilla, My Love*. By the way, it's everywhere you know, in textbooks, so lovely . . .
>
> From the beginning I knew we would be friends. I didn't know we would hang out, but the connection was an instant for me . . .
>
> I just found her serious. But, what I found mostly was that her writing was unbelievable to me—-so fresh, so pointed, so witty, so strong and also beautiful. There was no question ever in my mind about publishing anything she had written.[70]

Morrison continued, referring to her role as Bambara's lifetime editor, "Anyway I took it and did it—that one and the next one and the next one and the final one. . . . All of them, *Gorilla, My Love*, *The Salt Eaters*—all of those were titles that I put on her work. [Toni was] like me; I never have a good title. I was going to call [my later novel] *Paradise* [by the title of] *War* were it not for one of my editors," she laughed.[71]

Morrison described the manuscripts that Bambara submitted in such a way that it evoked the image of an abstract painting.

> When I say her manuscripts were a hoot, I meant that she typed them all out and then she would draw lines in red and green, pointing to changes. My assistant Eileen typed them and we would just pour over them and say 'what?' But she didn't revise the way other people do which is to re-type it. And then go back over it. Anyway, I found her manuscripts extraordinary.[72]

Morrison's commentary says a lot about her view of the aesthetic importance of Bambara's work.

In 1972, a week before Christmas, Gene Lewis hosted a gathering he termed a "Book Concert," to celebrate the publication of both *Gorilla, My Love* and poet Quincy Troupe's book *Embryo (1972)*. That night Bambara's story, "The Johnson Girls," was performed as a one-act play featuring Audreen Ballard, Barbara Carter, Hattie Gossett, Verta Mae Grosvenor, and Daisy Voight, who were also known to personify some of the Johnson Girls characteristics in real life. Cedar Walton, a renowned jazz pianist, was there with his trio at the Rafiki Restaurant on Bleecker Street for the late-night book party.[73]

Reviews regarding *Gorilla, My Love* were overwhelmingly positive. The critic in *The Saturday Review* wrote on September 18, 1972:

> These stories, fifteen in all by a young Black woman, are among the best portraits of a black life to have appeared in some time. Written in a breezy, engaging style that owes a good deal to street dialect, they are concerned primarily with children and manage to incorporate the virtues of such stories—zest and charm—yet avoid most of the sentimental pitfalls. Moreover they have resonance: their anger is a knife slicing through the entertainment, and it continues to cut when the stories are over.[74]

Bell Gale Chevigny hailed the characters in *Gorilla, My Love*, mostly adolescents and older females, who demonstrate tenderness and subtle invention. Chevigny wrote: "The stories are often sketchy as to plot, but always lavish in their strokes—there are elaborate illustrations, soaring asides, aggressive sub-plots. They are never didactic but they abound in far-out common sense, exotic home truths in life."[75] Chevigny, who had taught ex-offenders on parole in the Queens College SEEK program, found Bambara's characters to be cool and tough in proudly claiming their own authority. Chevigny was disappointed, however, that "the editor [Bambara] who challenged stereotypic sex roles in *The Black Woman* did not include more stories on black male-female relationships."[76]

Interestingly, when Bambara began teaching classes at Livingston College, Rutgers University, in its summer program, George Levine, the English Department Chair, did not know of Bambara's reputation as a serious writer. Levine valued Bambara's track record as teacher of first-generation college students. Bambara left City College to teach at Livingston in 1969 where she was offered an Assistant Professor position. Now Bambara continued her creative teaching approaches at Livingston, assigning students with field work in Harlem, the viewing of third-world films, the interviewing of elders, and the rewriting of European fairy tales to make them of greater interest to young black children.

While at Livingston College, Bambara deepened her understanding of African cosmology. In the 1960s, members of the Black Arts Movement were eager to move away from a strict adherence to the Leftist/Marxist wholesale discrediting of spirituality. By the 1970s, African-based religious practices such as those of the Yoruba were being adopted by African Americans interested in cultural ties that were non-Western. At Livingston as elsewhere, Bambara was never a public devotee to any political group or religious organization. Bambara's writings questioned allegiance to monotheism. Bambara appreciated multiple intellectual and spiritual emersions. Her search was to find the interconnections.

At Livingston College, Bambara met Jan Douglass, a dean at the newly opened college, who years later recalled how they immediately bonded as friends. As activist scholars, both Bambara and Douglass reached out to an array of student organizations that aimed to sustain open admissions policies, increase student and faculty diversity, and expand the curriculum to include more courses in African and Third World Studies. Douglass remembered the intensity of the times at the end of the 1960s. In 1972, Livingston College made headlines that reported stolen FBI files that confirmed FBI investigations of students alleged to be involved with participation in the Revolutionary Peoples Constitutional Convention organized by the Black Panther Party.[77]

About this time of intense student activism and uprisings in the neighboring black community in New Brunswick, Douglass recalled: "There were a lot of struggles. It was a crazy time. I remember the night I drove into town to bail out of jail a group of black students who had been scooped up by police because there were riots going on in the town."[78] Douglass remembered that while driving her car she was seeing things she never saw before. "Animals were jumping out of the woods. I did not know what was causing the disturbance. I didn't know who it was . . . the F.B.I. or whatever. . . . It was during the summer program and we arranged for everybody to go home. A student safety patrol found a basement room with cigarettes still smoking and police papers."[79]

Douglass recalled how critical Bambara's role and the role of her partner, Gene Lewis, had been in convincing the black students to seek safety away from the campus. "I remember Toni told Gene to come in to tell the kids to be careful because the police are surrounding the campus. And they listened to him."[80]

Reflecting on how Bambara immediately reached out to Lewis for assistance in their effort to protect the students on campus and how quickly Lewis responded in coming over from New York to Piscataway as soon as he received Bambara's call, Douglass added, "I do feel that she [Bambara] really loved him and that went on for a long long time—he was always available."[81]

In the midst of allegations surrounding the student crisis on campus, Bambara continued to be an advisor to black student groups and as she had at City College previously, Bambara won the respect of both students and faculty. In 1973, just before leaving Livingston, Bambara was unanimously elected Speaker of the Faculty Chamber. Calling Bambara "a person of distinction," the chamber voted confidence in Bambara's ability "to preserve those aspects of Livingston that ensure its multi-racial, multi-cultural quality."[82]

Earlier that same year, Bambara had received another letter that she surely treasured. Gwendolyn Brooks wrote to her from The Plaza on Fifth Avenue to let her know how pleased she was with Bambara's review of her most recent book of poetry, *Report From Part I*. In the letter, Brooks referred to Bambara as her "dear remarkable rich-minded golden-penned Toni."[83]

This chapter of Bambara's life ends with a trip to Cuba in the summer of 1973. The journey yielded important insights for Bambara, as she questioned the relevance of her own writing as an effective way to be involved in political struggle. Bambara traveled to Cuba with Robert Cole, Hattie Gossett, Barbara Webb, and Suzanne Ross. Ross, who remembered Bambara standing on her head, particularly when plagued with a headache, also recalled the black members of the delegation meetings with Afro Cubans. Ross believes that the feedback that came after Hattie Gossett's distribution of *The Black Woman* to Cubans helped Bambara to make links in her own mind about the relevance of her writing to political struggle.[84]

Bambara's literary and aesthetic interests were also fed on the mission. The itinerary included three days of meeting with the film institute, Instituto Cuban de Arte e Industria (ICAIC), where they watched *Lucia*. The film, directed by Huberto Solas in 1969, includes a focus on a Cuban woman entering the workforce after the revolution.[85] Bambara was also the center of lively debates about how the Club Tropicana was an anachronism that failed to promote revolution, with its floor shows of female dancers. Bambara was a part of discussions about alternative views on how the revolution opened the door for working-class people to enjoy the entertainment at a club that previously was restricted to an economically privileged class. In Cuba, as she did elsewhere, Bambara danced as Ross described in her memories of their nights at the Tropicana "wearing a delicate, short, black sundress, with small heeled black sandals. She had a very sensual and joyful side to her that she could thoroughly indulge."[86]

As her time in Cuba demonstrates, Bambara's life was a creative effort. Many who knew Bambara throughout her life testified to the joy she found in self-invention, a joy which was seamless with her work as a storyteller.

When she returned to New York from Cuba, Bambara returned to her flying-trapeze classes. Perhaps, it was the back-to-back book celebrations— three books in three years—or her new motherhood that had first prompted Bambara to take up the flying trapeze. Years ago, however, as an undergraduate

Queens College student, Bambara had written an unpublished short story about a young girl who studied flying-trapeze performances, and the girl's application of what she learned from these performers to her own life. At one point, in the story entitled "Dumb Show," the young protagonist says, "I had memorized through the years of trapeze watching, clowns, acrobats, each turn, each trick, each calculated slip, each spin that brought a gasp, each drop, near fall that held the heart until the point of bursting then released it, let it breathe again as they jumped from the rope ladder into the sawdust and bowed."[87]

Now Bambara was taking trapeze lessons at the Nicholas Kounofsky gym in New York. Like the character in "Dumb Show," the writer was flying perhaps inspired by the African flying myth that later appeared in one of her short stories or maybe because Bambara found this place of exercise ideal for contemplating her next move.

NOTES

1. Toni Cade Bambara, "On the Issues of Roles," in *The Black Woman* (New York: Washington Square Press, 1970), 123.

2. Claudia Tate (ed.), *Black Women Writers at Work* (New York: Continuum International Publishing Group, 1983), 14.

3. Toni Cade Bambara, "Working at It in Four Parts," Spelman Archives, Atlanta.

4. Anthony Heilbut, Interview by author, June 2011.

5. Art Goldberg, Interview by author, March 2012.

6. Louis Massiah, "How She Came by Her Name," in *Deep Sightings and Rescue Missions* (New York: Pantheon Books, 1991), 222.

7. Bell Gale Chevigny, Interview by author, March 2012.

8. Mary Doyle Curran, *The Parish and The Hill* (New York: The Feminist Press, 1986), 51–52. Originally published Boston: Houghton-Mifflin, 1948.

9. Toni Cade Bambara, John Golden Award Portfolio, Queens College Archives, New York.

10. Ibid.

11. Ibid.

12. George B. Parks, Letter to Miss Miltona Cade, May 21, 1958, Spelman Archives, Atlanta.

13. Ibid., 121.

14. Toni Cade Bambara, "Sweet Town," in *Gorilla, My Love* (New York: Vintage Books, 1972), 122.

15. Toni Cade Bambara, "Mississippi Ham Rider" in *Black and White in American Culture* (The University of Massachusetts Press, 1969), 218.

16. Jules Chametzky, Interview by author, April 2012.

17. Toni Cade Bambara, "Mississippi Ham Rider," in *Gorilla, My Love* (New York: Vintage Books, 1972), 54.

18. Ibid., 54.

19. Ibid., 56.

20. Toni Cade, "Something in the Wind," *The Paper,* City College of New York, April 25, 1968.

21. Interlocutory Judgment of Divorce, November 10, 1966, Spelman Archives, Atlanta.

22. Berny Horowitz, Interview by author, May 2012.

23. Ibid.

24. Ibid.

25. Bell Gale Chevigny, Interview by author, March 2012.

26. Ibid.

27. Ibid.

28. Ibid.

29. Ibid.

30. Ibid.

31. Thomas Leabhart, *Etienne Decroux (Routledge Performance Practitioners)* (London: T & F Books UK, 2009), 50.

32. Jack Anderson, "Etienne Decroux Is Dead at 92; Master of Modern French Mine," *The New York Times,* March 21, 1991.

33. Corrine Soum, *A Little History of a Great Transmission or Simplon's Tunnel* (London: Theater de L'Ange Fou & International School of Corporeal Mime, 1999), http://www.angefou.co.uk/published-work/simplons-tunnel.html.

34. Horowitz, Interview by author.

35. Goldberg, Interview by author.

36. Toni Cade Bambara, College Transcript, Spelman Archives, Atlanta.

37. Allen Ballard, Interview by author, April 16, 2008.

38. Ibid.

39. Toni Cade Bambara, "Working at It," Spelman Archives, Atlanta.

40. Amiri Baraka, "A New Introduction," in *Black Fire: An Anthology of Afro-American Writing*, edited by LeRoi Jones (Amiri Baraka) and Larry Neal (Baltimore: Black Classic Press, 2007), xvii–xx.

41. Ballard, Interview by author.

42. Toni Cade, "Realizing the Dream of a Black University," *Observation Post,* February 14, 1969.

43. Ibid.

44. Toni Cade, "Black Theater," in *Black Expression: Essays by and About Black America in the Creative Arts,* ed. Addison Gayle, Jr. (New York: Weybright and Tally, 1969).

45. Toni Cade Bambara, "Copyright Page," in *Gorilla, My Love* (New York: Vintage Books, 1972).

46. "Mailman Leaves Art Exhibit on Route," *New York Amsterdam News,* April 2, 1966.

47. Toni Cade Bambara, "Hammer Man," in *Gorilla, My Love* (New York: Vintage Books, 1972), 36.

48. Ibid., 40.

49. Ibid.

50. Toni Cade, "Geraldine Moore the Poet," in *Something Else,* ed. Leo B. Kneer (Scott Foresman and Co. 1970), 42.

51. Toni Cade Bambara, "The Children Who Got Cheated," *Redbook,* January 1970.

52. Harry Keyishian, Interview by author, April 2008.

53. Ibid.

54. Toni Cade Bambara, *The Black Woman* (New York: Washington Square Press, 1970), 1–7.

55. Ibid., 5.

56. Ibid., 123.

57. Bambara, *The Black Woman,* 7.

58. Ishmael Reed, "Pee Wee's Wreath," *The New York Times,* December 16, 1976.

59. Ibid.

60. Welton Smith, Interview by author, July 2000.

61. *Black Heritage: A History of Afro-Americans, Three Black Writers,* produced by Larry Neal, WCBS-TV, 1969. The Schomburg Center for Research in Black Culture, New York.

62. Ibid.

63. Toni Cade Bambara, "How She Came by Her Name," in *Deep Sightings and Rescue Missions* (New York: Vintage Books, 1996), 206.

64. Manthia Diawara, "Yeelen: Brightness," in *California Newsreel Catalogue* (San Francisco, California).

65. At Livingston College, Bambara's reading list for her black literature course included Marcel Griaule, *Conversations with Ogolemmeli: An Introduction to Dogon Religious Ideas* (London: Oxford University Press, 1965).

66. Toni Cade Bambara, "Black English," *The New York Times,* September 3, 1972.

67. Cheryl Chisholm, Interview by author, October, 2012.

68. Ibid.

69. Toni Morrison, Interview by author, March 2012.

70. Ibid.

71. Ibid.

72. Ibid.

73. "Gene Lewis Presents a Book," Poster. Courtesy of Hattie Gossett.

74. "Review of *Gorilla, My Love,*" *The Saturday Review,* April 18, 1972.

75. Bell Gale Chevigny, "Stories of Solidarity and Selfhood," *The Village Voice,* April 12, 1973.

76. Ibid.

77. *The Medium, Livingston College Newspaper,* April 8, 1971.

78. Jan Douglass, Interview by author, September 2010.

79. Ibid.

80. Ibid.

81. Ibid.

82. Hilda Hidalgo, Letter to Toni Cade Bambara, May 4, 1973, Spelman Archives, Atlanta.

83. Gwendolyn Brooks, Letter to Toni Cade Bambara, January 14, 1973, Spelman Archives, Atlanta.

84. Susan Ross, Interview by author, 2006.

85. Ibid.

86. Ibid.

87. John Golden Award Portfolio, Queens College Archives, Queens, New York.

FOUR

Cultural Worker on Southern Ground

> Suffice to say that I do not take lightly the fact that I am on the earth at this particular time in human history, and am here as a member of a particular soul group and of a particular sex, having this particular adventure as a Pan-Africanist-socialist-feminist in the United States.[1]

Despite the presence of strong student movements and progressive faculty leadership at Livingston College (Rutgers University), by 1974, Bambara's dream of transforming mainstream educational institutions into radical universities was fading. The cluster of Third World writers, faculty, and administrators that Bambara joined forces with at Livingston College included Nikki Giovanni, Sonia Sanchez, Hattie Gossett, Barbara Masekela, Pepsi Charles, Miguel Algarin, A.B. Spelman, Jan Carew, and Jan Douglass. Yet even this cadre faced inevitable cutbacks in Third World and Black Studies courses, and the implementation of stricter admissions policies that disproportionately shut out black and other students of color.

So, with the knowledge that she had a significant influence on students at both Livingston and City College in the years she had been teaching, Bambara would soon join a wave of others to become part of the reverse migration South that fed a bourgeoning southern Black Arts Movement. Once deciding to move to Atlanta, Bambara looked forward to developing ties with the historically black colleges that she hoped would provide greater possibilities for change. Bambara was disappointed to learn that some historically black colleges were less likely to reflect the ideas of the Black Arts and Black Power movements or the rising black feminist movement than some predominantly white institutions of higher learning. As a result, the writer and activist increasingly made the community much more than the campus her base for cultural work.

Bambara finalized her plans to move from New York to Atlanta in the mid-1970s. Now, Bambara recognized that there wasn't much more that she or any other member of the faculty could do to increase the likelihood that Livingston College would survive as a radical institution for social justice and change, so long as it remained part of the state-funded Rutgers University system.

Until her last days at Livingston, however, Bambara was a trusted advisor and mentor for countless Livingston students. As an advisor, Bambara created equitable faculty-student relationships, dynamics that she felt contributed to her own development as a teacher, person, writer, and mother as much as they nurtured her students.[2] Bambara sought to awaken students to an awareness of their own culture through Black Studies and to their own political power. In leaving Livingston after five years, Bambara knew she had influenced a cadre of students, who would continue their activism and cultural work once returning to their communities. Bambara had come to recognize her influence on students, sharpening their abilities to see their own gifts.

While at Livingston, Bambara had been accessible. She shared endless contacts, freely mined from her thick address book, to help students find jobs and resources. Her boundless imagination led her to create spaces that encouraged collaboration rather than competition among students. Her one-on-one conversations and group discussions included technical assistance and her classroom assignments addressed strengthening racial identity and pride.[3]

Now, Bambara was seeking a new environment for doing similar work. In addition to the opportunities that the South might provide in expanding her cultural work, Bambara had personal reasons for considering a move to Atlanta: Bambara also was seeking a safe and nurturing environment for Karma to freely play and grow up in. At one point, Bambara considered moving to New Jersey to purchase a home with other Livingston colleagues, in order to avoid the commute that added to long hours away from home and her daughter.[4] As Karma grew older, Bambara wanted her daughter to grow up in a place where she could walk the streets without stumbling over the drug paraphernalia that littered her Spanish Harlem neighborhood. Moving to Atlanta, where her mother had lived, presented itself as a possible alternative to living in New York.

In the 1970s, Atlanta attracted a new wave of writers, artists, musicians, and choreographers, as well as political activists who were still proud to call themselves black revolutionaries even after others who had once challenged American norms now turned their attention to their careers and involved themselves with mainstream politics. Unlike some of the nation's northern urban centers, burned out by riots and troubled leadership from cultural nationalist groups, a sense of optimism flourished in Atlanta as the growing reverse migration of African Americans to the South peaked. Atlanta's drawing cards included outgrowths of its historical black business community, affectionately known as "Sweet Auburn," a developing movement among black farmers to reclaim previously black-owned land, and the several historically black colleges that made Atlanta a black academic mecca in the eyes of many.

In 1974, Bambara was eyeing Atlanta just as its own Maynard Jackson Jr., became the nation's first African American mayor of a southern city. It was less than a decade after the passage of the Voters' Rights Bill and the same year President Nixon faced impeachment. Ten years earlier Jackson's mother, Irene Dobbs Jackson, had shown backbone as she demanded a library card and became the first black to desegregate Atlanta's public libraries.[5] While Maynard Jackson's most recognized first-term successes are often touted as rebuilding the Atlanta airport to make it the nation's largest, creating a new metro system, and designing a strong affirmative action program, the mayor's support for the arts also contributed significantly to bringing new life to Atlanta. Maynard's aunt, Mattiwilda Dobbs-Janzon (nicknamed Geekie), was an early trailblazer in operatic roles for black women worldwide, joining singers such as Marian Anderson in accomplishing distinguished firsts. Traveling from Europe, Dobbs-Janzon sang "He's Got the Whole World in His Hands" before an audience of 5,000 at Jackson's historic inauguration.[6]

In moving to Atlanta, Bambara—who, at 35, was the same age as the city's new mayor—hoped for personal renewal through increased time and space for her own writing. Bambara contacted friends in Atlanta, made appointments with astrologists, and made several exploratory trips to Atlanta before making a final decision to move there. While she had been pondering a move South for some time, the final moment of reckoning came when her friend Jan Douglass told Bambara that parking rates at a downtown lot near Macy's were $3 a day, a fraction of the standard $25 in New York. In the midst of reels of laughter, Bambara made the unexpected pronouncement, "Aha, I think this is going to work."[7]

In the long run, the former New Yorker depended less on cheap parking and more on the city's easy access to an international airport for quick and frequent getaways to make Atlanta a livable home base. Friends in New York, however, viewed Bambara's decision differently: How could she be leaving New York? Was she simply acting on impulse? Did she even have a job? About her friends' concerns, Bambara wrote: "In 1974, I resigned from a tenured professorship at Rutgers, side-stepped friends ready to commit me, packed up the kid and the household goods and moved to Atlanta to sit down. I sat. I wrote."[8]

Once making the decision to move South, Bambara knew that January 1, 1974, might be her last New Year's Day in New York for some time to come. She was reminded by a letter from Mary McDonald, another former Livingston College colleague, that her work already had an audience in the South. From McDonald's letter, Bambara learned of an artistic tribute to her there. McDonald explained that in an original theatrical production, young children dramatized two of the politically infused children's stories that Bambara's former Livingston students published in *Tales and Stories for Black Folks*

(1971).[9] As she had done with the work collected in *The Black Woman,* Bambara invited some of her undergraduate students to write for the anthology, thus providing an unusual opportunity for previously unpublished writers to appear in a book with authors such as Langston Hughes, Albert Murray, and Alice Walker. Developing vehicles for young writers and artists to be published remained a life-long mission for Bambara. As a teacher, Bambara wanted homework assignments to have real-life applications. In rewriting children's fairy tales, students were instructed to develop plans for bringing the stories to schools, day-care centers, libraries, churches, and other neighborhood centers. In *Tales for Black Folks,* Bambara reminded readers of the "great kitchen tradition" of storytelling that must be remembered.[10] The book is dedicated to family "and especially to our Young."[11] The book includes "The True Story of Chicken Licken," rewritten to describe Chicken Licken leading a march of animal farm mates to protest a policeman's bully club hitting her over the head—"the sky falling" as an erroneous police department alert claimed.[12] Another story turns "Billy Goats Gruff" into "Billy Goat's Turf," where collard greens bloom and the goats are victorious over the pig who tries to block their access to beloved collard greens.[13] One of Bambara's most popular short stories, "Raymond's Run," was first anthologized in *Tales and Stories for Black Folks.* "The children just love that book! When are you going to write some more stories for Black children?" McDonald asked in her New Year's Day letter to Bambara.[14]

That January, Bambara also learned about the continuing success of another one of her books, *Gorilla, My Love.* In a letter dated January 9, 1974, Bambara received positive news from her editor, Toni Morrison. Morrison wrote that *Gorilla, My Love* was to be reprinted and that similar to her own recently published work, *The Black Book, Gorilla, My Love* "is another thing living on beyond the four months the publishers allot to book life."

By the time Bambara visited Atlanta a few months later on her birthday—Monday, March 25th—the possibility of a move there was becoming a far more concrete idea. On this visit she and long-time associate Addison Gayle, who was then teaching English at Barnard College, delivered the keynotes at the 10 A.M. opening session of the "Fifth Annual Writers' Workshop/Conference" sponsored by the Ford Foundation and the English Department at Clark College.[15] As a presenter, Bambara joined panelists John Oliver Killens, who was then teaching at Howard University, and Sam Greenlee, whose highly acclaimed novel, *The Spook Who Sat by the Door,* was receiving critical attention as a newly released film. It was likely because of her long-standing interest in cinema that Bambara attended Greenlee's presentation, where he urged the Delta Sigma Theta Sorority to consider investing in the development of more black films. In her own talk and in workshops with younger students at the conference, Bambara asked conference participants to engage in writing as a way to promote new ideas and to create change.[16]

By the end of the spring, Bambara began reaching out to friends to see who might have an interest in her Spanish Harlem apartment. In a telephone call to her friend Valerie Maynard, artist, educator, and writer, Bambara or she asked Maynard about moving into her place on 124th Street between 2nd and 3rd Avenue. Although Bambara's question prompted some curiosity, Maynard, then a young and unknown artist, remembered telling Bambara that she could not afford it.[17]

When Sekou Sundiata, a poet who met Bambara when he was a student at City College, eventually moved into Bambara's spacious apartment, with its sliding doors, space for an office, outdoor garden with a greenhouse, and patio large enough for parties, he wondered who could have lived there before him. Unable to transport all of her belongings, Bambara had left behind floor to ceiling bookcases filled with books, enough to make a library. It was only when Sundiata began receiving countless pieces of mail addressed to Bambara that he realized that his former teacher lived there.[18]

While Bambara did not make time to fill out the postal forms to guarantee mail delivery, that summer she lovingly wrote her four-year-old daughter, Karma, who was staying with Bambara's mother in New York, humorous and thoughtful updates on postcards that a young reader could enjoy. In July 1974, on the back of a postcard from the Grant Park Zoo, Bambara or she wrote, "I will wait for you to come so we can look for a rabbit."[19] In another postcard, Bambara scribbled to Karma the following greeting on a postcard with Chaplin on a bicycle, with an apparent reference to Bambara's mother joining them in the move to Atlanta:

> Dear Karma, See the MONKEY ON THE BICYCLE? When you all come to Atlanta we will go to the zoo. I have seen lots of nice houses and yards . . . we will soon have a new home.[20]

Another time she wrote to Karma, "Do you want to plant flowers in our yard? I think that would be nice . . . see you soon."[21] The postcards pointed to early signs that Bambara saw an array of new possibilities for herself and her daughter in a move to the South.

According to Douglass: "We finally found a house that she liked. It wasn't very far from campus." The house, a modest compact one-family home, stood slightly elevated on hill with a small front lawn and adequate yard space for a garden.[22] The writer's new Mayflower Street home in Southwest Atlanta circled off of Cascade Avenue, which connected with streets leading to the Spelman, Clark, and Atlanta University campuses and was a short distance from where Douglass lived on Ozone Street. In New York, Bambara's primary social and work activities stretched across two states, New Jersey and New York, but in Atlanta, Bambara quickly settled into a neighborhood. There, she could easily visit with old friends, and she could meet up with new acquaintances like Susan Ross, a graduate student who was then working at the Institute of the Black World (IBW), the nation's leading progressive black think tank known for its publications, films, and conferences. Vincent Harding, former chair of Spelman's Department of History and Sociology, his wife Rose Marie, and a mix of other young professionals and academics also lived in the neighborhood. It had recently been transformed into a black community as a result of the white flight out of Atlanta in the previous decade.

But even in the midst of transition, Bambara sustained her commitment to activism. In the hot summer months during which she made her plans to move to Atlanta, Bambara flew to Alderson Prison, a minimum-security federal prison for women located in the Alleghany Mountains of West Virginia, 270 miles southwest of Washington, DC. There she would conduct writing workshops, lead discussions on her edited volume, *The Black Woman*, organize workshops among black and white inmates about black history and the black struggle in the United States, and link inmates to resources.[23] Known for housing celebrity inmates such as Billie Holiday,[24] Alderson Prison took the unusual step of establishing a creative writing contest and award in the name of Toni Cade Bambara, a radical activist. Also during that summer, as she prepared for the move south, Bambara made time to enjoy the jazz gigs in Manhattan that would be less accessible in Atlanta, and even to lecture, but she was disappointed that her schedule did not allow a return to Alderson Prison to present the Bambara Award. When Bambara frantically called to ask her friend and Black Arts Movement poet Sonia Sanchez to fill in for her, Sanchez immediately agreed to present the Bambara Award on her behalf.

Sanchez recalled the harsh conditions and maltreatment the women—many of them political activists—endured at the prison. "I flew in on a little plane and did a reading and talked with the women, but I was never invited back. I remember feeling that as we held hands in a circle at the end, there was a light there that they would be able to hold on to," Sanchez said.[25]

That year, the Bambara Award recipient, Estella Harris (later, Akua Kamau-Harris) wasn't at Alderson either, because she had just been transferred to an inmate facility in Kentucky as punishment for organizing a strike among female inmates to demand respect for their dietary choices—a protest that Bambara surely applauded.[26]

Missing Bambara's presence at Alderson, Kamau-Harris addressed a letter to Bambara to let her know how much Bambara's work with children and others in the community lifted her own despair. Kamau-Harris wrote, "I want to be able to make people move inside and out to the beauty of themselves as you do."[27] Bambara promised to ship the inmates a box of books, including copies of her own book, *Gorilla, My Love*.

Once relocating to Atlanta, Bambara invited Kamau-Harris to live with her and her daughter as Kamau-Harris searched for permanent housing for herself and her five children. "I couldn't believe I was just out of prison and living in the home of one of America's most important writers. She told me I could stay as long as I needed, but she drew the line when it came to taking in my five children even on a temporary basis," Kamau-Harris remembered with laughter years later.[28]

Several months later, Bambara also helped Kamau-Harris find employment as the teacher for a writing class for young children at Atlanta's newly opened Neighborhood Arts Center (NAC). When Kamau-Harris expressed doubt about her abilities to transition into the role of a writer and teacher at the

NAC, where widely known artists would be among her peers, Bambara confidently told Kamau-Harris, "You are a writer and a mother. That is all that is needed. You'll be fine."[29] Decades later, Kamau-Harris, who had become her close friend, continued to view Bambara's expression of confidence in her creative writing skills as a critical turning point in her life.

Bambara's residence immediately became a hub of activity. One weekend afternoon, associates from IBW, which Harding had previously headed, dropped by to welcome Bambara to her new community and to assist her in unpacking her truckload of boxes.[30] Howard Dodson—then director of IBW—and Jualynne Dodson, then a University California Berkeley graduate student working at IBW, joined others in helping Bambara unpack. Jualynne Dodson remembered walking into Bambara's house for the first time and immediately noticing the creative and the unusual purple-tiled kitchen floor. "I had never seen a floor that was purple in my whole life,"[31] Dodson laughed.

While the colorful twists of creativity were unusual, far more surprising to Dodson was Bambara's conversation. If Dodson had met some of Bambara's Livingston students or her prison inmate mentees, she might have been forewarned of the kind of probing questions Bambara soon interjected into her conversation:

> "So Jualynne, what are you going to do with your life?"
> "I beg your pardon? Did you just ask me what am I going to do with the rest of my life? WOW! I need to think about that!"
> "What about travel?" Bambara asked with an easy smile, comfortable filling in the prolonged silence that followed.[32]

"I had studied Spanish," Jualynne Dodson remembered, "but it was no longer with me. There was nothing in the trajectory of my life that was leading me to where I am now. At this point in time, I tend to be categorized as an African American sociologist who works in the arenas of the religion and culture of African descendants, particularly in the Spanish-speaking Americas. Bambara asked me the question and it pushed me to articulate something that I was not cognitive or conscious of prior to that point. In my fashion, I would say that Bambara was spiritually sent to me so that I would have to say what I did in order to make the work a real piece of my life. In other words, there was an ancestral or spiritual intervention that happened so that I could begin to see and take hold of the work I was to do; and that was to work inside the Spanish speaking Americas among African descendants."[33] Similar to others, Dodson's initial conversation with Bambara had an immediate impact and continues to inspire her scholarly and cultural work on religion and cultural traditions across the African diaspora nearly four decades later.[34]

Cheryl Chisholm, Bambara's former editor at Doubleday/Random House, remembered that Bambara offered her an influence of a different kind during a time of personal crisis.[35] Two years before Bambara's move South, Chisholm had moved to Atlanta from New York with her husband Charles Hobson, who organized the new mass communications department at Clark College. Although she was initially immersed in the whirlwind of social and political events swirling around the Jackson mayoral election, Chisholm, now the mother of a newborn, found herself withdrawing from Atlanta's bourgeoning social networks and becoming increasingly isolated. Chisholm was surprised to see an orange Volkswagen pulling into her driveway one day, breaking through the gloom.

Puzzled, Chisholm continued staring out the window and noticed Bambara jumping out her car and barging through her front door.

> "I've been wondering where the hell are you?" Bambara said without any formal greeting. "Why are you sitting in this house?"
> "I just had a baby."
> "Well, I had a baby too. What is going on?"[36]

More than 35 years later, Chisholm recalled the visit as "a little window opening—air, sunshine. Because I was so depressed I felt the light walk in when she came in."[37] In retrospect, Chisholm would view Bambara's visit and the conversations that followed as the beginning of an acceptance of her own calling to shift her career focus to work in film. Chisholm soon moved to Washington, DC, where she worked as a senior editor for Howard University Press and participated in what Chisholm remembered as a life-changing study group led by filmmaker Haile Gerima. Chisholm said that Gerima and Bambara both displayed a gift in successfully gathering people with similar interests and talents to study and work.

Years later, Bambara explained in an interview that she had observed her mother's interactions in similar "just do it" conversations with friends. She learned her mother's tactics, and was later able to use them to encourage ranks of cultural workers and activists—some in the early stages of identifying their life's work, others burned out from years of activism—to remember their passions and to act on their dreams. Bambara said that her mother, who she depicted as a "manger of intellectual resources," would ask of countless people, "What's the plan? And, folks would deliver it up."[38]

In Atlanta, as elsewhere, Bambara was free of formal ties to any one cultural, nationalist, Pan Africanist, Marxist Leninist, civil rights, or church group. As a result, she could easily move inside and outside the boundaries of various political camps raising questions, presenting ideas, and encouraging the work of a diverse group of artists and activists, mentoring in creative ways. Her home in Atlanta was a place where the writer and organizer connected individuals, the well-known and unknown, and created loosely formed networks. In her frequent salon-like gatherings, where lively conversations flowed over food and wine into the wee hours of the morning, Bambara had a way of organizing like no other.

Limitless in her energy to engage artists in ways that led to new creative works and to reignite activists burned out from years of community work,

Bambara's ways of seeing the gifts that were sometimes deeply buried in others—making the maps—helped others to overcome the pessimism and sarcasm that came in the aftermath of the tumultuous 1960s. Suicide, imprisonment of political leaders, assassinations, and untimely deaths all took a toll on the political movements that peaked in the 1960s. Withdrawal and the retreat from belief in the possibility of a 21st-century revolution in America led to agonizing debates about whether further investment in building new social political institutions or creating new cultural works would lead to measurable social change. Bambara, however, did not waver in her organizing work. Bambara listened to those in the community who wanted to use their creative gifts to foster social change and fostered self-confidence.

In "The Apprentice," Bambara captured her own boundless energy and commitment to encouraging others to commit to activism. In this short story, Naomi, a hip, fast-paced, action-oriented mentor who operates on minimal sleep, provides bountiful instructions to the young apprentice she is grooming as a community organizer. Following in Naomi's footsteps, the young apprentice has a hard time keeping pace with the seasoned activist, who moves through a whirlwind of rap sessions in every neighborhood setting imaginable, including the church, the city hall meeting, the tenants' meeting, the public housing hearing, and the old folks' home—where she raps while "mess[ing] around on the piano."[39] Decades after she wrote "The Apprentice," Bambara herself could be found turning a political rap session into a song fest as she played the piano and joined friends singing in the wee hours of the morning in a hotel lobby during Atlanta's Black Arts Festival.[40]

There are other reminders of Bambara in this story. At a late night stop at a take-out food joint, the apprentice becomes anxious thinking that Naomi will be literally on the car "stepping out on the hood with a bullhorn getting up a discussion about movies or something, on how we have to control Black images and stuff like that."[41] Instead, Naomi surprises her young apprentice with a less taxing neighborhood project, suggesting that The Regent (a theater of the same name as one of the cinemas Bambara frequented in her childhood Harlem), which was now showing *Cooley High,* would be perfect for running *La Luta Continua.* Naomi favored theater houses that featured double bills— key in drawing crowds not likely to come to see a film about the Mozambiquan liberation forces as a single feature. Only in Cuba was Naomi in conversation with someone who matched her own relentless energy for community work.

About Naomi in Cuba, Bambara wrote: " . . . she spent two whole days, or tried to, with this sister who was director of mental health, chairman of the journalism department, did voluntary labor on a construction brigade, had two kids and an invalid father, and liked to party ole Naomi to death in the all-night outdoor dance halls."[42] The character of Naomi seems to capture some of Bambara's zest as Bambara herself spent late nights dancing at the Tropicana in Cuba. Bambara also described herself at the peak of the revolutionary fervor of the 1960s when she wrote about Naomi: "She views everything and everybody as potentially good, as a possible hastener of the moment, an usherer-in of the new day. Examines everybody in terms of their input to making revolution an irresistible certainty."[43]

Chisholm remembered having the same sense about Bambara when first meeting her earlier in New York. Chisholm recalled:

> It wasn't that she looked at me and judged me an o.k. person and therefore she was going to connect with me. It was that was how she approached new people. She always assumed—and these are her kind of words—that everybody she met was down for the revolution. This is the late 60s, early 70s, so the political stuff is kind of petering out, right? But Toni was always building the revolution. Toni just automatically went forward to enlist every person she met in building the world she thought should exist.[44]

In "A Girl's Story," this author wrote a compelling coming-of-age tale about a young girl's trauma and isolation at the time of her first menstrual period. This story also depicted how a community mentor can be relied on for lessons about revolutionary freedom movements in Africa and can be a nonjudgmental listener at a critical point in a young girl's life. At a time when open conversations about menstruation were taboo and references to sexuality were closeted, Bambara uses a literary work to deliver a women's health activist message about the impact of adults, who show insensitivity to the need for social supports at this critical point in the life cycle. In the midst of a traumatic experience shrouded in shame and fear, Rae Ann, the story's narrator, learns she can turn to Dada Bibi to find the caring and support critical to restoring her own self-respect. Rae Ann receives a needed hug and finds comfort and strength in the conversation with Dada Bibi, a teacher who wears African wraps and shows Rae Ann how to make African maps out of clay and acrylic. In this short story, Bambara again illustrated the significance of the black woman as mentor.[45]

As an organizer, Bambara viewed independent black schools as one of the places that mentors could be most effective in developing intellectual curiosity and fostering cultural interests among black children. While in New York, Bambara had aligned herself with parents and school staff fighting for community control in Ocean Hill Brownsville. Bambara worked nationally with the Black Child Development Institute (BCDI) and assisted in the development of curriculum at independent black schools in Newark and Trenton, New Jersey.

Early on in Atlanta, Bambara addressed the importance of developing quality education models that included mentorship. In a talk sponsored by the Institute of the Black World at the J.F.K. Community Center, she stressed the importance of identifying international educational models in developing alternative educational institutions.[46] Grace Boggs, an Asian American woman married to activist James Boggs and the only Asian American to contribute to the anthology, *The Black Woman*, kicked off the conference the next day as the IBW keynote speaker. Including Boggs in the anthology is an early indication of Bambara's expansive definition of the term black. Bambara used the term black to refer to racial identity and to describe core aspects of culture across the African diaspora including music, dance, and an array of spiritual practices. Sometimes, the writer used the term black as a way to refer to political consciousness. At the conference, Bambara and Boggs had a rare opportunity to simply chat about political issues of mutual interest.[47]

When selecting a school for her daughter's education in Atlanta, it is not surprising that Bambara chose an independent black school for Karma to attend. Bambara first visited the Martin Luther King School, modeled after the freedom and liberation schools organized by the Student Nonviolent Coordinating Committee (SNCC) at the height of the civil rights movement, in a search for a school for her daughter in 1974.[48] Driving up to the front of the school for the first time in her orange Volkswagen, Bambara jumped out of her car eager to confirm that the school would meet her standards. Surprised to see the well-known African American writer whose works she often read in *Redbook*, Ama Saran, the school's head teacher, dashed out of her classroom to greet Bambara. Years later, Saran remembered running to the door thinking, "I couldn't believe I was looking at one of the best-known black writers in our time walk into the school's front door."[49]

During the years when Karma was enrolled at MLK, Bambara encouraged Saran and other mothers to extend the concepts valued at MLK by creating a women's circle of communal sharing of extended mothering and caretaking responsibilities. Karma's extended group of mothers and aunts included Bambara's friend Jan Douglass, Ama Saran, and activist-writer Leah Wise, whose daughters also attended the MLK School, often swapped responsibilities in providing overnight stays for their girls. Saran also recalled a young Karma—dressed in black tights and colorful ponchos, projecting a remarkably different style of children's dress, much more common in Greenwich Village than in Southwest Atlanta in the 1970s.[50]

While Karma attended the MLK School, Bambara voiced concerns about the reemergence of white supremacist groups in the South, which could lead to possible attacks on the school. At one meeting, Bambara argued for stronger actions to protect the day-to-day safety of the children, urging the school administration to develop blueprints on emergency escape routes, to map the physical interior of the walls in the school building and to schedule drills to execute escape plans, similar to fire and air-raid drills.[51]

In a letter on March 28, 1975, just a year after Bambara moved to Atlanta, Vincent Harding wrote friends of the IBW to confirm that the violent attacks on black organizations in Atlanta and elsewhere were escalating. Harding reminded IBW supporters that "reactionary forces often work together to disrupt or discredit movements for social change."[52] That spring Howard and Jualynne Dodson were shocked to find their pet dog in a loosely tied rope hanging from a tree on their property in an act that was feared to be white terrorism.[53]

Bambara not only met with parents and teachers to encourage structural changes and to advocate for greater parental and community involvement, the writer also came to the school on several occasions to read from *Tales and Stories for Black Folks*. Issuing politicized wake-up calls in her call and response version of "Goldilocks and the Three Bears," which Bambara renamed "The Golden Bandit,"[54] Bambara wanted fairy tales to be used to help children develop tools they could use to evaluate what is often presented to them without criticism. In Bambara's version of the fairy tale, Goldilocks is a burglar, vandal, and thief—not the frightened and innocent child that the fairy tale depicts.[55] Bambara sees no reason to make the blond-haired girl a heroine after she breaks into a home, destroys the furniture, and gobbles up their rice and peas and southern fried chicken. Telling her mama and papa that she was unjustly chased by a gang of bears made Goldilocks a liar as well.[56] As an activist and as a writer, Bambara believed that children had the capacity and the right to question the authority of adults.

Unlike some of the other mothers in her communal mothering circle of friends—who were more traditional in relegating children to what they considered to be age-appropriate activities that shielded them from what they defined as socially unacceptable behaviors—Bambara introduced her daughter to cultural events and meetings that others labeled as strictly for adults. One night when writer Pearl Cleage[Lomax], Bambara, and a few other mothers headed out to see a popular Blaxploitation film, Bambara decided to bring her daughter along.[57] Cleage, who was then Mayor Jackson's press secretary, remembered the sharp disapproval of the other mothers in their company when they realized Karma would be watching a film that celebrated black pride, but was troubling in its infusion of explicit violence and sex scenes. Cleage remembered Bambara's arguments that her daughter would see these movies eventually made sense. Cleage recalled that Bambara told her that "at least now, Karma is seeing these films through both of our eyes."[58]

On a panel with Cleage some years later, Bambara explained her point of view to a larger audience saying that books or television programs or movies normally considered adult material can provide important critical thinking opportunities for children. Bambara continued to emphasize the necessity of helping each growing child develop what she often called the "critical habit." Even in her role as a mother, Bambara questioned rules. With children, Bambara was a mentor who always strove to challenge norms. What she aimed to do was create environments where children would be eager to seek out their own truths through critical thinking.

Interestingly, however, when the acclaimed writer first came to Atlanta, she was not initially welcomed as a faculty member. Instead, she encountered substantial roadblocks. Soon after arriving in Atlanta, Bambara learned that the promise of a faculty appointment at Clark College, which she believed had been agreed upon, would not be honored. Even though there had been no signed formal contract before Bambara left New York, she did not understand how Clark could renege on its handshake, Douglass recalled.[59]

Chisholm had similar memories of Bambara's frustrations during her early months in Atlanta. Chisholm related that Bambara assumed that the black academic community would be enthusiastic about having a well-known black woman author in their faculty ranks. Chisholm said, "Bambara was baffled by the challenges she faced in seeking a college appointment."[60] About the general academic climate, Chisholm explained:

> It was very in-grown. Some of them were still teaching their courses as they had formulated them 20 years ago—smug and set in their ways. Bambara never went around saying she was this great writer—throwing stuff in people's face. Of course, the other side of her was the activism and some of them didn't respect either one—the creativity or the activism.[61]

There were exceptions, however, as academics like Richard A. Long, a prominent cultural historian, and Herbert Ross, a leading anthropologist, who were familiar with Bambara's writing were welcoming and helpful.

Long remembered having a chance to meet with Bambara shortly after she moved to Atlanta and recalled his first impressions of Bambara as positive. About Bambara's interactions with Atlanta's academic community, Long said: "I think she was always taken very seriously as an academic type person here in Atlanta. I was not aware that she was thought to be particularly bohemian or anything of that sort."[62]

At the time, Bambara was among the most recognized of a small handful of black woman writers to emerge from the 1960s; she also presented a strong curriculum vitae that included her promotion to Assistant Professor in the English Department at Rutgers, and guest lectures at major institutions across the country, including Duke University, where she was a Visiting Professor in the Duke University Division of Afro-American Studies.[63] In the fall of 1974, Bambara taught a course entitled "Introduction to Third World Literature." Commuting for one semester from Atlanta to Durham, North Carolina, on a bi-weekly basis, Bambara expected to receive a stipend of $3,700 and reimbursement for travel.[64]

In the syllabus for the course, Bambara described the class as an exploration of "the major tradition in the literature of the People of the Colored World—resistance."[65] Required novels to be read for the course included works by African American authors from the southern and northern regions of the United States as well as works by Caribbean, Latin American, African, and Asian writers in order to expand knowledge of how Third World writers respond to and resist efforts of colonialization.

Even though the course reflected objectives similar to classes taught at City College and Livingston College, Bambara's recent move to Atlanta created some challenges for her in organizing the readings for the course. In a letter dated August 23, 1974, to Walter Burford, Director of the Duke University Afro-American Studies Division, Bambara indicated that she would be forced to hand carry the shorter readings to be duplicated for the students which included "On Being Crazy," by W. E. B. Du Bois, "Good Morning, Revolution," by Langston Hughes, and "Urban Dream" by Victor Hernandez Cruz.

The writer closes her letter to Burford with a Bambara stamp of spontaneous humor which can be counted on to find lightness in otherwise serious moments. Her letter concludes: "Please pardon the sloppiness of this letter: am still in the process of locating boxes and dislocating shoulders. And look forward to a productive term."[66]

While Duke University found Bambara's teaching career compelling, what captured the attention of some academics in Atlanta were Bambara's bold and outspoken politics on race and gender, which were also central in her writing. She had little in common with some of the long-standing faculty members, who honored pedigree in the closely knit academic community. Some may have considered her lifestyle unconventional and found her rejection of the nuclear family implied by her decision to be a single parent unsettling. Bambara found an array of conservative values that promoted marriage and the nuclear family to be more deeply grounded in personal and societal interests of political power and social control than morality. Bambara wanted to freely express her creativity not only in her writing, but also in the way she dressed, the spiritual traditions she honored, and in her outspoken politics which addressed the rights of children, women, and elders—an agenda that was far more expansive than many of her academic peers at the time.

Bambara soon found an opportunity that provided the autonomy, freedom, and opportunity to do the work that mattered most to her: promoting writers and building networks between students, unknown writers, published writers, and scholars in order to connect art with the political in innovative and transformative ways. As she had done previously in *The Black Woman* and in *Tales for Black Folks,* Bambara was able to open doors to new writers and artists when she accepted an invitation to serve as the guest editor for a special edition of *Southern Exposure*. She continued to exhibit her masterful way of developing confidence among those who may not have previously recognized their creative talents. Published by the Institute for Southern Studies, the groundbreaking edition, entitled *Southern Black Utterances Today,* focused on southern black writing and visual arts. Bambara collaborated with her friend Leah Wise as project editor and mined her vast networks of artists, activists, and black scholars in a call for submissions for the special issue that was published in June 1975.

Bambara and Wise crafted a definition of southern black writing that was global, and included a number of essays that extended beyond the region. Clear that their definition of black writing was political, they wrote in their preface: "Blkriting is not always and only about writing. Frequently it's about flexin, clenchin, arresting mad underdevelopers. Sometimes it's smothered incense."[67]

As editors, Bambara and Wise identified more than 30 contributors for the 120-page issue that sold for $2.50, including internationally renowned black scholars, students from Atlanta's Frederick Douglass High School and SNCC activists. From the academic community Bambara's long-standing friend Addison Gayle Jr., then Associate Professor at City College in New York, contributed an essay on the significance of the South as an influence in shaping black literature. Beverly Guy-Sheftall, a pioneering black feminist thinker, coauthored "Images of Black Women" with Roseann P. Bell.

Atlanta-based Faye Bellamy, a community radio host and former SNCC activist, contributed a poem, "Being Me Is a Gas," that celebrated her grandmother and aunts, who provided love while taking care of business, selling beer and rooms. Writer, educator, archivist, and director for African and African American Studies at Emory University, Richard Long also contributed a poem to the special issue of Southern Exposure, "Hearing James Brown," and an essay on Pan-Africanism. Karma's teacher, Ama Saran, was invited by Bambara to review a children's book describing a Vietnamese boy's perspective on the role of children in their struggle to overturn ruling imperialist forces, and to comment on Lucille Clifton's All Us Come Cross the Water. Among the many poems in the thunderstorm of black writing and art that made up the journal's special edition was a poem from Kamau-Harris, the former Bambara Creative Award recipient, which called for "black love as fuel for the revolution."[68] In addition, the volume included a lengthy article by Wise focusing on her visit to China during the early days of the Cultural Revolution, accompanying a group of educators sponsored by the Guardian. Her detailed report mentioned health and education efforts such as a nursery school which encouraged children to develop habits in helping each other by designing nursery smocks with the buttons on the back. In many ways, the special issue of Southern Exposure captured the breath of Bambara's political and artistic interests.

During this time, the writer also agreed to an in-depth interview with Beverly Guy-Sheftall. Across two afternoons of conversation with Guy-Sheftall, who was among the first faculty members that Bambara met with at Spelman, Bambara reflected on her writing, her identity as a black feminist, and influences on her life as a writer. In 1974, Guy-Sheftall had only been teaching at Spelman for three years when she and her colleagues Roseann P. Bell and Bettye J. Parker decided to edit an anthology on black women in literature, Sturdy Black Bridges: Visions of Black Women in Literature—the first text of its kind in America. A decade later Guy-Sheftall would launch the first Women's Studies program at a historically black college.

With a few formal questions in hand, Guy-Sheftall drove to the writer's home for a conversation that became the first substantive interview with Bambara to ever appear in print.[69] This interview opened the way for subsequent conversations between the two over the several years that it took to finally find the African American editor, Marie Brown, to bring Sturdy Black Bridges to print in 1977. It was also the first interview for the groundbreaking anthology. Bambara's wisdom had a lasting impact on Guy-Sheftall and influenced the future direction of Guy-Sheftall's research and writing to chronicle black feminism.[70] In yet another instance, Bambara was a sounding board for ideas.

In response to Guy-Sheftall's insightful questions, Bambara argued for a united movement of women around the world that included Afro American, Afro Hispanic, Indo Hispanic, Asian Hispanics, and other women of color, who would address liberation issues not only for themselves as women, but also for all who are oppressed by colonialism, imperialism, and sexism. Bambara would amplify this call for political alliances among women of color throughout her life. Lamenting missed opportunities to form unions between black women and Puerto Rican and Chicano women in the 1960s, Bambara remained hopeful that unions among women focusing on liberation for themselves and their communities were still possible. Agitated by charges emanating from male-dominated political groups that argued that addressing chauvinism remained less of a priority than addressing racism, Bambara told Guy-Sheftall, "I don't know what they're thinking about because it's not as if you're a black *or* a woman. I don't find any basic contradiction or any tension between being a feminist, being a pan-Africanist, being a black nationalist, being an internationalist, being a socialist, and being a woman in North America."[71]

When Guy-Sheftall specifically asked Bambara if black women were any more in touch with the "black spirit"—something that Bambara argued would do more to shift political social movements in a positive direction than current political groups, who did not have ties with any specific spiritual practice—Bambara said: "No, I wouldn't say that black women or children or elders or men or any other sector of the community are any more in command of it [black spirit] or in touch with it than any other."[72] The writer's view that no individual or group or ideology provided the singular course for action contributed to her ability to be an effective mentor in the life of such a diverse array of people. This belief lies at the root of what became a lifetime mission to make interconnections between political and spiritual groups to create a more holistic approach to movements aiming to create social change.

Meanwhile, in the academic world, where status and rank sometimes mattered in ways that did not appeal to her own sensibilities, Bambara found at least some academic and social circles where she could align herself with more progressive forces in the kinds of equitable relationships that she relished. As the late fall holidays approached, Bambara received an invitation to a Thanksgiving dinner hosted by the parents of Susan Ross—Herbert Ross and Edyth Ross, both respected members of Atlanta's black academic community.[73] As part of the first wave of reverse southern black migration in the 1960s, Herbert Ross, longtime faculty member at Pennsylvania's Lincoln University, now hosted an annual pot-luck Thanksgiving dinner in Atlanta with his wife. With a bottle of wine in hand, Bambara and her daughter joined African students from Atlanta University, as well as an array of well-known scholars/activists, such as Hoyt Fuller and Jan Douglass, and members of Atlanta's social elite at the Ross Thanksgiving Dinner. Noted scholar Richard Long frequently surprised the crowd at the Ross's annual gatherings by bringing friends who happened to be in town, like Romare Bearden or James Baldwin.[74]

Although Bambara did not have a full-time job at Atlanta University, Bambara collaborated on projects with members of the Atlanta University faculty and was welcomed as a guest lecturer and workshop facilitator. In between formal workshops and classes on campus, Bambara met up with Dodson, checking in on her progress with teaching and her research on African American women, power, and the black church. Dodson laughed about how some of her attitudes had changed from their first meeting saying, "I was even comfortable wearing purple jumpsuits after getting over the purple floor."[75] Other female friends joined Bambara and Dodson in sessions that Bambara humorously entitled a class in "booty-ology." Dodson's laughter continued: "We would sit on the corner at a cross-roads between the schools of Atlantic University Center and analyze the physicality of guys walking by. The class is organized this way. Toni is the literature humanist and I'm the sociologist. On the 'ology' side we address how does our analysis fit or not into the social sciences. On the literature humanist side, we deal strictly with our responses and senses."[76]

If Bambara had prepared a syllabus for the course, she might have included Zora Neale Hurston, who was known to stop Harlemites in the street to tape measure their features in order to compare them with the dimensions of the features of specific African tribes as part of her anthropological studies at Columbia University.[77] For Bambara and friends, sitting on the block of Fair and Chestnut Streets, across from Clark College and Atlanta University and eating grapes, their free spirits were in full view and provided a counterpoint to those enrolled in studies with the aim of acquiring values and behaviors of the U.S. bourgeoisie. As the Black Pearl, a community store directly across from where they sat, blasted the Temptations' "Just my Imagination," these conversations were conducted with the straight-faced demeanor of scientists and humanists, who have gathered for an important study.[78] Once again, Bambara was suggesting a different vision of a person called writer, called teacher, or called mentor.

In Bambara's first year in Atlanta, 1974, new doors opened, presenting opportunities that she viewed as strengthening forces for the work she wanted to do, but there were also disappointments. Initially, Bambara had difficulty finding a job within the black academic community. When moving to Atlanta just as Maynard Jackson made his political ascendancy, which many believed had the capacity to shift political, social, and economic power in beneficial ways for the black community, Bambara never aligned herself with political forces that invested in mainstream party politics as the most effective strategy for change.

At the end of the day when coming home to 1556 Mayflower Street, Bambara returned to being a quiet neighbor who kept to herself and made time to write. For Mayflower resident Corrine Hudson, Bambara was not the famed writer or activist; she was simply a next-door neighbor. Hudson recalled only catching glimpses of Bambara as they greeted each other in the morning or at the end of the day across their adjacent yards. Decades later, Hudson was surprised to learn of Bambara's published books. Her most vivid memory of her former neighbor had to do with Bambara's decision to install a brick counter in her kitchen shortly after moving into her new house. Deciding to visit Bambara to inspect the work being done, Hudson recalled that they laughed about the shabbiness of the work as well as the workers.[79]

Bambara did not move to Atlanta to impress academics, political elites, or even next-door neighbors. In Bambara's first year in Atlanta, her heartbeat was in the many conversations she would have that repositioned ideas, developed critical thinking, and inspired creative passion.

NOTES

1. Toni Cade Bambara, "What It Is I Think I'm Doing Anyhow," in *The Writer on Her Work,* ed. Janet Sternberg (New York: Norton, 1980), 154.

2. Claudia Tate, ed., *Black Women Writers at Work* (New York: Continuum International Publishing Group, 1983), 19.

3. Ibid., 21.

4. Jan Douglass, Interview by author, September 2010.

5. Gary M. Pomerantz, *Where Peachtree Meets Sweet Auburn* (New York: Penguin Books, 1996), 246–48.

6. Ibid., 423.

7. Douglass, Interview by author.

8. Toni Cade Bambara, "Working at It in Four Parts," Spelman Archives, Atlanta.

9. Mary McDonald, Letter to Toni Cade Bambara, January 1, 1974, Spelman Archives, Atlanta.

10. Toni Cade Bambara, ed., *Tales and Stories for Black Folks* (New York: Zenith Books, 1971), 11.

11. Ibid., 5.

12. Linda Holmes, "The True Story of Chicken Licken," in *Tales and Stories for Black Folks,* ed. Toni Cade Bambara, 146–49.

13. Geneva Powell, "Billy Goat's Turf," in *Tales and Stories for Black Folks,* ed. Toni Cade Bambara (New York: Zenith Books, 1971), 144–45.

14. McDonald, Letter to Bambara.

15. "Clark Sponsors Writers' Meet," *Atlanta Daily World,* March 28, 1974.

16. Ibid.

17. Valerie Maynard, Interview by author, May 2010.

18. Sekou Sundiata, e-mail to author, July 2006.

19. Toni Cade Bambara, postcard to Karma Bene Bambara, July 1974, Spelman Archives, Atlanta.

20. Ibid.

21. Ibid.

22. Douglass, Interview by author.

23. Akua Kamau-Harris, Interview by author, July 2009.

24. Claire Hanrahan, "Alderson: Reclaiming the Vision," *Western North Carolina Woman* 1 (February/March 2003), http://www.seniorwomen.com/articles/articlesHanrahanAlderson.html.

25. Sonia Sanchez, Interview by author, May 2012.

26. Kamau-Harris, Interview.

27. Ibid.

28. Ibid.

29. Ibid.

30. Jualynne Dodson, Interview by author, September 2010.

31. Ibid.

32. Ibid.

33. Ibid.

34. Ibid.

35. Cheryl Chisholm, Interview by author, June 2010.

36. Ibid.

37. Ibid.

38. Kay Bonetti, "An Interview with Toni Cade Bambara," in *Conversations with Toni Cade Bambara,* ed. Thabiti Lewis (Jackson: University Press of Mississippi, 2012), 47.

39. Toni Cade Bambara, "The Apprentice," in *The Sea Birds Are Still Alive* (New York: Vintage Books, 1982), 28.

40. Amiri Baraka, "Toni," in *Savoring the Salt: The Legacy of Toni Cade Bambara,* ed. Linda Janet Holmes and Cheryl Wall (Philadelphia: Temple University Press, 2008), 112.

41. Bambara, "The Apprentice," 35.

42. Ibid., 38.

43. Ibid., 33.

44. Chisholm, Interview by author.

45. Toni Cade Bambara, "A Girl's Story," in *The Sea Birds Are Still Alive* (New York: Vintage Books, 1982), 152–65.

46. "Noted Writer, Educator, Addresses Education Forum," *Atlanta Daily World,* January 25, 1976.

47. Grace Lee Boggs, Interview by author, April 2010.

48. Ama Saran, Interview by author, June 2010.

49. Ibid.

50. Jan Douglass, Interview by author, September 2010.

51. Saran, Interview by author.

52. Vincent Harding, Letter, March 28, 1975, Manuscripts, Archives and Rare Books Division, Schomburg Center for Research in Black Culture, New York.

53. Jualynne Dodson, Interview by author, September 2010.

54. Toni Cade Bambara, "The Golden Bandit," in *JUMP UP AND SAY! A Collection of Black Storytelling*, ed. Linda Goss and Clay Goss (New York: Simon and Schuster, 1995), 219–22.

55. Ibid.

56. Ibid.

57. Pearl Cleage, Interview by author, April 2010.

58. Ibid.

59. Douglass, Interview by author.

60. Cheryl Chisholm, Interview by author, June 2010.

61. Ibid.

62. Richard Long, Interview by author, April 2011.

63. Toni Cade Bambara, Letter to Walter Burford, August 23, 1974, Box 1 Folder 13: Bambara, Toni Cade, 1974–75, University Archives, Duke University.

64. Ibid.

65. Third World Literature B.S. 150, Fall 74, Box I, Folder 13. University Archives, Duke University.

66. Toni Cade Bambara, Letter to Walter Burford.

67. Toni Cade Bambara, Special Issue Editor, "Preface," in *Southern Black Utterances Today*, Volume III, Number 1 (Atlanta: Southern Exposure Press, Spring/Summer 1975).

68. Akua Kamau, "Our Black Love Is Fuel for the Revolution," in *Southern Black Utterances Today* (Atlanta: Southern Exposure Press, 1975), 60.

69. Beverly Guy-Sheftall, Interview by author, August 2010.

70. Ibid.

71. Beverly Guy-Sheftall, "Commitment: Toni Cade Bambara Speaks," in *Conversations with Toni Cade Bambara*, ed. Thabiti Lewis (Jackson: University Press of Mississippi, 2012), 10.

72. Ibid.

73. Susan Ross, Interview by author, September 2010.

74. Ibid.

75. Dodson, Interview by author.

76. Ibid.

77. Vernon J. Williams, *Rethinking Race: Franz Boas and His Contemporaries* (Lexington: University Press of Kentucky, 1966).

78. Dodson, Interview by author.

79. Corrine Hudson, Interview by author, April 2011.

FIVE

From Atlanta to Vietnam

I don't know how to chart the evolution of my creative interest. Suffice to say
that the lens has widened, the scope broadened, and the demands on myself have
increased.[1]

While rejecting the label writer as much too narrow for describing the work
she did, Bambara was placing a lot of her energy into writing. In an important self-revelatory moment, Bambara admitted that her public persona
sometimes included "a penchant for flamboyant performance" and a ten-
dency to "exaggerate to the point of hysteria."[2] In contrast, about her writing
Bambara explained: "I write for the same reason I keep track of my dreams,
for the same reason I meditate and practice being still—to stay in touch with
me and not let too much slip by me. I would be writing whether there were a
publishing industry or not, whether there were presses or not, whether there
were markets or not."[3]

Shortly after moving to Atlanta, Bambara began writing some of the short
stories that would appear in *The Sea Birds Are Still Alive*, published in 1977.
Unlike some of the stories that appear in *Gorilla, My Love*, some written when
she was much younger, the stories written in Atlanta emerged from the political experiences of the 1960s and 1970s. While *Gorilla, My Love* is marked by
humorous stories that include young girls as narrators, several of the stories
in *The Sea Birds Are Still Alive* are more serious in tone, particularly those
stories that center on the work of seasoned political activists. But Bambara as
a writer was not simply interested in her characters' political acts; Bambara

explored their humanity and inner workings as she delved into their spirits. Not only do readers come to know these characters as revolutionaries, but these are activists who are also neighbors, lovers, and family members who plant gardens, hang out on the block, light candles, and sing.

Just as the arc of her writing expanded, Bambara's community work intensified through involvement with specific neighborhood organizations. Offering an array of art classes, dance programs, craft, and writing programs, the Neighborhood Arts Center (NAC) officially opened its doors in the refurbished Peter Bryant Elementary School in May 1975.[4] Now, Atlanta was home to a neighborhood arts institution with a mission to bring a highly diversified arts program to Atlanta's black working class. In the early 1970s, Atlanta continued to be plagued by a racially divided arts community, with most white art patrons frequenting Atlanta's downtown arts museums while the black middle class gathered to appreciate art holdings in the collections of historically black colleges. When the NAC opened its building next door to low-income housing projects in the working-class Mechanicsville community, it immediately became a cultural beacon.

During this time, Bambara unexpectedly became involved with cultural and political work of a different kind. In the spring of 1975, Arlene Eisen, an anti-imperialist and woman's liberation activist who was teaching at New College, San Jose State University, contacted Bambara to invite her to join a women's delegation to meet with the Viet Nam Women's Union in Hanoi.[5] Eisen, the author of *Women of Viet Nam,* had been a guest of the Women's Union on a previous visit to Vietnam.[6] Her book documented the history of women's oppression and liberation in the context of the country's wars against French and U.S. occupations. Bambara's book, *The Black Woman,* makes a revolutionary call for a unified struggle for "liberation from the exploitive and dehumanizing system of racism, from the manipulation and control of a corporate society, liberation from the constrictive norms of 'mainstream' culture."[7] This call resonated with Eisen. Years later, Eisen explained, "We saw the struggle for women's liberation tied to the struggle to defeat imperialism—I think Toni did too. We had read Toni's book, *The Black Woman,* and thought it was important to have her perspective as a militant black woman represented on the delegation."[8] As usual, Bambara welcomed opportunities for international travel that might enhance the black community's own struggles for liberation.

In 1971, a 10-person Vietnam Mission on Reconciliation, which included civil rights activists Dorothy Cotton, Bernard Lafayette, and Bishop Paul Moore, the priest who headed the Episcopalian church Bambara's family briefly attended in Jersey City, had traveled to Vietnam along with an array of other progressive groups.[9] The feminist mission to Vietnam also was historic. Other members of the 1975 feminist delegation included Laura Whitehorn, an activist with the radical white student organization the Weathermen/ Underground, who was later jailed. Whitehorn knew Bambara from reading her writings, and had included *The Black Woman* on her syllabus as a teacher at the Boston-area Cambridge Women's Liberation School.[10] Eisen also invited Donna Futterman, health activist, later internationally renowned for her medical work in HIV-AIDS care in South Africa and New York, and Pam Costain, founder of the Minnesota socialist feminist union, to be part of the unique delegation.[11]

Before leaving for Vietnam, Eisen arranged for a meeting among the group's members to better understand their mission. During their orientation, Eisen suggested that Bambara serve as the delegation's leader. Bambara later reflected, "Anybody who has ever gone abroad with a delegation knows how hard it is to establish a collective habit with folks who are products of this society in which narcissism itself is an obsession and individualism is raised to some kind of metaphysical principle. But we managed in two days to establish some ground rules for how we would operate as a group."[12]

Remembering their New York meeting, Whitehorn recalled years later, "Our little delegation was composed of three white women, all of us anti-imperialist radicals or revolutionaries from middle-class backgrounds, and Toni. She had her work cut out for her."[13] Bambara's guidance included reminding the group to avoid tendencies to romanticize the Vietnamese people as "quaint and exotic,"[14] and she encouraged the delegation to report accomplishments as well as internal problems the nation faced. Whitehorn also recalled that Bambara "had to apply large doses of her particularly intelligent brand of common sense" in shaping the direction and work of the delegation.[15] Plus being a masterful storyteller, Bambara uniquely interacted with members of the Viet Nam Women's Union through the many stories she told about the American experience when they finally arrived in Vietnam that summer.[16]

In the interim between Eisen's invitation for Bambara to join the delegation and the group's date of departure, Bambara used the time to write and edit some of the short stories that later appeared in *The Sea Birds Are Still Alive*. Years later, Bambara explained, "I sat down and wrote and that became *The Sea Birds*. Most of those stories had not been published; been hanging around the house, and they were completed during that spring and summer."[17] Bambara's house guest, Kamau-Harris, who was still looking for permanent Atlanta housing after her release from Alderson Prison, remained in Bambara's home to house sit while Bambara was in Southeast Asia.[18]

A week before leaving for Vietnam, Bambara finally received some good news about a position at Atlanta University for when she returned from Southeast Asia. In a letter dated July 14, Robert Detweiler of Emory University informed Dr. Richard Long, then Director for African and African American Studies at Atlanta University: "I am pleased to tell you that Dr. Ekman from NEH [the National Endowment of the Humanities] has formally approved our request that the $7500 half (including benefits) from NEH funds originally designated for Gloria Blackwell be used to pay Ms. Toni Cade Bambara for part time faculty employment in the Interinstitutional Program, based at Atlanta University, during the 1975–76 academic year."[19] The modest offer made it

Delegation relaxes in Hanoi's Reunification (Thong Nhat) Park transformed by Ho Chi Minh from a dumping ground for household waste to a popular destination with lake adorned by gardens, fountains, paths and statues. L-R: Donna Futterman, Minh of the Vietnam Women's Union, Laura Whitehorn, and Bambara with Pam Costain, kneeling in front, July 1975, Spelman Archives, Atlanta. Courtesy of Karma Smith.

possible for Bambara to leave Atlanta with a commitment in hand for academic work when she returned. Bambara could travel knowing there would be at least one source of guaranteed income when she returned, providing some sense of relief.

Flying out of JFK airport in New York, the delegation traveled with a host of supplies and antiwar materials to demonstrate solidarity with the liberation fighters in Vietnam. Wanting to increase solidarity between black organizations in the United States and liberation forces in Vietnam, Bambara suggested the role of "mailman" for herself as she carried letters from the Institute of the

Black World, the February 12th movement, H. Rap Brown, and prisoners. In previous meetings with the group, Bambara discussed how black organizations rarely had the same opportunities as white leftist groups to carry messages directly to the Vietnamese people.[20] Bambara viewed part of her personal mission as increasing international understanding of the fact that aggressive revolutionary groups in the United States also faced highly repressive tactics that included surveillance and violence.[21]

Although Bambara refused to accept a formal role as the group's leader, she represented the delegation in tenuous negotiations with customs officers in New York, London, Paris, India, Bangladesh, and Vietnam where, as Whitehorn recalled, "Toni worked her magic to make some of the interactions look smooth as silk." The group was attempting to pass a huge suitcase, filled with illicit medical supplies from the San Francisco Women's Health Collective, without the luggage being confiscated before it could reach the mothers and babies whose lives depended on it. Their suitcases were also filled with injectable valium that was efficacious in stopping convulsions that women exposed to Agent Orange during pregnancy would experience during childbirth, resulting in the death of mother and baby.[22] Years later, Whitehorn said she watched as Bambara employed a mixture of grace, humor, and street smarts in theatrical ways during her airport negotiations. "Dressed in African cloth and African head-wrap, Toni took charge at every stop, alternately smiling and glaring at customs officials and airline employees, widening her eyes to coyly ask that the suitcase be boarded on the plane by the functionary in question—but only with great care, please," Whitehorn recalled.[23] For Bambara, the mission was to make certain that the lifesaving medications crossed the borders into Vietnam. In fact, the delegation delivered the medications to the hospital and that visit to the hospital was the high point of their time there.[24]

On July 21 when the delegation arrived in Vietnam for their 10-day visit, Vo Thi The and her assistant Tran Thanh Tuyen led the Women's Union in greeting Bambara and other members of the delegation with hearty thanks for making the visit, presenting them with flowers, and enchanting them with an unusual concoction of beer and pineapple juice that quickly became Bambara's favorite. Bambara was reminded of the loving hugs of welcome that were routinely extended by southern American black women. Coming from a small family with few known extended family members, Bambara welcomed what must have felt like the love extended at a family reunion. While in Vietnam, Bambara paused to make informal notes in her notebook:

In our semi-formal sit down talks with women from various branches of the women's union such graciousness—such attentiveness to each person's disposition. Frequently, for example, one of the delegates would be speaking at length and the Vietnamese would pay attention to the other members of the delegation. Clasping your hand perhaps, or shifting a chair closer to you, pouring you tea, fanning you with their fan. You may not be the center of attention, making a presentation, but the gestures said, you matter, you are cared for. I don't know that I ever saw anyone use a fan or hat to shield or cool themselves without first fanning someone else.[25]

In meetings with the Vietnamese women at handicraft co-ops, agriculture co-ops, and infant schools, as well as the Institute for Protection of Mothers where their hand-carried and carefully protected antibiotics and anticonvulsants were delivered, Bambara made notes for future speeches that sounded like testimonies delivered in church, in which she spoke about how women "shared their next-to-nothing things and their more-than-hoped-for wealth of spirit."[26] And the Vietnamese women, similar to the women she knew back home in Atlanta, were spinners of miracles, "pulling gardens out of rocks and taking entrails and garbage and making cuisine, and taking a peanut and inventing 20,000 products,"[27] bringing to mind the genius of George Washington Carver.

As expected, Bambara took extensive notes in Vietnam, even during the movies she watched in theaters there, which celebrated the Vietnamese victory and provided striking images of citizens assuming social responsibility. Bambara must have chuckled to herself as she jotted down tidbits of conversations she overheard from women in the audience who talked back to the movies, like a character that might have appeared in one of her early Harlem stories in *Gorilla, My Love*. Also, in Vietnam, Bambara had appreciated the late-night meetings with Cuban construction workers where she'd learned about their building and stocking chicken farms and dairies, as well as constructing a 620-bed hospital and a hotel. The visit to Ho Chi Minh's house, which Bambara called "a huge Johnson, palace, mansion monster,"[28] returned her to thinking about the international ties between social movements, as she learned that Ho Chi Minh was said to have been reading *Negroes with Guns*, Robert Franklin William's groundbreaking book defending the right of black people in America to bear arms, on the day he died.[29]

Out of all the conversations Bambara and the other women heard, one topic drained them emotionally more than others. Those were the stories of fierce interrogation and torture heaped upon women through counterrevolutionary torture quotas.[30] Bambara wanted to expose the practices of police in South Vietnam whose torture mandates were similar to routine traffic-ticket quotas in the United States, where police were expected to issue so many tickets per week. Women told the delegates about broken bottles pushed into their vaginas, beatings with electrical prods, and physical attacks with water hoses—all examples of the abuse experienced by the women that Bambara would later bring to her fiction in *The Sea Birds Are Still Alive*. Writing in notebooks and journals or even supportive conversations at the end of the day did little to relieve the unbearable pain Bambara and her colleagues felt when hearing of the women's suffering firsthand. What they heard made it impossible to relax or sleep. Even if they had known the vocabulary that would have been needed to translate the women's stories of the injuries that resulted from rape, molestation, and beatings into the kind of clinical terms used by doctors to objectify a patient before performing surgery, this would not have been enough to lift their own anger and sorrow. At one point, Bambara turned to theatrical devices when she quickly transformed their hotel room into a theater for a healing improvisation session that lasted late into the night.[31] Tapping into her own wit and humor, Bambara directed the delegation to gather props that included glasses of champagne, and to carefully prepare frozen chrysanthemums floating in the hotel bathtub.[32] Reminiscent of the late night productions that she had staged in her downtown New York apartment decades ago, Bambara was convincing in her role as a visiting professor "whose sexy demeanor promised way more than he could deliver," as Whitehorn remembered, smiling years later about Bambara's portrayal of a male professor.[33]

On July 30, the delegation began their return trip to New York, which included extending a one-day stopover in Laos into a five-day stay, in order to accommodate the schedule of a representative from the Student-Workers Alliance who they hoped could provide them with valuable insights about the ongoing war there.[34] Later, Bambara wrote: "For example, we would stay up all night pooling our information and trying to figure out what questions would be crucial to ask, questions that would break it all open for us. We would then call [the representative from the Student-Workers Alliance] up, lay out the questions and between three o'clock when he had to be at the hospital and three-twenty when he had to run an open-air education seminar, he would dash into the lobby, lay the answers on us and then swiftly move out again."[35]

About the entire trip, Bambara concluded:

> The summer of 1975 was a very good time to be in Vietnam. The people were celebrating the 45th anniversary of the Vietnam Workers' Party which was established in 1930 and which has as its first political thesis equality between men and women. Just as the Party was established in February of 1930, so, too, the women's organization was encouraged to form. And out of the many early organizations—Women Against Imperialism, Women for the Defense of the Country, a lot of patriotic bourgeois women's groups as well as rank and file worker's groups—there finally emerged the Women's Union. So the Women's Union was celebrating its 45th anniversary as well.[36]

At the JFK Airport, Bambara extended farewells that would prove to be final, as she would never see any members of the delegation again. Even so, members of the delegation continued to be influenced by Bambara's writing and her powerful presence throughout the trip. When Whitehorn was arrested in 1985 and served a lengthy prison sentence as a result of accusations surrounding her work with the Weathermen/Underground, all her possessions were ransacked and seized by the FBI, but the government did not have the power to destroy Bambara's influence.[37] Whitehorn wrote: "One thing Toni had clearly drawn from our trip was a sense of the ancient nature of the Vietnamese revolution—the depth of dedication of the Vietnamese people to keep fighting for independence and freedom over thousands of years. . . . I think Toni saw that in Vietnam more clearly than I did because she had such an appreciation for the generations of struggle Black people had already waged without 'burning out,' 'moving on' or whatever those phrases are that people use to describe people who used to be active radicals and then one day stopped."[38]

Over the years, Eisen continued to encounter Bambara's lasting work and legacy, especially her writing exposing the lies about the murders of Atlanta's black children in the 1980s, and her international reach into this century. More than 30 years after their Vietnam visits, while working as a roving lecturer in advanced English classes at the University of Havana, Eisen learned that their Cuban professor had assigned Bambara's short story "The Lesson." The story sparked animated debates among the students about poverty and racism in both the United States and Cuba.[39] Translated into multiple languages, Bambara's works would eventually be read by students across the globe, but in 1975, the students who most often interacted with her lived close to her Atlanta home.

Returning to Atlanta in time to attend the NAC's closing summer program festival on August 31, Bambara immersed herself in teaching, proposal writing, assisting with administrative tasks and organizing events at NAC. In between meetings, Bambara dabbled in her own artistic interests, painting in oil, acrylic, and watercolors. Sometimes bringing her sketchbook from home, Bambara also used pencil and ink to release the images previously locked in her imagination. At times, Bambara returned to her piano-playing, pulling from stacks of sheet music that included popular Broadway tunes and jazz standards. In her teaching at NAC, Bambara was also sharing her experiences from Vietnam and what she learned about the courage of Vietnamese women who stood in battle to defeat American imperialism. For Bambara, the winning guerrilla warfare tactics executed by women in struggle had potential application throughout the world for reshaping the political realities of oppressed people.

As NAC's first writer-in-residence, Bambara was appreciated for the attention her affiliation with NAC brought to the center locally and nationally. Even though the widely published author insisted on not being headlined above others working at the NAC because of her publications or international name recognition, she was among its most popular teachers when the fall program opened.[40]

As Bambara, sometimes wearing a colorful gele, moved through the school's corridor that housed NAC's hallway gallery, which included gifts from Romare Bearden of his prints, she found at NAC the cultural diversity that often was missing in mainstream academic institutions. For example, the community center tapped resources such as musician Williams Jennings, who instituted a jazz study program at NAC long before most white or black higher institutions of learning; cultural worker Alice Lovelace, who collaborated with Bambara in creating daring new blue prints for increasing resources for emerging writers in the NAC community; and poet and community activist Ebon Dooley, who remembered Bambara's nonconformist spirit as a significant influence in "keeping us honest" and "giving room for creative energy to breath"[41] Spike Lee, a student at Morehouse at the time, was one of the early students who dropped in at NAC. Decades later Bambara wrote about Lee's 1980s film *School Daze,* which was set on a southern black college campus during homecoming week. For the volume on Lee's films which Lee edited, Bambara tapped her experiences on Atlanta's campuses to unravel Lee's film *School Daze,* which she argued reflected some of the elitist, sexist, and homophobic behaviors of the fraternities and sororities that the film depicted.[42]

At the same time, Bambara made her first formal presentation on the summer's trip to Vietnam at the School of Social Work on the campus of Clark College.[43] That fall afternoon Bambara arrived on campus early enough to use the bulletin board in the back of the room to mount pictures and display artifacts that included a pin from the Women's Union which Bambara treasured. With her daughter Karma in tow, Bambara spoke to students, faculty, and community in a lecture cosponsored by the Institute of the Black World. Her friend Jan Douglass was in the room to introduce Bambara foremost as a cultural worker, but also as a prolific writer with published writings on women, children, education, and black language.[44] Fliers promoting the event mentioned that Bambara was teaching one course at Atlanta University, "Approaches to the Study of the Contemporary Black Woman," as a visiting lecturer.[45]

A little after 4 P.M. at Wright Hall, Bambara began her lecture with praise and remembrance for the elders she met in Vietnam. She told the audience:

> I was just composing a letter the other night trying to thank them for a gift that they gave me. They gave me back my grandmother. In the sense that being in the presence of these women renewed your whole love affair with your grandmother and with all those other women that we know, you know, who kept on keeping on. You're in the presence of Vietnamese women for five minutes and you recall, yes, Harriet Tubman, right Sojourner Truth. They gave me back my grandmother.[46]

In her talk that afternoon, Bambara won smiles from the audience as she used her unpredictable wit to paint an unforgettable characterization of revolutionary leaders as strikingly handsome and sexy men. "Isn't it interesting to compare the look of Third World heroes to the leaders of the 'advanced' world? Ho, Cabral, Lumumba, Che, Nyerere, Fanon, Malcolm, Fidel, Stokley, Camillo Cienfuegos. The health, the smile, the organic vibrancy that comes across. They so fine! Now just compare faces like that, just the look if you will, with the Big Business Thugs."[47] Bambara always found interesting ways to make certain that her talks were not lofty and related to the experiences of her diverse audiences. A year later, "Viet Nam and Black Struggle: Two Revolutions in the Making," an article based on Bambara's October talk at the School of Social Work, appeared in the publication *Black World View.*[48]

Douglass, who fondly refers to herself and Bambara as being "hanging girlfriends," remembered how deeply moving the travel to Vietnam was for Bambara. Once returning from Vietnam, Douglass recalled Bambara being absorbed with finding historical parallels in the struggles of blacks in the United States with the struggles of the Vietnamese. For some years to come, this trip marked Bambara's most significant opportunity to do the kind of work that she yearned to do as a part of international travel: building coalitions, meeting with cultural workers, and aligning with women's groups. This kind of activity had characterized Bambara's earlier visit to Cuba, as it did the Vietnam trip now.

When Bambara spoke about the Vietnam experience and its implications for the black community on radio talk shows, television, and on campuses, she began to integrate selected readings from early drafts of *The Sea Birds Are Still Alive* into her talks. About the early readings of *The Sea Birds Are Still Alive,* Bambara commented:

> When I got back, one of the tasks I had was to deliver this information to my constituency. I decided to do it the way I knew how to do. I wrote a short story in seven sections. I would read a section, then we would have music, [and] somebody would get up and read the greeting cards that the children had made. Then I would read another section based on stories I had been told, then someone would show some slides and posters, then I would read another section. Like jazz. It went on like that. That story line became the title story in *The Sea Birds Are Still Alive.* Very oddly, the first time I ever heard it on radio, the person read it, and then had music, then read it, etc. I thought it must really lend itself to that kind of orchestration.[49]

While energized by travel, reports to the community on Vietnam, and the readings that followed, Bambara knew that it would be sometime before *The Sea Birds Are Still Alive* appeared in bookstores. Meanwhile, Bambara continued to send the short stories that eventually appeared in *The Sea Birds Are Still Alive* out to magazines and academic journals, sending a copy of "The Organizer's Wife" to her New York friend John Henrik Clarke, writer, activist, and long-time City College professor. On his recent visit to Atlanta to speak on the importance of the "The Black Radical Tradition," Clarke had promised to assist Bambara in getting "The Organizer's Wife" published. On December 17, Bambara wrote Clarke, a member of the editorial board of *Freedomways* magazine, to commend him on his talk and enclosed her short story.[50]

In his letter of response to Bambara on the day after Christmas, Clarke mirrored Bambara's optimism about creating a new social order that would not only reshape the black experience in America, but also humanity as a whole, and was enthusiastic about the possible publication of "The Organizer's Wife" in *Freedomways.* While he promised to present the short story for discussion at *Freedomways'* editorial meeting in the next two weeks, Clarke warned his friend that there would be no compensation even if the story was published. He bluntly wrote, "We are very pleased to have the story and to know that you thought of *Freedomways* considering the fact that it has been years since we have had the funds to pay for material."[51]

Although "The Organizer's Wife" was not published in *Freedomways,* it became the lead story in *The Sea Birds Are Still Alive.* Another story from *The Sea Birds Are Still Alive,* "Witchbird," first appeared in *Essence* magazine, reaching Bambara's favorite authenticating audience—black women—a year before the book was published.[52] Famed actor and activist Ruby Dee gave life to "Witchbird" in her perfect rendition of the spunky attitude and swagger of the story's narrator, on the groundbreaking public television series she hosted with Ossie Davis, increasing access to Bambara's work.

Nevertheless, the year concluded with another disappointment. In the early months of her work at NAC, Bambara's commitment remained strong, but the writer and activist began to be troubled by early signs that NAC's board might be too willing to make compromises on program content to satisfy funders. At the annual NAC fall retreat, where Bambara made arrangements for her daughter to accompany her, hints of discord were evident even amid the relaxed setting of the South Carolina Sea Islands. In an end of the year letter to all NAC staff, director Sandra L. Swans wrote: "How is our creation (NAC)? What is its future? Where is it going? . . . As we move into 1976, a questionable year for all who live in America, I hope you will strive to make your links as strong as possible in all the chains you are a part of and realize that without a vision and dedication to make that vision a reality, WE will perish."[53]

Interestingly, it was Swans who would leave NAC before the end of the following year—and Bambara with her, leaving behind NAC's writer-in-residency job. Bambara would align herself with the revolutionary fervor that Swans expressed in heated political disputes that erupted between Swans and the NAC board, whose opposition was headed by the more practical fund-raising-guided politics of Shirley Franklin, who would later become the first female mayor of Atlanta. Although Bambara left her writer-in-residency position at NAC in less than a year, Bambara supported NAC as an important cultural institution as long as the organization existed. She also sustained her close friendship with Swans, dedicating *The Sea Birds Are Still Alive* to Karma, Mama Swans, and a host of Karma's other "mamas."[54]

This last collection of short stories reflected Bambara's determination to make certain that the political ideas of the 1960s have vibrancy in the 1970s and benefit from the challenging lessons learned at the peak of the 1960s revolutionary movement. What unites many of the stories in *The Sea Birds Are Still Alive* are their political messages, boldly stated along the themes of liberation, transformation, and what it means to be human. In this collection, Bambara again features female characters that refuse to be victims in personal relationship and confront sexism, capitalism, or imperialism through liberation struggles as the title story of *The Sea Birds Are Still Alive* best illustrates. Two of the stories, "The Sea Birds Are Still Alive" and "The Organizer's Wife," the original story title for the collection, also speak to the significance of home—past, present, and future—for those committed to liberation struggles.

In the story "The Sea Birds Are Still Alive," Bambara first describes home as a place of loss—as in its Vietnamese setting, where the successive colonial forces of the Spanish, French, Japanese, and American occupations of the country brought about tragedy—"the old songs gone, the dances forgotten, the elders and ancient wisdoms put aside, the memory of home scattered in the wind."[55] But home is transformed again when reclaimed as a place for sustaining newly found humanity. Bambara wrote about a liberation fighter returning to his village: "It was a good time in history to be on the earth, to be on the boat going home. He leaned way over, examining the holes below that bled rust with each grumble of the engine, each turn of the wooden paddles. Then he straightened, back stiff with the conviction that he, like many others going home now, was totally unavailable for servitude."[56]

In the "Organizer's Wife," Bambara wrote about home in the future in a way that linked the experiences of activists in the rural black south with liberation fighters in Vietnam and elsewhere. In this story, home is where farm workers are organizing to hold onto their farm land. The narrator of "The Organizer's Wife" is a woman whom Bambara later described as being different from the women who usually peopled her stories, people who were more like herself: "very big-mouthed, verbally energetic and generally clear as to what they're about doing because their mouth is always announcing what they're doing. That story came out of a curiosity. What do I know about people like that? Could I delve into her? The story took shape around that effort."[57]

As a mother and political activist, however, Bambara could draw from some of her own experiences in shaping this character. In this story, Virginia, the narrator, is an organically oriented, breastfeeding mother who washes her infant in the morning dew and carries her baby on her back while sustaining her vision of home in the future. Although she considers leaving her community, Virginia, like the characters in "The Sea Birds Are Still Alive," continues to find strength for the fight as she envisions home as a transformed place while still in the midst of struggle. Virginia sees victory as is reflected in Bambara's following passage:

> Home in the future. The future here now developing. Home liberated soon. And the earth would recover. The rain would come. The ancient wisdoms would be revived. The energy released. Home a human place once more.
>
> The bones spoke it. The spirit spoke, too, through flesh when the women gathered at the altar, the ancient orishas still vibrant beneath the ghostly patinas some thought right to pray to, but connected in spite of themselves to the spirits under the plaster.[58]

These words are spoken by a woman in the American South, but could have been spoken by characters in liberation struggles set in stories in numerous other places around the world. What links stories in *The Sea Birds Are Still Alive* are the resilient voices of Bambara's characters and themes of resistance.

Another example of how Bambara united voices of political struggle across the globe can be found in "The Long Night."[59] In this story, Bambara describes the kind of attacks that members of the Liberation Army and the Black Panther Party faced in the United States in a way that resonated with the devastating stories of torture she heard from women during her visit to Vietnam. While the "Long Night" describes a police assault on what appears to be a black urban community, the narrator's struggle to not cave in could have been the experience of a woman freedom fighter in Asia, Latin America or Africa. Rather than depict activists as superheroes or saints, Bambara's revolutionaries face the frailties and fears that make them human.

About the narrator who closeted herself in her apartment bathroom to protect herself from randomly flying police bullets, Bambara writes:

> She would tell. They would beat her and she would tell more. They would taunt and torture and she would tell all. They'd put a gun in her eye and she would tell even what there wasn't to tell. Chant it. Sing it. Moan it. Shout it. Incriminate her neighbors. Sell her Mama. Hawk her daddy. Trade her friends. Turn in everybody. Turn on everything. And never be the same. Dead or alive, never be the same. Blasted from her place.[60]

In writing about an activist whose posters spoke of Harriet Tubman, whose files included negatives of university campus agents, and who identified her Afro pick as a possible instrument for guerilla warfare, Bambara succeeded in drawing parallels between women guerilla fighters in Vietnam and the narrator in the "Long Night" who is trapped in a setting that evokes the experience that members of the Black Panther Party and other groups faced during the black revolutionary movement in the United States. In the 1960s and 1970s, COINTELPRO, established by the FBI, targeted black power and some civil rights groups in a clandestine program, which included eavesdropping, intimidation, and assaults on organizational leadership in efforts to thwart their influence. At one point, the Black Panther Party's community agenda included free breakfast programs, health clinics, campaigns against police brutality, and a militant assertion of the right to self-defense. A decade before *The Sea Birds Are Still Alive* was published, Fred Hampton, a Black Panther community leader, was killed when police riddled his apartment with bullets.[61]

When *The Sea Birds Are Still Alive* was published in 1977, one of the first reviews that Bambara read was written by actor-activist Ruby Dee. While "The Organizer's Wife" was never published by *Freedomways,* a review filled with exuberant praise for the book in which it was published eventually did appear there. Dee writes:

> FIRST OF ALL, beneath the extraordinarily gifted writer, Toni Cade Bambara, there has to be a very much involved and deeply caring Black human being. In her collection of short stories, *The Sea Birds Are Still Alive,* she brings blurred, ill-defined ideas and characters into sharp focus. She writes like a fine poet who

makes every word count because there's so much to say. I believe her work requires the reader to come half-way equipped with sensitivity to the importance
and dimensions especially of the black perspective and experience in America
since the 1960s. . . .

Oh yes—*The Sea Birds Are Still Alive* is definitely about revolution—all kinds
of revolutions; and after I'd stopped rereading so much of the book I concluded,
as Toni Cade Bambara puts it, "Being a revolutionary is something else again. I'm
not sure I'm up to it, and that's the truth." However, she sure makes me want to
keep on trying.[62]

Reading an advance copy of this review, Bambara cried.[63]

Margo Jefferson, the reviewer for *Newsweek*, also found beauty in *Sea Birds*,
"where the writing is more like a jazz improvisation than a structured linear plot," creating wholeness with "the imaginative fullness of a good novel"
that is "apt to create a world so precise in geography and tone that each
tale seems a chapter rather than a separate story." The reviewer compares
Bambara's work to Grace Paley's collections of short stories where lives and
neighborhoods overlap.[64] The review also includes a photograph of Bambara.
This time the camera snapped her in yoga-like meditative poise, another reminder that Bambara had declared the 1970s as a time for self-development
and self-instruction.

Years later, Margo Jefferson remembered the meeting at *Newsweek* when
her editor was determining what books would be reviewed for the magazine's
upcoming issue. The editor had held up the book *The Sea Birds Are Still Alive*
and dismissively quipped, "Who cares?"[65] That moment helped feed Jefferson's
determination to see the brilliance of Bambara's book receive its due through
a review in the influential publication.

At 37, even before *The Sea Birds Are Still Alive* appeared in bookstores, Bambara was one of the more widely read and known black women writers in
America. Her stories appeared in a range of publications including *Redbook*,
Essence, and *The Black World*. Her commentaries could be read in the *New
York Times* as well as in prison inmates' newsletters. Her books were reviewed
in the nation's leading mainstream newspapers and in publications that targeted radical black scholars.

Barbara Mahone's review of *The Sea Birds Are Still Alive* in *First World* addressed both the political and the more intimate relationships found in this
collection of stories. About Bambara's second collection of short stories, Mahone observed: "She writes with great versatility in both style and subject
matter—about weary women, distant fathers, radical children, true lovers,
spirited elders, and die-hard revolutionaries—coloring our perspectives of
Black life and bringing us closer to each other."[66]

In March 1976, on the day before Bambara's birthday, the Los Angeles
Hollywood Review reported that an earlier one of her short stories published
in *Gorilla, My Love* was reaching a diverse audience through Kres Mersky's

one-woman show, "Kres Mersky at the Codfish Ball." The review applauds Mersky's performance of Bambara's "late-in-life, but not to be counted out black woman trying to stave off the grave."[67]

More than 25 years later, Mersky, a white actor, recalled reading "My Man Bovanne" for the first time in the feminist anthology *Bitches and Sad Women*. "I was deeply moved by Bambara's writing about an older black woman who wasn't allowing age to take away her right to make decisions about her life. This was a woman who knew how to assert herself within her family and with everyone else."[68] Mersky's decision to give voice to a Harlem black woman through a stage performance of "My Man Bovanne" was unusual in the mid-1970s. Mersky, who never met Bambara, sent her the *Hollywood Reporter* stage review with a short note: "The show is going great. Everyone loves 'My Man Bovanne!'"[69]

Another one of Mersky's plays performed along with "My Man Bovanne" came to the attention of a cultural icon of a different kind, Richard Pryor. In another story in "The Codfish Ball," Mersky reenacted a story as a lesbian in a deeply disappointing love relationship. After viewing the tape of Mersky's performance, Pryor met with Mersky to work out an agreement for airing her performance on his new television show scheduled to debut in the early 1970s. Only when Pryor threatened to cancel his television show did the television producers agree to air a watered-down version of Mersky's sketch. Mersky said that was only one example of how her one woman performance portraying a lesbian created a political stir and was subject to censorship. On the other hand, Mersky, a young white woman in her mid-20s, portraying a mature black woman as depicted in Bambara's short story, received only praise from racially diverse audiences.[70]

Bambara did not see Mersky's performance, but that summer Bambara went to New York to review Ntzoke Shange's highly controversial work, *For Colored Girls Who Have Considered Suicide/When the Rainbow Is Enuf*; the review was published that fall in America's leading feminist magazine, *Ms*. While some black male critics wrote vitriolic reviews damning the play for Shange's betrayal of the black community through stereotypic portrayals of black men and super-heroic black women, Bambara praised the work. In a review entitled "For Colored Girls—and White Girls Too," Bambara cheered the play: "Blisteringly funny, fragile, droll and funky, lyrical, git down stompish, the play celebrates survival."[71] Again, Bambara spoke strongly as a black woman, fearless about jumping into a fray and standing up for the voices of black women.

Meanwhile, on a personal level, Bambara was heeding Atlanta's clarion call as she increasingly valued the time and space for introspection and writing that life outside of New York provided. About her trip to New York in a letter on July 13, Bambara described the surprise that her opportunities for writing and activism were making it easier for her to make Atlanta home than she initially expected as long as she stayed away from campus politics. Perhaps most rewarding was the time and space southern living allowed for pursuing new interests:

> Well. Nothin much to report from this end, kiddo. Been reading newspapers to workers in the factory. Shooting little films about kids. Cutting the grass. Daydreaming about a larger house so I can consolidate my work under one roof. Karma's doin well. A hellafyin kid. She keeps me honest. Trying to stop smoking, change a lotto habits and stay off the campus.
>
> Was up to New York a few weeks ago to review Ntozoke Shange's "For Colored Girls Who Have Considered Suicide/When the Rainbow is Enuf." Loved it. The play that is. N.Y. scared me a bit Everyone seems to've been knocked off balance by the bank takeover, the CUNY closure, lack of jobs. Seems to be no popular people strategy. The music, though, is more energetic than ever. Hard to imagine ever returning there for anything other than a quick trip. Which shocks me—I've always loved New York. Most exciting town I've ever been to/imagined—
>
> Lemme get out here and hoe some onions and get some kinda dinner together.[72]

Bambara had entered a new season in her life. Not only was Bambara spending more time in her own garden, but she more frequently jumped into her Volkswagen to travel the country roads for chats with southern black women who reminded her so much of the women she met in Vietnam. Bambara's future works of fiction would be rich in images of women who she visited, women who Bambara later described in her fiction as having ways "To talk with the lemon grass, enlist the cooperation of eucalyptus" and hear "Eyebright in the underbrush calling. Bladderwort singing. Calamus around the salt marshes."[73]

Not surprisingly, Bambara still avoided identifying herself strictly as a writer. While compelled to write, Bambara projected a different persona from many renowned writers. Defying stereotypic images of writers who prefer the Ivory Tower or demand seclusion, Bambara relished a different image. Rather than cast herself as a celebrity writer, she "wanted to venture into the wilds of deep rivers and ocean bottoms" as she reflected: "My image of myself, on the other hand, despite my breakthrough from my bourgeois training that promoted 'literaphilia' as a surrogate for political action and 'sensibility' as a substitute for social consciousness, was that of a somnambulant oyster in whose tissues irritating gritty something-or-other was making sleep and daydreaming a lumpy affair."[74] However, Bambara found Atlanta to be ideal for delving more deeply into herself. Bambara wrote: "In Atlanta, in the still waters of my landlocked hermitage, I was eager to find out what pearly thing might become available when the oyster was shucked."[75] In fact, in her first couple of years of living in Atlanta, the oyster was shucked, and then came *The Sea Birds*.

NOTES

1. Claudia Tate, "Toni Cade Bambara," in *Conversations with Toni Cade Bambara*, ed. Thabiti Lewis (Jackson: University Press of Mississippi, 2012), 59.

2. Ibid., 54.

3. Ibid.

4. "Neighborhood Arts Center Scheduled to Open in May," *Atlanta Daily World*, April 24, 1975.

5. Arlene Eisen, Interview by author, September 2012.

6. Arlene Eisen-Bergman, *Women of Viet Nam* (San Francisco: Peoples Press, 1974).

7. Toni Cade Bambara, *The Black Woman* (New York: Washington Square Press, 1970), 1.

8. Arlene Eisen, Interview by author.

9. "Report of The Mission on Repression in Vietnam, Fellowship of Reconciliation," August 17, 1970, Manuscripts, Archives and Rare Books Division, Schomburg Center for Research in Black Culture, New York.

10. Laura Whitehorn, Interview by author, August 2001.

11. Eisen, Interview.

12. Toni Cade Bambara, "Vietnam Trip," Manuscripts, Archives and Rare Books Division, Schomburg Center for Research in Black Culture, New York.

13. Whitehorn, Interview.

14. Ibid.

15. Ibid.

16. Ibid.

17. Toni Cade Bambara, "How She Came by Her Name," in *Deep Sightings and Rescue Missions* (New York: Vintage Books, 1996), 234.

18. Akua Kamau-Harris, Interview by author, July 2009.

19. Richard Detweiler, Letter to Dr. Richard Long, July 14, 1975, Spelman Archives, Atlanta.

20. Bambara, "Vietnam Trip."

21. Toni Cade Bambara, "Vietnam and Black Struggle: Two Revolutions in the Making," *Black-World-View* (June–July 1976): 6–13.

22. Whitehorn, Interview by author.

23. Ibid.

24. Ibid.

25. Toni Cade Bambara, "Untitled Vietnam Transcript," Manuscripts, Archives and Rare Books Division, Schomburg Center for Research in Black Culture, New York.

26. Ibid.

27. Ibid.

28. Bambara, "Vietnam Trip," Manuscripts, Archives and Rare Books Division, Schomburg Center for Research in Black Culture, New York.

29. Ibid.

30. Bambara, "Vietnam and Black Struggle: Two Revolutions in the Making," 13.

31. Whitehorn, Interview by author.

32. Ibid.

33. Ibid.

34. Bambara, "Vietnam and Black Struggle: Two Revolutions in the Making," 6.

35. Bambara, "Untitled Vietnam Transcript."

36. Bambara, "Vietnam and Black Struggle: Two Revolutions in the Making," 7.

37. See Safiya Bukhari, *The War Before: The Life Story of Becoming A Black Panther Fighting for Those Left Behind*, ed. Laura Whitehorn (New York: Feminist Press, 2010), the introduction written by Whitehorn describes the influence of the liberation struggle in Vietnam on organizing activities of the Black Panther Party and other radical activist movements in the United States.

38. Whitehorn, Interview by author.

39. Eisen, Interview by author.

40. "Neighborhood Cultural Festival Planned At Art Center, August 30," *Atlanta Daily World,* August 22, 1975.

41. Ebon Dooley, Interview by author, 2005.

42. Toni Cade Bambara, "Programming with School Daze," in *Five for Five: The Films of Spike Lee* (New York: Stewart, Tabori and Chang, 1991), 47–55.

43. "School of Social Work to Faculty, Staff and Students, Invited to a Lecture." School of Social Work, Memo, September 18, 1978. Robert W. Woodruff Library, Atlanta University Center Archives/Special Collections, Atlanta.

44. Douglass, Interview by author, September 2010.

45. Memo from "School of Social Work to Faculty, Staff and Students."

46. Bambara, "Vietnam Trip."

47. Ibid.

48. Bambara, "Vietnam and Black Struggle."

49. Massiah, "How She Came by Her Name," 234.

50. Toni Cade Bambara, Letter to John Henrik Clarke, December 17, 1975, Spelman College Archives, Atlanta.

51. John Henrik Clarke, Letter to Toni Cade Bambara, December 26, 1974, Spelman College Archives, Atlanta.

52. Toni Cade Bambara, "Copyright Page," in *The Sea Birds Are Still Alive* (New York: Vintage Books, 1982).

53. Sandra Swans, Letter to Toni Cade Bambara, December 31, 1975, Spelman College Archives, Atlanta.

54. Toni Cade Bambara, *The Sea Birds Are Still Alive* (New York: Vintage Books, 1982).

55. Ibid., 76.

56. Ibid., 76–77.

57. Beverly Guy Sherftall, "Commitment: Toni Cade Bambara Speaks" in *Conversations with Toni Cade Bambara*, ed. Thabiti Lewis (Jackson: University Press of Mississippi, 2012), 13.

58. Toni Cade Bambara, "The Organizer's Wife," in *The Sea Birds Are Still Alive* (New York: Vintage Books, 1982), 17.

59. Bambara, "The Long Night," in *The Sea Birds Are Still Alive* (New York: Vintage Books, 1982), 94–102.

60. Ibid., 98.

61. Jeffrey Hass, *The Assassination of Fred Hampton: How the FBI and the Chicago Police Murdered a Black Panther* (Chicago: Lawrence Hill Books, 2011).

62. Ruby Dee, "Review: The Sea Birds Are Still Alive," *Freedomways* (Summer 1977): 102–4.

63. Beverly Guy-Sheftall, "Commitment: Toni Cade Bambara Speaks," 17.

64. Margo Jefferson, "Blue Notes," *Newsweek Magazine,* May 2, 1977, 76.

65. Margo Jefferson, Interview by author, June 2011.

66. Barbara Mahone, "A Handsome Family Quilt," *First World* (May/June 1977): 40–42.

67. "Kres Mersky at the Codfish Ball," *Hollywood Review,* March 24, 1976, Spelman College Archives, Atlanta.

68. Mersky, Interview by author, March 2011.

69. Kres Mersky, Note to Toni Cade Bambara, March 24, 1976.

70. Kres Mersky, Interview by author, March 2011.

71. Toni Cade Bambara, "'For Colored Girls'—and White Girls Too," *Ms* 5, no. 3 (1976): 36.

72. Toni Cade Bambara, Letter to author, July 13, 1976.

73. Toni Cade Bambara, *The Salt Eaters,* 152.

74. Toni Cade Bambara, "Salvation Is the Issue," in *Black Women Writers (1950–1980),* (New York: Anchor Books, 1984), 42.

75. Ibid.

SIX

Making Dreams Work

Dream work too makes impatient with linear literary convention and with conventional narrator postures—as omniscient mind, as witness, as participant. Both dreams and mediation [meditation] hint at another possibility—the narrator as medium, the camera eye as permeable.[1]

For Bambara, dreams were a way to see new possibilities. When involved with community organizing, Bambara rejected notions that visions of global change and transformation were far-fetched illusions or fantasies that would never see the light of day. Similar to human rights activists who spark worldwide social and political movements, this writer could see dreams for change as a force for shaping new realities.[2] In Atlanta where she began writing novels, Bambara explained that entering a dream state was critical to the work she was doing. In fact, the author described that the writing process sometimes required her to transition into a sort of medium who received stories through dreams and other states of altered consciousness versus thinking of herself as the creator of the story. In her everyday life, Bambara also found dreams to be a reliable source of guidance. The activist-writer kept a dream journal and encouraged others to do the same in many of the workshops that she facilitated.

In the mid-1970s, as her southern gaze deepened, Bambara turned her attention to writing her first novel: *The Salt Eaters,* the only novel of hers to be published in her lifetime. In the novel, the central character, Velma Henry, a burned-out 1960s' activist, enters a dream-like state in a healing session,

where she ultimately claims health as her right and finds wellness and wholeness within herself. A community-based healer, Minnie Ransom, guides her
through this transformative healing process surrounded by elders and spirits
at a community infirmary.[3]

In this work of fiction that rings with poetry and wisdom, Bambara addresses familiar themes from her previous short stories, such as the importance of memory, cultural identity, and activism. Another similarity between
The Salt Eaters and Bambara's short stories is that the central characters are
primarily women. But now, unlike the majority of her previous work, the acclaimed short-story writer chose to set her first novel in the South.

Bambara presented other new themes in The Salt Eaters as well, embodied
in its challenge to political activists and spiritual adepts to leave their separate
camps and unite their forces—creating mind, body, and spiritual wholeness
within themselves and in their communities. In addition, Bambara recognized
a need for healing in the black community from the traumas of the fractured
movements of the 1960s that took a toll on an alarming number of artists
and activists. This novel proposes creating a force of political wholeness in yet
another visionary way and that is through the work of a performance group of
women that Bambara named the Seven Sisters. This diverse group of women
of color—including sisters of the corn, rice, plantain, and yam—is a group
that Bambara saw as a potential model for a real-world effort to unify women
of color movements across indigenous communities.

What also distinguished Bambara's first novel is that while Bambara like
other black women novelists continued to celebrate the black experience,
Bambara simultaneously introduced a wide range of cultural images and
spiritual traditions in her novel that extended beyond the cultural experience of many urban and rural black Americans. In The Salt Eaters, Bambara
delved into exploring a culturally diverse array of healing traditions and
disciplines.

Among the many mainstream reviews of The Salt Eaters, John Leonard's
review uniquely captured the vastness of Bambara's symbolic landscape and
raised the fundamental question that he believed emanated from her work.
In his New York Times book review, he argued that Bambara's point of view
underscored the interconnections of spiritual beliefs and practices.[4] In The Salt
Eaters, Bambara made a call to see the interconnections and truths expressed
in diverse spiritual practices rather than only touting spiritual practices emanating from the African diaspora or any other race or ethnic group for that
matter. Writing in the New York Times, Leonard provided a sample of the diverse symbols, secular and spiritual, that Bambara tapped into when writing
The Salt Eaters:

> Consider the "woman-charged culture of Dahomey," the mamba priestesses of
> the Vudon and the Amazons. Consider, as well, the saints, the loa, the dinns
> and the devas. Think about the fire rites of macumba, condomble, obeah, sango,
> lucumi, santeria, winti and voodoo. Focus on the letter "Y": the wishbone and

the slingshot and the water-witch wand and the fork in the road. What if all systems—I Ching, thermodynamics, astrology, numerology, alchemy, metaphysics, everybody's old myths—are interchangeable?[5]

While Bambara was clearly a cultural visionary, she wanted the process of creating wholeness to be a step toward empowering individuals and communities to awaken to their abilities to make immediate real-life changes in the world. In the midst of exploring timelessness and dimensions of outer space, frequented more often by avant-garde jazz musicians and abstract painters than by her contemporary black women writers, Bambara was awake to political and social realities.

Prior to beginning the intense writing required to complete her first novel, political and social realities kept her involved with work—strengthening networks for black writers whose works were also calling for change. Bambara was a critical force in the development of the Southern Coalition of African American Writers (SCAAW), this organization was in the forefront of making Atlanta a base for a new Black Arts Movement in the South. In local public schools, Bambara also spent time working with high school students interested in the creative arts. Whether in a workshop in her home or organizing a conference for southern black writers and artists, Bambara demonstrated her commitment to transformation and there was increasing recognition of her influence in Atlanta.

In the winter of 1977, Bambara was in Atlanta's spotlight as she joined others from Atlanta's arts community in receiving the city's first Jubilee Bronze Award. In a televised broadcast of the awards ceremony, Bambara was introduced as an influential writer and was recognized for her community contributions, particularly her work with children. The awards ceremony recognized black artists who were contributing to the arts in Atlanta through community service.

On February 18, Bambara arrived at Channel 30, Atlanta's public television station, stylishly dressed in a long slinky black dress with a flower, signature of Billie Holiday, neatly tucked into her crowning 1960s' afro.[6] That night the MC identified Bambara as a short-story writer and surprisingly also introduced her as a prolific poet even though the few poems of hers that were published appeared in print nearly 20 years ago. Nominated by Michael Lomax, director of Atlanta's Bureau of Cultural Affairs, who continued to champion Bambara long after her formal employment at the Neighborhood Arts Center (NAC) ended, Bambara was the only nominee in the writing category, in contrast to categories such as dance and the theater arts, which were competitive.

In a ceremony that focused largely on Mayor Maynard Jackson's administration's success in extending the reach of the arts into the community, Bambara's brief comments had a different focus. Unlike the others, who accepted their coveted awards with speeches that included appreciative listings of family members, coworkers, and mentors of influence, Bambara made her expression of gratitude brief. Conveying her serious-mindedness with a gaze reminiscent of a 1960s' political street rapper, Bambara's thin shimmer of a smile signaled her appreciation of the recognition. Bambara simply told the audience that she was accepting the award on behalf of the children, "precious resources whose very presence on the earth is a continuous source of inspiration."[7]

Even as The Bronze Jubilee Award spotlighted Bambara's accomplishments as a writer, she was once again entangled in a web of negotiations in seeking a position at an Atlanta college. After teaching briefly at Clark College, Bambara was in negotiations with Spelman College, Atlanta's preeminent college for black women. After living in Atlanta for three years, Bambara continued to hope for a position as writer-in-residence for the 1977–78 academic year. The writer was disappointed by Spelman's slow-moving pace and by the institution's refusals to honor her salary request of $7,000 for the academic year.[8]

Just a year before, the Spelman campus had erupted as hundreds of students and faculty, led by Millicent Dobbs Jordan (Spelman professor and aunt to Mayor Maynard Jackson), organized protests that encompassed a range of actions—including holding the Spelman Board of Trustees and its chairperson Marian Wright Edelman captive at their meeting. The 26-hour protest included demands to rescind the Board's nomination of Donald Stewart, a white man, to the presidency of Spelman.[9] The protest, which aimed to have a black woman named to the position of president, had become so heated that interventions from Rev. Martin Luther King, Sr. and Congressman Andrew Young were needed to help restore calm to the campus.[10] Now, a year later, Stewart was involved with discussions to have Bambara introduce the school's first course focused on black women writers.

As negotiations at Spelman stalled, Bambara accepted an invitation from Howard University to give the keynote address to the Third National Conference of Afro-American Writers, where the theme explored "Black Writers and Their People: Craft and Consciousness."[11] In her speech, Bambara challenged the audience to begin a process of effectively moving forward from the 1960s to the 1970s without losing the momentum of the previous decade. More and more, she was involved with focusing attention on creating movements that connected the political with the metaphysical. Rather than seeing black people as victims of oppression, Bambara expressed her undying optimism to the audience of writers, academics, and students, pointing out: "We are now in a period of healing, study and self-development. Some see the trend as retrogression; I find it quite interesting. . . . If the hallmark of the last quarter century was revolution, a shifting of global empires, the understanding and the rejection of the American empire, plus the rise of the national consciousness, then the hallmark of this quarter is the transformation of the knowledge gained and the energies developed."[12]

While in Washington, Bambara also met with Jacqueline Trescott of *The Washington Post*. In their early morning interview, the writer described an array of activities that she had prioritized for herself. Along with developing her own filmmaking skills and wanting to create her own film company, she also intended to organize among workers to create farm cooperatives in the South. Bambara, who was participating in dream analysis groups in Atlanta, told Trescott of wanting to conduct dream analysis sessions with parents and children as well.[13]

Puffing on a cigarette, Bambara once again revealed her lingering ambivalence about her move to Atlanta, which provided an encouraging environment for writing, but suffered from cultural gaps in the eyes of the former New Yorker. Trescott reported that one of Bambara's complaints about Atlanta was limited access to jazz: "As she scrunches up her pear-shaped face, makeupless under a flyaway Afro, she asks, 'do you know there are only four bass players in town?'"[14] Bambara relished her New York roots. Coming to terms with life in Atlanta, a city that was lacking the cultural diversity that fed her spirit in New York, required the author to sometimes seek cultural nurturance elsewhere.

Still in need of a job, Bambara returned to Atlanta from Washington where she continued to pursue negotiations with Spelman College. As always, however, Bambara would be cheered by the growing support for her work and writing. When catching up on her mail after returning from DC, Bambara was delighted to find a letter from Tran Van Dinh, now a professor at Temple University, letting her know he had begun reading *The Sea Birds Are Still Alive* as soon as he had received the book. Van Dinh, by now an internationally recognized Vietnamese author whose books included writing on anticolonial struggles in Vietnam, wrote his friend:

> I started immediately with *The Sea Birds Are Still Alive* when a student of mine (a Black woman whom I am advising on her work on Paul Robeson) came into my office and saw the book. She was excited that I read your work and was impressed that I even knew you. She is a great admirer of yours and has read all your works. She thinks and I concur with her that you "are the greatest woman writer on this earth" and that "included Vietnam," I added.[15]

As weeks passed with no resolution to the Spelman negotiations, Bambara wrote a detailed letter to Stewart on June 10, where she requested an immediate follow-up to their last meeting held in February, as well as "a confirmation letter in the form of a contract by June 30th."[16] In addition to seeking $7,000 for the nine-month teaching contract, Bambara also requested an estimated $1,000 for six film rentals and other materials for the course.[17]

Although these salaries were less than what Bambara had been accustomed to receiving at the state-supported Rutgers University, Beverly Guy-Sheftall, a Spelman graduate who had begun her academic teaching career at Spelman College six years earlier, recalled that her starting salary in 1971 was $7,500 for the entire year and that the salary Bambara was being offered at Spelman— the same amount for one semester of teaching—was within the standard salary range at the time.[18]

Bambara's friend Jan Douglass recalled her involvement with the President of Spelman, Donald Stewart, in finally reaching a settlement with the author. Douglass said, "The Stewart family is like extended family. When Don Stewart became president of Spelman, I went to Don to see if he could help and he and Michael Lomax, director of Atlanta's Cultural Affairs Office, worked out something. They found some money and she became author-in-residence at Spelman College."[19]

In August, having finally reached an agreement with Spelman, Bambara immediately canvassed the community to begin promoting the noncredited course, which was open to all. Through visits to senior citizen centers, community centers, and tenants' groups, Bambara circulated posters and flyers produced by the NAC and Atlanta's Bureau of Cultural and International Affairs, which under the direction of Michael Lomax provided funds to support Bambara's salary. The writer also helped to prepare press releases for the local black newspaper to encourage the community to attend the seminars that would be meeting on Tuesday and Thursday nights from 5:30 to 7:30 P.M., a time intended to be convenient for those with jobs to attend.[20] By then, the title of the course had been renamed "Images of Black Women in Literature and Film." The cutting-edge political films scheduled to be screened included Lucia, a Cuban-produced film depicting Cuban women in various historical time periods; La Luta Continua, a picture whose subject was Mozambique's struggle for liberation; Bush Mama, which captured the heightening consciousness of the welfare mothers' movement in the United States; and The Battle of Algiers, which focused on the revolutionary movement in Algeria to increase awareness of global political change.[21]

In early September, when the course had only been in progress for a few weeks, Bambara received a note in which her friend E. Ethelbert Miller, a scholar and also an accomplished poet, recommended that she set aside some time to read the book African Folk Medicinal Practices and Beliefs of the Bambara and Other Peoples, by Pascal James Imperato, a physician and public health scholar. According to Miller, the book described how the Bambara of Mali believed in reincarnation and recognized supernatural causation of illness.[22] Imperoto's research also documented the importance of diviners, herbalists, charm makers, fortune-tellers, spirit mediums, and spirits such as the most powerful spirit Faro, "master of the spoken word" in the belief system of the Bambara people.[23] Interestingly, these were topics Bambara was exploring in her research and writing.

In responding to Miller, Bambara wrote: "Dear E. Hey thanks so much. I'm ordering it now. Funny. Am doing a Book of Baths with a friend (rituals, recipes, remedies, seduction scenarios, what have you) and I just started laying out all the Sudanese water baths and clay picks and sand baths and stuff the old folks in my family used to talk about. And here you come with the Bambara [people of Mali] book right on time. Thanks again."[24] Bambara did submit a proposal for a collection of short stories entitled, The Book of Baths a few years later.[25] The book was never published, but most of the stories intended for the book eventually were.

The Imperato book probably contributed to her preparation for teaching her course on black women at Spelman College as well. What was initially intended to be a course that focused on black women writers expanded to include film and an array of works written on and about black women. The course content included discussions focusing on holistic systems of healing which paralleled the research Bambara was doing in preparing for her writing project.[26]

For Angelle Cooper, then an undergraduate student at Spelman College, however, what was most memorable about the seminar that Bambara taught was being introduced to Bambara's writing and hearing Bambara read from her own work. Years later, Cooper remembered that as an undergraduate student she had been totally unfamiliar with Bambara's writing. Hearing Bambara read one of her own short stories, "Gorilla, My Love," had an immediate impact. Cooper said, "I remember that story speaking to me. I remember running back to my dorm room to copy every word of the story and mailing it back home to my mother and sister in Philadelphia. This was before copying machines and I couldn't afford to buy the book. I had no idea whether the book would be easy to get or if it was in the library. I just knew that I had to share this story with my family back home. Copying the story word for word was the best way I knew how to do that at the time."[27]

The response of Spelman students and community members to the course made it seem, at least for the moment, that the struggles to implement the course had been worthy of the frustration the writer had entailed. Now, Bambara's publicized position on the Spelman campus added to the attention she was receiving in Atlanta as a speaker at conferences and as a resource to students elsewhere. In December, Bambara participated on a panel and in an open forum that reflected her interests in the value of recognizing Black English not as a dialect, but as a language. A flyer that asked, "Our Language Patterns, and What, if Anything, to do About Them?," promoted the panel's first iteration at Georgia State University in November, as well as its second appearance at Clark College in December.[28] Bambara would join Gloria Blackwell, from the Clark College Department of Social Work, and others to discuss these issues. As a writer, Bambara's short stories are often recognized as hallmarks for the dignity embedded in her mastery of articulating black urban voices that are free of the stereotypic black dialect that is often depicted with dropped "g's" and so-called slang. Bambara's interest in working with younger students in the community also continued as she assisted in developing a new creative arts program for Atlanta's high school students that would include classes in photography, mass communications, drama, poetry, contemporary design, music, and creative writing.[29] The dedication of the first and ongoing editions of the student creative writing journal WE (Writer's Education) mentions Bambara, along with Mayor Maynard Jackson, and David Kidd, the high school instructor, as a source of inspiration. The second issue of Potlikker, edited by NAC's writers-in-residence Ebon Dooley and Kamau-Harris, also recognized Bambara's contributions in Atlanta's black arts community.[30]

The semester ended with Bambara providing the keynote address for the more than 100 women who attended a December women's conference at a local community center where "Role Alternatives for Black Women: Where to From Here in the Black Freedom Struggle" served as the theme.[31] Bambara's friend Jualynne Dodson, who was now director of the Research Center of the Atlanta University School of Social Work Research Center and one of the primary organizers of the conference, planned workshops on law, health, and politics.[32] Bambara opened her keynote speech with the wake-up call, formatted as questions, that she often used at the beginning of her talks, reminding audiences to consider the significance of the present moment and challenging them to commit themselves to political action by bringing the attention of the audience to the particular moment of time by naming the specific day of the specific month of the specific year.[33]

Bambara freely expressed her optimism about the possibilities for transformation. Regarding the probing series of questions that Bambara used in opening her speeches, Dodson concluded: "In a practical fashion, it helps you to reposition yourself as to who you are and to the fact that each period in which you live is an important and dynamic time to be on the planet given the work that we all must do to help produce a humane world."[34] Even now, Dodson reported that she still uses Bambara's eye-opening series of questions in beginning her own speeches.[35]

In an undated letter to her mother that probably was written about the same time in the mid-1970s, Bambara expressed a similar spirit of optimism about being alive at the end of the 20th century, a time when the fruits of liberation struggles in Africa and Cuba could be observed. In mentioning recent presidential elections and again referring to the significance of the particular moment in time, the writer makes a light-hearted reference to recently elected President Jimmy Carter whom she humorously refers to as Tom Sawyer. (When writing her master's thesis, "The American Adolescent Apprentice Novel," which she completed more than a decade earlier, Bambara's literary analysis included frequent references to Mark Twain's fictional characters.) While wary of mainstream politics, Bambara appears to be enjoying life. In this loving letter to her mother, Bambara is even optimistic about finances:

The upswing in readings/lectures should hold me till this grant comes through in Spring (light a candle for me, or pray, or put my picture under a pyramid, or work some roots or whatever it is you do) and the royalties come in summer. It still looks good. Solid. Got a new collection brewing in the dark of my bottom drawer. Never dreamed I'd have so much to say. I don't know what folks mean when they talk about writers' "block." I can't keep up with myself. Have taken to napping for an hour in the afternoon and sleeping a short spell at night cause I'm so busy jumping up every few minutes to draft another story. A sister around here that does illustrations is eager to collaborate on some children's books. I wanna too. Soon's I clear off at least one desk. I guess as soon as I get the novel out the way I'll do a few of those . . . Yeh. Yeh I like this life I'm leading. Now all I need is a dude I can talk with and laugh with. Just finished too the second draft of the SNCC film I mentioned. I hope that comes through, cause I want to script/ do films in about five years time. Never did finish that film I was working on, but will get back to it next Spring I suspect.

What's happening with you? I never realized how many folks had met you. Seems like everyone I run into says "how's your Mama doing' or 'I hear about your mother. She sounds like a "groove" and blah, blah. Keep me posted.'

Well. Now that Tom Sawyer's been elected, should be interesting to watch the developments of the South's attempt to push for economic hegemony in the country/world. Whole new conglomerate/finance group rising to rival the Rockefeller, Morgan, Mob-Union-Midwest groups. Can't figure out what effect it all'l [will] have on us folks, but would imagine some education dough'll be floating to this state. Hell, look what happened to the universities in Texas, particularly in Austin, when Johnson got in. I blew the polls. Wanted to cast my vote for Peter Camejo the only candidate with a humane platform and a sound analysis of this country. . . . Oh well. In our lifetime. This is the last quarter of the 20th century. As an erstwhile basketball fan and an ex-baseball spectator, you know what can happen in the last quarter. I'm optimistic. That is, realistic. The world is changing rapidly. 25 years is a long spell. Look at the changes on the Continent from 1956 to 1976. Or Cuba in those 25 years. Or the whole power configuration in the world in 25 years. The more I travel, the more positive I judge the American people. The "myth" of democracy and justice and fair play and all that still looms large in the imagination. And the fascist forces I'm beginning to see, are really quite small—-powerful, seductive, in key places, but really not all that Big or they would not have to lie so brazenly and thoroughly to the people. In our life, I hope you plan to be around for the 21st century, Mama, cause it is gonna be beautiful. Take good care of yourself.[36]

In January 1978, however, Bambara did face challenges. Fully expecting to teach Part II of the Black Women in Literature course in the spring semester, Bambara did not anticipate that the course would be cancelled. The agreement as Bambara understood it was for her to restructure the course formerly entitled "American Writers in Literature" into a course on black women writers—filling a gap in the Spelman curriculum. More than a week into the semester, with no books ordered or classroom space assigned, Bambara recommended that the students seek an independent study rather than risk taking the course with her and not receive credit. In a letter where Bambara also mentioned her own health problems, Bambara wrote that she no longer had an interest in investing "further time and energy pursuing the matter. So at this point in time there is no course."[37]

Years later, Beverly Guy-Sheftall remembered the series of events that led Spelman to abort the Black Women in Literature course that Bambara had proposed. "What I recall, and I never did understand it, is that there was an issue about her teaching a black women writers class, as if there was no academic reason for doing this. Now what I don't know is if it was a money issue and they used an ideological argument to cancel the class, or whether it was an ideological issue from the beginning."[38] What Guy-Sheftall clearly recollected decades later, however, is that for the most part English Department members were not familiar with Bambara's writings and that they raised questions about the legitimacy of a course that focused on black women writers. Still with disbelief and disappointment in her voice, Guy-Sheftall said, "They certainly were not aware of the *Black Woman*. And I'm not even sure they were aware of her books of short stories." Finally, the writer's resurgent optimism prompted a solution as she told Guy-Sheftall, "Hell, I'll just hold the workshop in my home."[39]

More and more, Bambara's home became not only a space for writing that required seclusion, but also a space that invited gatherings of students, writers, filmmakers, and activists. By then Bambara had moved from Mayflower to a one-family house at 991 Simpson Street, elevated high enough on a hill to see the downtown skyline and just a short downhill walk to fried-fish sandwich restaurants, chicken wing shops, and other small businesses that catered to the working-class neighborhood. It was not far from the Vine City community, where long-standing SNCC activist Donald Stone and others joined Julian Bond to improve housing and work conditions in the 1960s.

What Bambara's editor Toni Morrison remembered about that time was corresponding with Bambara about the subject of a new manuscript, this time the editor's own. Years later, Morrison recalled with laughter that while Bambara liked the new book, it simply wasn't her style. Morrison explained:

> There's somewhere in the world the manuscript of *Song of Solomon* that I sent her. I don't know whether she wrote me this or told me—she said she sent Karma to a neighbor to stay while she got some fish sandwiches. And she got on the couch and read the manuscript and she wrote all over it. And she wrote things like, "Yeah, we know that" or "hurry up." You know, that's like her because she does not wait for the lame or the halt or anybody who isn't there. You know she really moves you fast. If you don't get it, well. So . . . She's writing all over the manuscript, contesting things.[40]

In May 1978, Bambara received the good news that Morrison would be the invited commencement speaker at Spelman. Once the writer learned that Morrison also would be doing a reading at the President's House at Spelman College, she rushed to order copies of *Song of Solomon* for the handful of Spelman students who frequently gathered at her home for spirited discussions about their own writing and the works of other black writers.[41] Having read the *Song of Solomon* in galleys, Bambara was well equipped to facilitate lively discussions with the Spelman students about Morrison's latest book. Taronda Spencer, then a student at Spelman College, smiled as she recalled the excitement generated by the book. Spencer, later the archivist for Spelman College, remembered, "While my classmates struggled with understanding the book and its symbolism, we had Toni guiding us through our reading of Morrison's masterpiece that was hot off the press at the time."[42] In 1978, Morrison also was named distinguished writer by the American Academy of Arts and Letters and *Song of Solomon* was the first book by an African American writer to be listed as the main selection in the Book-of-the-Month

Club since Richard Wright's *Native Son* in 1940. The novel also was winner of the National Book Critics Circle Award that year.[43]

On May 20, the night before the graduation, Bambara and Morrison spent a relaxed evening at the home of then married couple, Pearl [Cleage] Lomax and Michael Lomax, not far from Bambara's place. Years later, Cleage attached special significance to the evening. "I was already in awe of *The Bluest Eye* when my friend and sister writer Toni Cade Bambara brought Toni Morrison over to my house for dinner. Terrified of burning the roast chicken or scorching the bottom of the cornbread, my only memory of the evening is asking her to sign my copy of her novel and enjoying her pleasure in the French vanilla ice cream we had for dessert. I still have the book." Signing Cleage's copy of *The Bluest Eye*, Morrison thanked Michael and Pearl "for the well spent evening."[44]

Recalling details of the evening, Cleage said: "It took a long time for me to feel comfortable that night. For the most part, Toni Morrison was pleasant, but aloof." Cleage was part of Mayor Jackson's administration and her books would later become best sellers. About Bambara and her presence in the Atlanta community, Cleage said, "Her house was the gathering place. We used to call it the 'witch's house' because of the steep staircase. I don't think I ever heard Toni say a bad word about anyone. That was not part of her critique. She was part of a community of black women writers who cared about other writers."[45]

The night of the dinner was without complications, but suggestions that Morrison receive an honorary degree from Spelman erupted into debates similar to the ones surrounding Bambara as writer-in-residence. When Donald Stewart was named president of Spelman, he had become the first to institute honorary degrees, and he suggested that Morrison be the first to receive one from the college. Guy-Sheftall explained that because of protest from some members of the English faculty, Stewart decided to hold an impromptu faculty vote and learned that some faculty members found the writing of Morrison deeply offensive.[46] Some members of the English Department faculty and the honorary degree committee objected to aspects of Morrison's previously published works such as *The Bluest Eye* and *Sula*. Guy-Sheftall remembered that some considered Morrison's writing to be "vulgar" or "inauthentic."[47] Whether Bambara knew about the debate is unclear, but the discussion provided another indication that some members of the English Department were in need of an awakening to the literary value of contemporary black writers who were influenced by the cultural revolution of the 1960s. On the other hand, Bambara may have found the troubling incident a good reason to laugh and a reminder to keep to her pledge of avoiding campus life.

Over the next several months what Bambara expressed excitement about was her mother's imminent move to Atlanta. That year, Bambara's mother, Helen Cade, moved from New York to join Bambara in Atlanta and settled in Bambara's former home on Mayflower Street. Now Karma had an in-residence grandmother so that Bambara could more freely travel and spend late nights writing. At the end of July 1978, Bambara sent her mother an update regarding the planned move to Atlanta, and filled her in with news about promising opportunities for support for her future writing. Bambara wrote:

Dear Ma,

   Have fixed up the house except for kitchen. Bathroom will be operable as of tomorrow afternoon. Have already moved in and set up the books, paintings, etc. Acme Movers (can you believe that) will move me Thursday morning, Aug. 3rd. Having the gas, elec, water, phone turned off in Mayflower house the next day. Gas, elect. phone are on in Simpson (phone ringing at 2 spots. though they keep threatening I may not be able to keep same number . . .
   I hope to get set-up in a week's time. Got to get some manuscripts out and find a job. Have used up all the loan money I took out and am hugging bottom of savings. But phew what a relief to be in the place at last. Hope to be able to get at least one book contract by Sept.[48]

Finances remained challenging as a result of no longer teaching at Spelman College, but Bambara found ways to continue the field work she needed to do to prepare for writing. By now, the writer was deepening her research on traditional healers, root workers, and interpreters of dreams by making trips to New Orleans to visit with ritual specialists who had mastered traditional healing practices. Leah Wise, another one of Bambara's several friends who worked at the Institute of the Black World and coedited the special edition of *Southern Exposure* with Bambara, remembered some of the explorations. Wise recalled how Bambara followed Zora Neal Hurston's path in visiting different medium folks in Louisiana as she learned about various folk traditions: "I remember her telling me about laying on someone's couch as a part of an experiment that allowed her to be free and fully dive into the experience."[49] Freedom of thought and political movement were critical to Bambara's well-being. Free of academic ties, the author had more space and time for her chosen work.

Part of Bambara's ability to sustain an independent writing life in Atlanta related to the fact that Atlanta continued to draw cultural workers to the city—for some, Bambara's presence and activism in the city was part of the draw for the artistic and intellectual community. A long-standing friend of Bambara's who resettled in Atlanta was Hoyt Fuller, former editor of *Negro Digest* and *Black World*. A decade earlier in Chicago, Fuller played a significant role in developing the Organization of Black American Culture (OBAC). The Artists Workshop of OBAC became internationally renowned for its street mural "Wall of Respect," which inspired the title of one of Bambara's short stories.[50] Some of Bambara's earlier short stories had been published in these leading black magazines. Soon after Fuller moved to Atlanta, Bambara was leveraging her position as a Board member of the Coordinating Council of Literary Magazines (CCLM), a membership service organization of noncommercial literary magazines, to encourage CCLM funding for *First World*.[51] Bambara quickly became an editorial advisor to *First World*, along with Maya Angelou.

A year earlier, in the spring of 1977, Bambara wrote Fuller to plead with him to submit an application for funding from the CCLM. In an effort to convince Fuller to prioritize submitting a proposal, Bambara writes: "We've already made a strong case for [First World] and some [money] is currently being argued over about for earmarking." Bambara adds, "We've got strong Blk/3rd World—'scuse me, 1st world—representation on the Board and on grants selection committee. As you may recall from a quick chat we had last Fall, I got on the Board mainly to insure [First World] funding, to monitor [money] in interest of black publications around the country. So do pulezze [sic] apply."[52]

Bambara was promoting Atlanta as the black arts mecca of the South in other ways as well. For example, Bambara was involved with establishing Atlanta as a venue for black writers' conferences and promoting the campuses of Atlanta's several black colleges as ideal meeting places for publishers and black writers from across the country. The CCLM's meeting at Spelman College is one example. Hosted by English Department Chair Richard A. Carroll, CCLM met in Spelman's Sister's Chapel Auditorium and the John F. Kennedy School Auditorium that same year and attracted CCLM panel participants who were part of Bambara's circle, including Ishmael Reed, Ebon Dooley, and Pearl Lomax [Cleage]. At Spelman's CCLM Conference, Bambara moderated a workshop on "How to Find Money for Literature."[53] This is also one of many examples of how Bambara sustained ties with Spelman College in ways that supported the organizing work she continued to do in the black arts community.

Bambara also became involved with the development of a new organization for cultural workers, the SCAAW, which the writer helped to form. When SCAAW's founding president Alice Lovelace championed forming the organization, Lovelace chatted frequently with Bambara when working to develop the organization's tenets that included challenging elitism among black writers, encouraging published and non-published writers to form mutual networks and reminding black writers to remain engaged in their communities. SCAAW also aimed to acquaint writers with their audiences, to introduce them to publishers, book agents, and booksellers, as well as to provide a creative atmosphere in which to develop their writing skills. Very soon, plans were in the making for a regional writers' conference in Atlanta.

Wanting to avoid organizational leadership titles, Bambara promoted collective leadership models rather than hierarchical organizations that are more easily dominated by singular figures. Lovelace remembered that even when Bambara was working vehemently to promote organizations like SCAAW, she declined having her own name headlined on SCAAW's brochures, conference programs, or any other publicly distributed materials.[54] Nevertheless, the author's name succeeded in attracting resources to new cultural efforts in Atlanta.

In the fall of 1978, Bambara helped to shape the organization's first conference. Lovelace explained, "Bambara promoted a different sensibility about writers. She often said there is no such thing as a 'writer.' Instead, there are dancers who write, secretaries who write. Painters who write. Anyone who is in the world can be a writer."[55] At the conference that attracted 140 people, Bambara moderated one of the writers' workshops. Hosted by the NAC where Bambara also continued to have strong ties, the conference program included international scholar Hoyt Fuller as a speaker and a workshop where Earl Graves, the New York editor of *Enterprise Magazine,* was a panelist.[56] Bambara could see that SCAAW was reaching its goal of becoming a national and international marketplace of ideas and material resources for black writers in the South.

In SCAAW's second year of existence, Bambara continued to function as an influential SCAAW advisor and as elections chairperson. That year, SCAAW's conference was hosted by Clark College where program speakers included a number of Bambara's associates and friends such as Gwendolyn Brooks, Addison Gayle, Haki Madhubuti, Nikki Giovanni, Tom Dent, Pearl Cleage, Richard Long, and Sonia Sanchez. At the conference, Bambara chaired a panel on "Dealing with Major Publishers," which included Phil Petry, *Black Enterprise* editor, and focused on strategies for writers to publish their work through mainstream presses, alternative publishers, and self-publishing.[57] Because of Bambara's growing interest in the significance of dreams and the power of the mystical, Bambara also may have suggested the two other panels on SCAAW's program that year, "Using Dreams to Unlock and Unblock the Creative Self," and "Using Astrology as a Tool for Self-Understanding." Lavada Bibbs, President of the Society for the Advancement of the Spiritual Arts & Sciences, led both of those workshops.[58]

Just as Bambara increased awareness locally and internationally of the importance of Atlanta's new stream of political black writers, she also promoted community organizers collaborating with psychically adepts in some political efforts. Now, however, in the midst of her diverse organizing work, Bambara also heeded her own call to do more of the writing she had come to Atlanta to accomplish. This activist was ardent in organizing among Atlanta's cultural workers' community, but soon the writing of her first novel would become the centerpiece of her life. Teaching and living in Atlanta had facilitated research on alternative healing systems. And, Bambara later explained that the skeleton of the novel that became *The Salt Eaters* can be found in her notes for a short story she was developing in her earlier years in Atlanta. Bambara said that *The Salt Eaters* was initially developed in the 1970s as a short story that centers on a Mardi Gras Society, which decides to reenact a slave insurrection.[59] Bambara later wrote that it wasn't until several years later that the writing of the story entered a new dimension, a dimension previously unknown to her that allowed her to write her first novel when the story began speaking to her more as a dream.

Years later, Bambara provided specific examples of having experienced writing *The Salt Eaters* in an altered state of consciousness. She explained, "Some of the characters began speaking Portuguese, I don't speak Portuguese. I had originally set it in some place like New Orleans, or kind of like Galveston [Texas] and the scene shifted, so I went with it and wrote it out."[60] Bambara also described the writing of *The Salt Eaters* as a kind of "self-remembering." She explained, "I'm acutely aware of a dialogue that is going on between me and the characters which are conjured. I am acutely aware of myself as a reader. I actually am aware of the relationship between what's going on in my head and what I can do with my hands, and that is not the state that I normally walk around and fry the eggs in."[61] This comment reflects how she differentiated the writing of *The Salt Eaters* from the writing of some of her short stories, which required smaller amounts of her time. Only when Bambara realized that the story was exploring far too many themes and included too many characters to be confined to a short story did *The Salt Eaters* begin to take shape as a novel.[62]

The process of writing *The Salt Eaters* acted as a passage-way to acceptance of the admittedly hard work of writing a novel. That process required that Bambara establish firm boundaries so that she could do concentrated writing.

In an unpublished autobiographical sketch that Bambara entitled "Working at It," Bambara described how she entered a dream-like space for writing her first novel.[63] As if preparing for a sacred performance, Bambara created writing space for *The Salt Eaters* by taking time to clear her writing table and freeing herself of assignments and routine tasks that would interfere with writing. She began to be more in touch with her own internal self as she centered and claimed her writing space from within as well. Bambara wrote:

> In the winter of 77/78, while pursuing an idea that would not stay put within the parameters of the short story form and broke loose to become the novel *The Salt Eaters*, I recognized finally that writing was not only a central activity in my life, it was the center at which everything also converged or revolved around. I was a writer. I took three days out to review the backlog. I noted amongst the published work and overstuffed folders and notebooks a process, a chart. I listened to my contradictions, to my duplicities of feelings; probed beneath the smooth camouflage of words for tell-tale droppings. Writing is like dreaming, I was discovering. To grow you have to take risks. Dreams confront. Characters do too.[64]

Writing her novel was different from anything she experienced when writing short stories: it felt similar to receiving a spiritual call. Bambara explained, "I had to put the novel aside twice, but finally one day I'm walking out in the woods that some folks here call a front yard, and I slumped down next to my favorite tree and just said, 'Okay, I'm stepping aside, y'all. I'm getting out of the way. What is the story I'm supposed to be telling. Tell me.' Then I wrote *The Salt Eaters*."

As *The Salt Eaters* opens, Velma, a burned-out 1960s' activist who attempted suicide, is seated on a stool in a healing circle and is asked the question which is at the core of the novel: "Are you sure, sweetheart, that you want to be well?"[65] The question is raised by Minnie Ransom, a renowned healer in the community, who wears "a flouncy dress tied by two types of kente cloth," is adorned with 50 pounds of silver bangles, carries the scent of coconut in an afro tucked under a turban, and is sometimes directed by her spirit guide, Old Wife. Ransom has extraordinary powers, including the ability to cure cancer. This hip-dressing Afro-centric centurion is free of ties to any specific religious practice or tradition. Ransom's patient Velma has overextended herself in meeting the needs of the community and the needs of her husband and family, sacrificing her own needs for personal time and restoration. Velma has even tried to rescue others from the repeated exploitation of grandstanding civil rights leaders who exploit the grassroots, particularly women and children. Similar to the sexist issues that Bambara writes about in *The Black Woman,* the black male civil rights leaders who Velma encounters in *The Salt Eaters* accomplish little more than promoting themselves as heroes of the people.

The journey to wellness in *The Salt Eaters* requires that Velma make choices including claiming the right to her own health. Ransom makes it clear, however, that her patient is not alone on her journey to wellness and wholeness. There are an array of healing forces in her midst which include timeless spirits such as the ancient mud mothers dwelling in million-year-old caves, haints, and orishas that float in and out of the healing circle. There are also real-world healing forces such as clairvoyants, elders, and wise women who surround Velma in the circle of healing.

Similar to healing traditions across the African diaspora, Bambara also evoked color as a source of healing power. In the *The Salt Eaters,* yellow sometimes intermingled with white, is a color that signals healing possibilities. Community members who frequent the infirmary learn that they don't have to read the notices on the bulletin board to know that a healing is taking place, since seeing the old-timers wearing yellow and white was as much an announcement of the healing ceremony as a circled date on a calendar. The old-timers come in their yellow shirts, smocks, slacks, dresses, and sometimes sprinkle yellow in the pink chiffon flowerets in their hats.[66] Yellow also is dominant in the healing room itself, whose tiles are yellow mixed with white.

The power Bambara attributed to dance is multicultural as is the name of *The Salt Eater's* eccentric dancer—formerly Tina Mason, now "Geula Khufu." In this name Bambara evoked the mighty Egyptian pyramids as well as Hebrew culture. The teacher as the name suggests wants her students—three black women, Lebanese, Greek, and Pakistani women along with one Chinese woman—to root themselves in their sacred traditions and in the pelvic movements found in the dances of each of their cultures as she counters amnesia by whispering the word "Remember?"[67]

Drawing examples from her own life, Bambara also employs music as a powerful instrument for combatting amnesia and aiding in recovery. All of the remembered sounds of her mother's classical and jazz piano, her father's spoken word in Harlem and the bebop she heard in Greenwich Village explode in *The Salt Eaters*. By interconnecting the names of Wagner, Coltrane, Ornette Coleman, and Dexter Gordon, Bambara creates a musical score within the novel that includes the "pittitt tibaka bata" of small drums and the "rada rada booming from the park," which are then smothered by "the strains of Dexter Gordon's 'Tower of Power' blasting from a jukebox."[68] The din of nature—lightning, thunder, rain, and a shaking earth—also contributes to the vibrations that enlighten and encompass the healing ritual.

The healing ground Bambara creates for Velma is an infirmary built right after the Civil War.[69] As part of the Academy of the Seven Healing Arts, the Southwest Community Infirmary built by the Free Coloreds of Claybourne after the Civil War shares land with what was once a Masonic Lounge and Fellowship Hall, but now aims to unite martial arts, medical arts, and the arts and humanities. The academy has its own Wall of Respect of the Academy, the community's most important monument, and is located in the southern town of Claybourne, a chakra center that is also home to a transchemical plant.[70] An ancient tree outside the infirmary frequently has pots of water hanging from its branches, carried there by Ransom to honor the ancestors.

In *The Salt Eaters,* the principled Ransom employs her skills and power to welcome Velma to a healing place where Velma can reclaim her intuitive gifts and make choices about the work she wants to do. Throughout the healing ritual, forces of the universe springing from trees, rainbows, gardens, fountains, loa (spirits), flowers, old roots, and the new moon rescue the once bleeding, thrashing, and hallucinating Velma. "Body/mind/spirit out of nexus, out of tune, out of line, off beat, off color, in a spin off its axis, affairs aslant, wisdom at a tangent,"[71] Velma requires a powerful intervention.

In the awaited climactic moment of healing, "The sky is lit by tomorrow's memory lamp."[72] Velma is "replenished like the Lady Rising from the Sea."[73] Velma is aglow in "two yards wide of clear and unstreaked white and yellow."[74]

After publication of *The Salt Eaters*, Bambara explained that the initial idea for creating the healer Minnie Ransom emerged from her wanting to confront Ishmael Reed's characterization of Minnie Yellings in his novel, *The Last Days of Louisiana Red*.[75] Reed describes Minnie Yellings as the Queen of the Moochers who fails to follow in the footsteps of her more spiritually righteous father who studies the Gumbo in New Orleans.[76] When asked to review Ishmael Reed's *Louisiana Red*, Bambara was appalled to find that Reed did not provide any guiding principles for Minnie Yellings. She explained, "So I thought I should 'ransom' Minnie, and the book evolved around my concern about the split between medicine people—healers or whatever you want to call them—and the politicians, historians, and so on."[77]

The question critics, such as her friend Reed and others, have asked of *The Salt Eaters* is: will Velma's healing be a lasting one? In *Airing Dirty Laundry,* a collection of critical essays, Reed identifies part of Velma's illness as an addiction to the mimeograph machine, the primary tool for organizing and outreach at the time. Reed wrote:

> Though Velma is healed at the end of the book, one gets the feeling that it won't be long before she's back at the mimeograph machine; the moral of that book seems to be that as soon as one oppressor lets up, another one takes his place, and while the foes in the abolitionist novel and those of folklore were as easy to identify as the devils in morality plays, the modern villain may be the father of your child.[78]

Bambara must have been aglow like Velma at the novel's finish, but the question before Bambara was similar: will she have the resurgence needed to continually battle the bite of corporate power and racism and to find cures for social, environmental, and other diseases that plague her own community, particularly the most troubling amnesia?

In her novel, however, this writer does not invest her hope for the future in a singular activist. In *The Salt Eaters,* Bambara envisions an alliance of the women of color, the Seven Sisters, being a powerful guiding political and cultural force as well as a futuristic model of wellness and wholeness. The name of this alliance evokes the Seven Sisters of the Pleiades, the constellation credited with guiding sea travel from time immemorial and legendary for providing direction for the building of ancient temples such as the Great Pyramid of Egypt, the Temple of the Sun in Mexico, and the Pantheon in Greece.[79] The influence of the Seven Sisters is noted in an array of mystical traditions, stories, legends, and sacred texts including the Bible.[80] The number seven also gives the constellation numeric power as seven is a symbol of totality and wholeness, that is, the seven days of the week, the seven colors of the rainbow, and the seven root chakras of the body.[81]

Now, with the manuscript completed, Bambara continued to be replenished by her cultural work in the community and at home. In March 1979, during the week of her 40th birthday, Bambara hosted a SCAAW reading for Sonia Sanchez at her home. At the time, Sanchez was spending a week as writer-in-residence at Spelman.[82] A month earlier, Bambara had hosted a similar event for her friend Ishmael Reed.[83] As Sanchez dazzled the group with readings from *We Be Word Sorcerers,* Kristen Hunter (who was then writer-in-residence at Emory), Donald Stone, Jan Douglass, and Hoyt Fuller listened. Always determined to encourage emerging writers, Bambara invited Joyce Winters, a new assistant editor for *First World,* along with poets Melanie Rawls and Osker Spicer, to read as well.[84]

That night Fuller used a nickname for his friend which Bambara feared was already more widely known than she wished. In a note to Fuller after the memorable night, Bambara writes: "My number one daughter explained very carefully to my number two daughter that the tall man had called Mama Toni a 'saucer,' on account of he knows Mama Toni is fixin to fly. So now, thanks to your un Atlantan accent Hoyt, I am known around here as the The Saucer.

Can I live! As it turns out, several of my peers as well are saying 'saucer.' Now. If only you can take a tip from the Romans ('Good morning, citizen, Carthage must be Destroyed!') and start another trend . . . we will rise above this mess and fly again. See what you can do."[85] The misnomer may have arisen from the word "sorcerer" being bounced in and out of conversations after Sanchez read from the *We Be Word Sorcerers* volume at the evening salon Bambara hosted.

As the summer of 1979 began to transition into autumn, Bambara continued business as usual, making final edits to *The Salt Eaters* while also contributing to political action. When Sojourner South, a network of 150 black women based in Atlanta, began organizing an anti-apartheid poster campaign, Bambara offered support.[86] During that year, the United Nations International Year of The Child, Bambara supported other events that the Sojourner South organization sponsored including one of the anti-apartheid marches held in downtown Atlanta. Chaired by her friend Jan Douglass, Sojourner South also aimed to increase awareness about the plight of tortured and murdered African children living under oppressive regimes. In an informal circle of eight women, Bambara focused on male-female and family relationships, the environmental racism movement developing in Georgia, and read drafts of *The Salt Eaters*.[87] Bambara also frequented another weekly women's circle focused on dream analysis with friends, such as Jan Douglass, Pat Carter, and others.[88]

On August 27, 1979, Bambara submitted the manuscript of *The Salt Eaters* for publication, noting the positioning of the planets in the cosmos, which was "finally in the second and third years of the Last Quarter."[89] The book was edited under Leo's double moon.

At this point, dreams, ancestral spirits, and astronomical influences are significant in Bambara's life and writing. In *The Salt Eaters*, Bambara has been described as a "politicospiritual healer" in a "literary laying on of hands" to help cure the culturally ill[90] through similar metaphysical forces. Years later, Eleanor Traylor, who Bambara credited with understanding *The Salt Eaters* better than she did herself, also described Bambara's novel as having healing power. Traylor added, however, that the challenge for the reader is to surrender to the novel's healing forces. Traylor explains:

> The entire meaning of the novel rests upon the question of Velma's healing and that cannot be told, it must be shown. We must believe that she is healed and that believing demands of us the plunge that Velma takes. It is the demand of this narrator for that plunge that captures my heart and requires my whole head. It is one of the most daring demands that any narrator can make because how do we know that Velma is healed? How do we know that? We only know it if we do what the narrator is risking, and the narrator risks having us determine who Velma is. Who is Velma? Well, Velma is me.[91]

Unlike some other later reviews of *The Salt Eaters* in the mainstream media, scholar John Edgar Wideman recognized the emphasis Bambara placed on creating wholeness among women like the Seven Sisters who transform themselves and in that process transform the world. Similar to scholar Traylor's reading of the work, Wideman argued that Bambara is writing about much more than the healing of Velma Henry. Wideman wrote about the impact of *The Salt Eaters*: "She makes us understand that what is at stake in Velma Henry's journey back to health is not only one woman's life but the survival of the planet."[92]

In "At the Still Center of A Dream," the mixed review of *The Salt Eaters* that Anne Tyler wrote for *The Washington Post*, she claims that Bambara's characters are seen as if in a dream. Anne Tyler writes: "In dreams, a single detail from one scene can pivot the dreamer into another scene, something unrelated, incongruous in waking life but in sleep possessed of a logic all is own. The transition is so seamless that the dreamer hardly notices."[93] Tyler, however, did not find any dream logic in *The Salt Eaters*, only too many characters and lack of connections that made the book difficult to follow.

In a letter to Bambara, poet Adrienne Rich was interested in the challenges of finding meaning in the book's dreams and signs. Rich writes that there are interesting "signs to be mapped through the confusion, such as how the image of the dowsing rod and the slingshot and the forked stick, resonate from the Y in Y-bird?"[94] In her published review of *The Salt Eaters*, Rich who self-identified as an anti-racist, lesbian and feminist, defined what she believed to be Bambara's primary concern in writing the novel:

> The poison exuded by white power and racism is the "snakebite" which can be neutralized by judicious salt-eating and salt-poultices; but Bambara's real concern, if I understand her rightly, is the poison of the serpent, the madness that circulates in the bloodstreams of the oppressed, causing them to destroy themselves and each other, take on the oppressor's values, forget their traditions, devalue their own powers. There is, in *The Salt Eaters*, enormous concern with finding again what "amnesia"—that potential disease of all people whose history and traditions have been forcibly stolen—has erased of the usable past.[95]

In *The Salt Eaters* Bambara made numerous calls to women of color— surely, one of the most significant being for women to claim wholeness. Bambara's call for women of color to create wholeness within themselves must be viewed as a powerful antidote to burnout and complaint that far too often was the consequence of tireless struggles to overcome political, social, and economic inequities. Bambara viewed self-care and self-remembrance to be as revolutionary as political acts, that is, making time for one's personal craft, creating alliances among women of color, remaining deeply rooted in one's own cultural traditions, recognizing a woman's power to speak for herself, while making choices that foster a deeper relationship with one's inner-self as critical to well-being. Rather than assign responsibility for health solely to medical practitioners, Bambara imagines health beginning with self and supported by a range of caregivers including midwives and healers rooted in cultural traditions. These issues are occasionally discussed in scientific journals, but more often discussed among health activists and scholars in the public health and women's health community. *The Salt Eaters* as well as other works of Bambara's fiction are important because she uses her storytelling craft to make an important holistic case for empowering self with health within the annals of literature.

Writing would always be a political act for Bambara, but it could also be a source of joy, particularly when she viewed her writing as demystifying existing sources of power and suggesting new relationships and alliances for change. This Bambara succeeded in doing in the writing of *The Salt Eaters*. Three years after completing *The Salt Eaters,* Bambara continued to reflect on the monumental significance of completing her first novel and what was required of her to do so. In a letter to her cousin Carole Brown, Bambara wrote:

> Yeah, writing is hard work ain't it. Requires a selfish get-the-fuck-outta-my-face hardheaded obsessive no-I-don't-want-to-take-a-break-to-see-a movie determination. I'm continually amazed that I have any friends at all, Carole, cause I have thrown people bodily out of my house for walking in uninvited and unannounced trying to "rescue" me from work. And [I am] continually amazed that I can put in long, rigorous hours at the desk and have no more than 2 good pages to show for it. What keeps me going, among other things, is that I am determined to learn how to write, to master forms, push the language to its limits. It used to be a part time past time soon's-I-get-a-minute sort of thing. Then when "Salt" grabbed hold of me, writing became more and more a central activity. It is now a compulsion. And a joy. And my unction. And THE thaang. Was telling some little PH.d sic PH.d child the other day who's been in my face wanting to do a lit bio—girl, I've only just begun to hit my stride, check back with me in 5 years and we'll talk.[96]

Around the time she wrote to her cousin, Bambara told writer Claudia Tate in an interview that she viewed her responsibility as a writer to be a truth-teller. As in *The Salt Eaters*, Bambara again made an interconnection between the political and the spiritual. She explained, "We have rarely been encouraged and equipped to appreciate the fact that the truth works, that it releases the Spirit, and that is a joyous thing."[97] Having recently completed her first novel, Bambara joyfully saluted herself as a writer and so would others.

NOTES

1. Toni Cade Bambara, "Salvation Is the Issue," in *Black Women Writers*, ed. Mari Evans (New York: Anchor Books, 1984), 43.

2. For a discussion on dreams as prophetic and transforming, see Barbara A. Holmes, *Dreaming* (Minneapolis: Fortress Press, 2012), 79–92.

3. For a discussion of Minnie Ransom's laying on of hands as a traditional healer in the African context, see Gay Wilentz, *Healing Narratives: Women Writers Curing Cultural Disease* (New Brunswick: Rutgers University Press, 2000), 70–72.

4. John Leonard. "Books of the Times," *The New York Times*, November 27, 1981.

5. Ibid.

6. Bronze Jubilee Awards. Video Cassette, 1978. Schomburg Center for Research in Black Culture, New York.

7. Ibid.

8. Edward E. Riley Jr., Letter to Donald Stewart, June 16, 1977, Spelman Archives, Atlanta.

9. "Spelman Protestors Granted 'Amnesty' By Trustees Board," *Atlanta Daily World,* August 20, 1976.

10. "Spelman Trustees Vow to Reconsider Decision to OK Dr. Stewart as Pres." *Atlanta Daily World,* April 29, 1976.

11. Jacqueline Trescott, "Black Writers in the 70s," *The Washington Post*, May 6, 1977.

12. Ibid.

13. Ibid.

14. Ibid.

15. Tran Van Dinh, Letter to Toni Cade Bambara, May 12, 1977, Spelman Archives, Atlanta.

16. Toni Cade Bambara, Letter to Mr. Donald Stewart, June 10, 1977, Spelman Archives, Atlanta.

17. Ibid.

18. Beverly Guy-Sheftall, Interview by author, August 2010.

19. Douglass, Interview by author, September 2010.

20. Toni Cade Bambara, Letter to Donald Stewart, June 10, 1977, Spelman Archives, Atlanta.

21. "Spelman Plans Movies on Black Women in Literature," *Atlanta Daily World,* November 3, 1977.

22. E. Ethelbert Miller, Letter to Toni Cade Bambara, September 7, 1977. Courtesy of E. Ethelbert Miller.

23. Pascal James Imperato, *African Folk Medicine: Practices and Beliefs of the Bambara and Other Peoples* (Baltimore: York Press Inc., 1977), 34.

24. Toni Cade Bambara, Note to E. Ethelbert Miller, undated. Courtesy of E. Ethelbert Miller.

25. Toni Cade Bambara, Outline of chapters, Book of Baths, Spelman Archives, Atlanta.

26. Richard A. Carroll, Letter to Tom O. Cullen, June 24, 1977, Spelman Archives, Atlanta.

27. Angelle Cooper, Interview by author, April 2010.

28. "Stamp Out Bad English?" Flier, Spelman Archives, Atlanta.

29. "Creative Arts Program Going Strong in Atlanta," *Atlanta Daily World,* October 9, 1977.

30. *Pot Likker,* vol. 1 no. 2, eds. Ebon Dooley and Akua Kamau (Atlanta: Neighborhood Arts Center).

31. "Key Women Participate in Workshop at JFK," *Atlanta Daily World,* December 15, 1977.

32. Jualynne Dodson, Interview by author.

33. Ibid.

34. Ibid.

35. Ibid.

36. Toni Cade Bambara, Letter to Helen Brehon, undated. Courtesy of Walter Cade III.

37. Toni Cade Bambara, Letter to Donald Stewart, January 25, 1978, Spelman Archives, Atlanta.

38. Guy-Sheftall, Interview.

39. Ibid.

40. Toni Morrison, Interview by author, March 2012.

41. Taronda Spencer, Interview by author, April 2011.

42. Taronda Spencer, Interview by author, April 2010.

43. *Conversations with Toni Morrison,* ed. Danille Taylor-Guthrie (Jackson: University Press of Mississippi, 1994), xvi.

44. Pearl Cleage, Interview by author, April 2010.

45. Ibid.

46. Guy-Sheftall, Interview by author, August 2010.

47. Ibid.

48. Toni Cade Bambara, Letter to Helen Brehon, Courtesy of Walter Cade III.

49. Leah Wise, Interview by author, May 2001.

50. Toni Cade Bambara, "The War of the Wall," in *Deep Sightings and Rescue Missions* (New York: Vintage Books, 1996), 57–66.

51. Toni Cade Bambara, Letter to Hoyt Fuller, April 1978. Archives Research Center, Atlanta University Center, Robert W. Woodruff Library, Atlanta.

52. Ibid.

53. "CCLM Sponsors Literary Conference in Atlanta on November 17 & 18," November, 1978 Archives Research Center, Atlanta University Center, Robert W. Woodruff Library, Atlanta.

54. Alice Lovelace, Interview by author, January 2002.

55. Ibid.

56. Conference Agenda, 1978 Writers Conference, Spelman Archives, Atlanta.

57. Ibid.

58. Ibid.

59. Beverly Guy-Sheftall, "Commitment: Toni Cade Bambara Speaks," in *Conversations with Toni Cade Bambara,* ed. Thabiti Lewis (Jackson: University Press of Mississippi, 2012), 19.

60. Kalamu ya Salaam, "Searching for the Mother Tongue," in *Savoring the Salt: The Legacy of Toni Cade Bambara,* ed. Linda Janet Holmes and Cheryl Wall (Philadelphia: Temple University Press, 2008), 60.

61. Ibid.

62. Ibid.

63. Toni Cade Bambara, "Working at It in Four Parts," Spelman Archives, Atlanta.

64. Ibid.

65. Toni Cade Bambara, *The Salt Eaters* (New York: Random House, 1980), 3.

66. Ibid., 11.

67. Ibid., 166.

68. Ibid., 200.

69. Ibid., 120.

70. Ibid., 153.

71. Ibid., 49.

72. Ibid., 293.

73. Ibid., 292.

74. Ibid., 295.

75. Ishmael Reed, *The Last Days of Louisiana Red* (Champaign: Dalkey Archives Press, 2000).

76. Ibid.

77. Paula Giddings, "Toni Cade Bambara on Her First Novel: A Call to Wholeness from a Gifted Storyteller," *Encore* (June 1980), 48.

78. Ishmael Reed, *Airing Dirty Laundry* (Boston: Addison-Wesley, 1993).

79. Munya Andrews, *The Seven Sisters of the Pleiades: Stories from around the World* (North Melbourne, Australia: Spinifex Press Pty Ltd, 2004), 7–59.

80. Ibid.

81. Ibid.

82. Chris Singelton, "SCAAW Host Reception for Poet Sonia Sanchez," *Southern Coalition of African American Writers Newsletter* 1, no. 5 (1978), 1.

83. Ibid.

84. Ibid.

85. Toni Cade Bambara, Letter to Hoyt Fuller, Archives Research Center, Atlanta University Center, Robert W. Woodruff Library, Atlanta.

86. "Sojourner South Protest Apartheid," *Atlanta Voice*, September 15, 1979.

87. Carpenter, Interview.

88. Jan Douglass, Interview with author, September 2010.

89. Toni Cade Bambara, *The Salt Eaters* (New York: Random House, 1980), iii.

90. Charles A. Frye with Charlene Harper, Linda James Myers, and Eleanor W. Traylor. "A Symposium on Toni Cade Bambara's The Salt Eaters," *Contributions in Black Studies* 6: Article 4, 1983.

91. Ibid.

92. John Edgar Wideman, "The Healing of Velma Victory," *The New York Times,* June 1, 1980.

93. Anne Tyler, "At the Still Center of a Dream," *The Washington Post,* March 30, 1980.

94. Adrienne Rich, Letter to Toni Cade Bambara, September 6, 1980, Spelman Archives, Atlanta.

95. Adrienne Rich, "Review: The Salt Eaters," *New Women's Times,* December 1980/ January 1981.

96. Toni Cade Bambara, Letter to Carole Brown, December 11, 1982. Courtesy of Carole Brown.

97. Claudia Tate, "Toni Cade Bambara," in *Conversations with Toni Cade Bambara,* edited by Thabiti Lewis (Jackson: University Press of Mississippi, 2012), 53.

SEVEN

In the Sun, Resplendent

To write is to shape, to discover or re-create a pattern in nature that can be trusted to sustain. There is so much disorder, carelessness, dissipation and chaos peddled as information, truth, need, that everybody ought to get into pottery, make rock gardens, write poetry. . . . One would find, I think, a sense of order by using the ordering impulse to "let through" that more basic design, that design within which the perceivable world operates, that lost design, that underlying natural design.[1]

In April 1980, Bambara's first novel, *The Salt Eaters,* arrived in bookstores and received an avalanche of critical attention. The attention that came from mainstream and alternative press reviews led to numerous invitations for Bambara to promote the book from colleges, bookstores, and grassroots organizations, including progressive and women's groups. This was an exceptional time, as Bambara positioned herself to be recognized and celebrated as a writer, even if only briefly.

When *The Salt Eaters* was published in 1980, Toni Morrison, Toni Cade Bambara, and Alice Walker shared a platform as the most recognized black women fiction writers to emerge in the United States in the 1970s. Toni Morrison, who served as editor of *The Salt Eaters,* left Random House shortly after doing so to devote more time to her own writing. At the time *The Salt Eaters* was published, Morrison's three published novels were *The Bluest Eye* (1973), *Sula* (1974), and *Song of Solomon* (1977), the latter winner of the National Book Critics Circle Award; her book *Beloved* (1987) would later win

Women activists strengthen forces in the Black Belt at the Federation of Southern Cooperatives Meeting in rural Eppes, Alabama. L–R: Myrtle Glascoe of Mississippi, Billie Jean Young of Alabama, Faye Bellamy of Atlanta, and Bambara also living in Atlanta, 1983. Courtesy of Billie Jean Young.

the Pulitzer Prize. Meanwhile Walker's works of published fiction at the time included *The Third Life of Grange Copeland* (1970), *In Love and Trouble: Stories of Black Women* (1973), and *Meridian* (1976). Walker had also edited a collection of the works of Zora Neale Hurston, *I Love Myself When I Am Laughing,* in 1979. Unlike some of the radical black women poets who remained with alternative presses in the 1960s and 1970s, Morrison's, Walker's and Bambara's early works were published by mainstream publishers and were marketed not only to feminist and Afrocentric audiences, but also to general American audiences in the early 1970s.

In the early 1980s, a *New York Times* critic identified Toni Cade Bambara as one of a small handful of black female writers who had not fallen "out of style according to a phase of the cultural moon."[2] Other black women writers on the short list identified by the *New York Times* as "the black exceptions" were "a brilliant Toni Morrison, a strong angry Toni Cade Bambara, Alice Walker and Paule Marshall."[3] When *The Salt Eaters* was published, Bambara was in the sisterhood of the best-known contemporary black female writers at the time.

Bambara, Morrison, and Walker were also significant in that they shared a concern for recognizing the works of writers that had been lost, forgotten, or not yet recognized. Walker, for example, unearthed Zora Neale Hurston's writings in the 1970s and Morrison contributed to the new black renaissance of writers emerging out of the 1960s in her role as a Random House editor who supported publication of new black writers' works. These black women writers were also considering screenplays for films which were eventually developed. Although none of Bambara's fiction was ever commercially produced as a feature film, some of her stories were scripted for television and Bambara was beginning to expend significant amounts of creative energy in assisting and developing film projects. These failed to make it to the screen in the early 1980s, but through her ties with radical grassroots organizations and writing workshops, Bambara demonstrated an undying commitment to strengthening resources and linkages for nascent filmmakers as she had done previously for emerging writers.

Demonstrating her commitment to the political work of radical students, Bambara visited the University of Alabama in Tuscaloosa to develop the first-ever conference on black women in the South at the beginning of 1980. Monica Walker remembered her anxiety about the responsibility of guiding such a luminary writer through the series of appointments and meetings planned for her that day, but Bambara was typically accessible and respectful of students and as eager to learn from them as they were to learn from her.[4] In the midst of developing conference plans, Bambara allotted extensive time to meet with students and to design strategies for increasing diversity among faculty and students. One of Bambara's primary principles in her organizing work on campuses was to create collectivity and to unite forces that could more effectively create institutional change in concert. She also was a role model for faculty who were seeking to break through rigid hierarchical relationships between students and faculty. In meeting with students, Bambara opened doors for students to access speakers like Bernice Reagan, founder of the music group Sweet Honey in The Rock, and to invite other nationally renowned scholar-activists to participate in the conference program.[5] Walker recalled her first meeting with Bambara: "From the very first moment that I met her—not knowing much about her—she was like the Angela Davis. She had this huge afro and she was also the most personable person I had ever met. It was so easy talking to her because she was so easy going in her conversation. She was curious. She interviewed you the whole time you were with her."[6]

After a day of nonstop intense meetings, Walker and another student activist, Stella Shade, drove Bambara back to her hotel expecting her to be eager to retire. Instead, Walker and Shade spent the entire night in the car, holding conversations that ranged from the highly political to the very personal. "We talked until sunrise," Walker laughed years later. "Somewhere around 6:30 that morning Toni decided to go to her hotel room for some sleep. At some point we may have gone to a restaurant for take-out coffee. I remember I dozed off at different points and so did Stella so it must have been Toni who always kept the all-night conversation going."[7] Walker also explained how the first meeting with Bambara was a life-changing event. As she recalled, "For the first time in my life I was seeing myself as a world citizen rather than simply as a rural black woman. Toni sent me out on a journey toward curiosity. I started thinking about my life in terms of BT and AT: Before Toni and After Toni."[8]

In February 1980, Bambara returned to Tuscaloosa to participate in the conference that she had helped students and faculty organize on her first visit to the University that year. The groundbreaking conference had been named "Black Women in the South: Retrospects and Prospects." Speaking at the conference, Bambara urged young black students to not only address race and gender issues on campus, but also to organize vehicles for rural black women in Alabama and Mississippi to confront economic, health, and political concerns in the communities where they lived. Bambara's work at the conference influenced students to join with activists to form the first rural network of its kind for southern black women, the Southern Rural Women's Network (SRWN), which held its first Conference at The Federation of Southern Cooperatives in Epps, Alabama. Organized in 1967 by black sharecroppers, the Federation was historic in its efforts to increase landownership and economic rights among black farmers. When the SRWN met in Epps more than a decade later, cosponsors included Rural America, the Alabama Center for Higher Education, the Mothers of Many, and the Alabama Coalition against Hunger.[9]

Bambara facilitated several workshops in Epps, including one entitled "The Health and Sexuality of Women." Addressing farmers, civil rights workers, quilt makers, and health workers who joined former organizers of the University of Alabama Black Women's Conference, Bambara called on black women to be concerned with their physical, mental, spiritual, and educational health. In her talk, Bambara suggested that women "use all forces afoot in the universe—political, martial, economic, physical, metaphysical, spiritual, psychic, creative, sexual" to address their political, spiritual and physical well-being.[10] In so doing, Bambara was making a tangible call in the political organizing sphere that mirrored the mission of the multidisciplined Seven Arts Academy described in *The Salt Eaters*. Bambara told the rural women activists who gathered at Epps that achieving wellness in a racist and sexist society was critical and challenging. Bambara summoned the women "to build immunization systems, to resist germs, bad ideas, inflammatory images, crippling dogma, decadent values and other diseases."[11] She also challenged them to develop an independent and freeing sense of their own political will through exercising informed choices. For Bambara, informed choices involved "the recognition/study/analysis/critique of all forces afoot in order to build immunity to the disordering disease this society inflicts."[12]

Decades later, Ishmael Reed alluded to the synchronicity found between Bambara's writings and her activism when he wrote about *The Salt Eaters:* "Much of the book is devoted to this healing process and seems to suggest that for a black woman in a racist, sexist society, strength can be found in binding with other women in organizations and secret societies: 'the mud sisters,' 'daughters of the yam,' and the Seven Sisters."[13]

A few years later, the Black Women's Health Project launched its national self-help group initiative at a landmark conference at Spelman College in Atlanta. Early on, Bambara espoused a view of women's health that was holistic and boldly embraced political, cultural, and social factors as part of the wellness paradigm. While the Black Women's Health Project developed a model that centered on peer supports and increasing access to quality health care within mainstream medicine, Bambara also included diverse culturally based health practices, dream analysis, dance, music, loyalty to one's craft, and astrology as valid components of a wholeness and wellness.

In Bambara's opinion, to battle the constant mental, social, and political assaults that black women faced from within the black community and in the larger society, a powerful and comprehensive tool chest was needed to fight health threats. While Bambara maintained relationships with activists in the Black Women's Health Project, she was not an active member. In general, Bambara avoided affiliation with existing groups as a base for activism and more often acted as a catalyst for the creation of new groups that included cultural work as part of its mission. In the long run, Bambara was an independent free spirit with little patience for internal organizational politics even within progressive groups.

At black women's political conferences, Bambara made opportunities to meet with artists who integrated the political within their own creative work. In Tuscaloosa and in Epps, Bambara met with activists and students to encourage their artistry. In formal and informal discussions about progress they were making on their own writing, Bambara encouraged women to develop social contracts where they would check in with each other on a regular basis regarding progress they were making in their work.[14] Billie Jean Young, a writer and SRWN organizer, remembered how Bambara not only inspired her to self-publish a first book of poetry but also contributed to her confidence to write what became her highly acclaimed one woman show, *This Little Light of Mine: A Dramatization of the Life of Fannie Lou Hamer,* in the 1980s. Hamer, a fiery voting rights activist and civil rights leader, died of breast cancer in 1977 at age 59. The words on Hamer's tombstone, "I am sick and tired of being sick and tired," have motivated countless black women health activists.[15]

The spring of 1980 was an eventful time for Bambara. Less than a week prior to the publication of *The Salt Eaters,* Bambara received a letter from the editors of *Redbook* magazine dated March 25th—her 41st birthday—indicating that her short story "Mama Load" was a finalist in the National Magazine Awards competition, along with 60 other writers from magazines,

such as *The New Yorker, Antaeus, Atlantic,* and *Playboy.*[16] Beginning with
"Raymond's Run," which had appeared in *Redbook* nearly 10 years earlier,
Bambara's short stories and essays appeared in the popular women's magazine six times prior to its publication of "Mama Load." Other progressive
writers published by *Redbook* included Dr. Benjamin Spock, a staunch anti-
Vietnam War protestor whose column on parenting challenged generations
of expert advice and empowered mothers. Anthropologist Margaret Mead's
cultural commentaries were also regular features in *Redbook.* In November
1969, among the hundreds of stories *Redbook* received was Lucille Clifton's
short story, "Magic Mama," which *Redbook* chose to publish at a time when
only one other of Clifton's stories had been published in *Negro Digest.*[17]

Bambara's short story, "The Mama Load," is narrated by a newly divorced
woman who is recovering from her marriage to her former husband Sonny,
whom she divorced after he announced his extramarital love affair. In the divorce
settlement, "Sonny got all the Coltrane albums and cash money" and the wife
seeking justice ends up with "custody of the kid," Karen and Sonny's "nutty
mother," Rosetta.[18] Rosetta is not a typical aging mother-in-law as she designs
costumes for the dance "troupe of senior hussies" that she organized.[19] Meanwhile, even the solace the newly divorced narrator finds in her writing craft
is disrupted by the free-spirited, wine-drinking Rosetta, who literally over-
crowds her daughter-in-law's manuscripts on the kitchen as she makes outfits
for Verdi's Othello or Davis's Purlee.[20] While the typically strong-minded outspoken narrator that is so often the center of many of Bambara's short stories
is weighed down by her circumstances, she refuses to be a victim. When facing
the judge in divorce court, the spirited narrator belts out a strongly worded
feminist proclamation like a popular blues singer making a comeback: "This
is my time. 'Cause you see, Your Honor, I wasn't raised to be some caretaker
or thief in the night. For that matter, I was raised to flat-out state my case and
take my space. That's how my daddy and mama raised me. . . . It's my time
now."[21] At the divorce hearing, the story's narrator rises like Bambara herself
might have done during her own divorce hearings years ago, refusing to back-
step when she tells the judge, "You know what Mao says, Your Honor, and
Bobby Seale too. So I mean to seize my Jam now."[22]

Not surprisingly, the self-assured narrator is a woman with southern roots.
The narrator's strength is traced back to her own mother, a healer and a storyteller who relished eating earth. Unlike the "mama load" in Bambara's story,
the narrator's mother wasn't being kept by others; she herself was an independent woman who kept the faith, kept up a garden, and was the rock of the
family.[23] The narrator's mother is the kind of woman who would be comfortable in the company of Minnie Ransom, the healer in *The Salt Eaters,* who also
cherished hills of rich earth for eating, a passed-on African ritual that pregnant
African American women continued to safe-keep as a practice for generations,[24] particularly in the rural South. Elders in Bambara's stories speak to the
value of traditions rooted in black culture.

Interestingly, it was the diverse *Redbook* readership that provided the most voluminous and treasured written feedback to Bambara's published short stories, more than any other magazine or journal audience. About "Mama Load," Leila Bronson in her letter to the editors at *Redbook* wrote, "Then I read 'The Mama Load' that tells it like it is [sic], not only for divorced Negro women but many of us white women as well."[25] While "Mama Load" resonated with *Redbook* editors as one of its two best stories published that year, it did not enter the winner's circle in the National Council of Magazines short-story competition, Bambara learned just as *The Salt Eaters* hit bookstores on April 1.[26]

With the novel now in bookstores, Bambara's month of April began with travel to Mississippi, New York, and New Jersey and ended at home at the Neighborhood Arts Center (NAC) with a reading and book signing.[27] On April 15, the writer was among the speakers at the 1980 Fine Arts Festival, along with muralist Nelson Stevens and actor Ossie Davis; the Olatunji Drums of Passion also performed.[28] Bambara then flew to Colgate College for a book signing hosted by poet and faculty member, Mae Henderson, before catching a plane to New York in order to provide a talk in Newark, New Jersey, at the University of Medicine and Dentistry of New Jersey (UMDNJ).[29]

At UMDNJ, midwives, mothers, activists, and other health-care workers gathered to celebrate the opening of a birth room at University Hospital, a new teaching hospital in Newark. What local women truly wanted was a setting for labor and birth that would support birth as a normal and natural event with minimum medical intervention. In the view of the Chair of the Department of Obstetrics and Gynecology at the time, low-income inner-city women were plagued with far too many physical, mental, and social woes to be cared for in settings where they themselves could have responsibility in the decision-making that would affect their own labor and birth experiences.[30] Already on the road promoting *The Salt Eaters,* Bambara readily agreed to be the keynote speaker at the birth room's opening and in her talk tied prevalent themes in *The Salt Eaters* with issues facing black women and families demanding greater choices in their health care. Meanwhile, hospital administrators were impressed that one of America's leading black fiction writers was making an appearance at University Hospital in the midst of her book tour. While living in Atlanta, Bambara became increasingly interested in Deep South midwives who sustained African-based practices and rituals in their practices when women gave birth at home. At the medical school in New Jersey, the writer had a rare opportunity to celebrate contemporary midwives who continued practices that were similar to Bambara's fictionalized midwives.

At the opening of the birth room, Bambara commented on the contrast between the sterile labor and delivery room, and the birth room—where the décor included African cloth on the labor and birthing bed, a handmade wooden cradle for the newborn to sleep in, and a rocking chair for mothers who chose to have their babies rooming in with them. While addressing the audience, Bambara grabbed a piece of white chalk to draw concentric circles on the medical school blackboard to illustrate the importance of remaining centered in oneself, in the community and in nature. Her union-organizing principles appeared to underlie her emphasis on the importance of health-care workers joining with mothers and the birthing families to create a holistic birthing environment that supported women who practiced emotional and mental centering during the labor process through breathing, massage, mantras, and music. Bambara also referenced breastfeeding support groups, single mothers' alliances, midwife associations, and home birth groups as important resources for the community. But it was the theme of centering that had the most direct ties to concepts Bambara explored as critical to creating wellness in *The Salt Eaters*. In reference to the principle of center-ing as more than a preparation for prayer or meditation—as it is sometimes referred to in religious practices, Bambara explained that centering was part of a process in creating wholism within self and community:

> Everything in the book, the way it's structured, the avoidance of a linear thing in favor of a kind of jazz suite, the numerous characters, the potter and the masseur, everything becomes a kind of metaphor for the whole. We have to put it all together. It deals with all the senses and also different kinds of ways to meditate, different kinds of ways to tap into the center. The masseur, in my mind, is the other half of the potter, in the sense that to raise the clay you've got to get the clay centered. The potter's wheel is part of the whole discussion of circles, prayer circles and being in a circle. The masseur says, "My dance is my meditation."[31]

In June, Bambara traveled to Tuskegee, Alabama, where she provided the centennial address at Tuskegee University's ceremonial unveiling of the mural "I AM BECAUSE WE ARE," a Tuskegee commissioned work by activist painter Nelson Stevens, which provided another opportunity for Bambara to reflect on the theme of the responsibility of artists working in the black community.[32] Bambara knew Stevens from his contributions to the Chicago Outdoor Mural Movement, including his work on the revolutionary 1967 "Wall of Respect." About involvement of the community itself in the process of Stevens's work, Bambara told the audience: "His 40 murals to date, executed most usually with students and community workers, immediately arrest the attention of our pri-mary or foremost critics—the passerby folks of the neighborhood who witness daily the building up of statements through color, line, rhythm, texture, and home-based iconography."[33]

Just as Bambara used her words to carry the sound of jazz, Stevens' images not only captured the eye but also spoke to the ear in what Bambara labeled the mural's musicality. In particular, Bambara pointed out that the George Washington Carver panel in the mural had "the ingredients that give rise to the polyrhythmic climate that sees the foot tapping."[34]

What also mattered to both Bambara and Stevens was a process of work-ing that kept the artist community-based and visible. In her talk at Tuskegee, Bambara recognized images and symbols that Stevens wore as he worked in community spaces as symbolizing healing and good fortune, resonating with references to African religion and African American culture found in *The Salt Eaters*. Working in the heart of the black belt, Bambara wanted the audience to also see Stevens projecting the images of the diaspora even in the clothing he wore such as the "official master artist outdoor mural hat (the one with the blue snake carrying pyramids on its back)" and the "clamped ace deuce on his head."[35]

Bambara likened Stevens who wanted his work to be socially responsible to the untiring liberation work of Harriet Tubman. Bambara explained: "When Harriet Tubman crossed the border, she might have sat down for a leisurely cup of coffee, might have draped a shawl around her shoulders and settled comfortably into the hearth-side rocker, humming out the rest of her days. But she didn't. She took responsibility for what she knew—that there is no life of honor to the 'I' when the 'we' are penned up and down pressed."[36]

In her short story, "The War of the Wall," Bambara returned to the theme of the value of community artists doing their work within the community's view. The author described an artist transforming a wall they used for pitching pennies and playing street games into a canvas for her artistic work as alarming to the neighborhood. Since the children of Talbro Street have claimed the wall for themselves, they go to war to keep their space.[37] The Talbro Street children and some of the neighborhood adults are astounded by her behavior, which they find discourteous and disrespectable. For example, this artist fails to recognize the importance of greeting elders and has shocking food preferences. Possibly a vegetarian, she questions ham hocks in the greens, cheese in the macaroni, hard-boiled eggs in the potato salad, and sugar in the iced tea.[38] When the adults finally see her work, they are in awe. This artist who works outdoors may have found acceptance because she engaged with the community and her art is in full view of the neighborhood, rather than being tucked away in a museum.

By the fall of 1980, with the book launching of *The Salt Eaters* having passed its peak, Bambara increasingly allocated more time to the medium she had been passionate about since childhood: film. It would be another 10 years before Julie Dash would become the first black woman to have her work *Daughters of the Dust* shown in major mainstream theaters in the United States. Based on the inquiries she was receiving about her own scriptwriting interests and translating *The Salt Eaters* into film, Bambara had every reason to believe that she would see her own work rendered in film much sooner. Bambara's typical optimism kept her focused on creating the work rather than being deterred by the barriers that historically prevented black filmmakers from access to wide audiences, with only a few historic exceptions such as Oscar Micheaux.[39]

A decade earlier a young generation of revolutionary filmmakers at the UCLA film school made their mark by mixing images of revolutionary urban uprisings emanating from the African American community with Afrocentric symbols reflecting cultural practices throughout the African diaspora. Although the films were restricted by budget, the strident political messages emanating from their visuals, music, voices, and settings were as cutting-edge as Bambara's mixing of cross-cultural spiritual practices and musical sounds in her literary texts such as the repetitive rhythms in the downbeat of gospel and soaring jazz chants to create a soulful canopy akin to the spirit found in the works of the UCLA filmmakers. Bambara noted that radical black students succeeded in making film a place of insurgency where struggle was not only documented, but also evoked. Later, Bambara's independent film work built on the tradition of insurgent filmmakers who like the visual artist Stevens, empowered the community through the cultural and political images in their works. Earlier, Bambara's writings in *The Black Woman* and *Gorilla, My Love* influenced the young filmmakers in the 1970s, particularly women of color.

Dash, who described Bambara as "my hero," recalled Bambara's earlier influence:

> In the 70s, [friends and I] would gather in a dormitory room, sitting around reading *Gorilla, My Love*. We were so famished at the time for that kind of acknowledgement as young women that we used to kind of act it out and read it aloud in the dorm. We read her, Toni Morrison, Nikki Giovanni, and Ntozaki [Shange]'s *For Colored Girls*. It fed us and nurtured us. That's all we had—we didn't have those kind of images on the screen. At the time, rarely would you see a black face [on screen]. Television shows and movies were made to explain us to other people. I felt like I knew her [Bambara] and she knew me and she was speaking directly to me, but I never imagined that I would ever meet her.[40]

Years later, Dash and Bambara would finally meet in Atlanta.

Paul Carter Harrison, who wrote the Obie-award-winning play *The Great MacDaddy* and the groundbreaking *Drama of Nommo,* and also conceived and directed Mario Van Peebles' *Ain't Suppose to Die a Natural Death*, wanted to bring a different set of new images to the big screen. Immediately recognizing the imaginative big-screen film possibilities of *The Salt Eaters,* Harrison wrote to Bambara, which initiated conversations for a possible collaboration. Years later, Harrison explained that the production failed to happen because Hollywood studios simply did not see money-making potential in translating *The Salt Eaters* into film. On May 1, 1980, a month after *The Salt Eaters* landed in bookstores, Harrison wrote Bambara a compelling letter that included arguments for placing *The Salt Eaters* among the most heralded classics in literature and unveiled the beginnings of a bold plan to bring *The Salt Eaters* to mainstream American movie houses:

> Dear Toni:
>
> We have never met formally. We do share, however, many friends in common. Thereby, I have taken the liberty of calling you Toni in deference to a strong sense of familiarity—*albeit* we have never met. I have just finished reading your new book, THE SALT EATERS. Here too, I discern a mutuality of

interest in ritual and myth amongst the folk, though you may not be familiar with my own works (i.e. THE DRAMA OF NOMMO, or the play, THE GREAT MACDADDY).

THE SALT EATERS is a very intriguing work. In fact, it is a remarkable accomplishment in both novelistic style and content. It resonates with the mythic heightening of folk-life found in Yeats, a ritualistic animation of character induced by a Joycian stream-of-consciousness, and the magical/spiritual word-force (as implied in THE DRAMMA OF NOMMO) of all the heavy/heady horn-players –Moody, Dexter, Parker, Coltrane, et. al.

As a result, this work seems clearly inspired by the hidden meaning of the black experience, and eschews the sentimentality of social realism found in Faulkner, or even Baldwin (however much I might admire the latter). It seems to me (as well as Larry Neal) that you have your "chops" on a potentially new formalism in the aesthetics of the black-novel; an authentication of vision/style pioneered by Toomer in the Twenties, resurrected by Lindsay Barret (SONG FOR MUMU) in the early Sixties, and advanced by such writers as [Charles] Johnson (FAITH AND THE GOOD THING) and perhaps even Toni Morrison. You have, thus, been able to create from the peculiar experience of Afro-American life a work which is intelligent, witty, and *very* hip!

Now, I've made these observations of THE SALT EATERS because, firstly, I was very moved by the book. Secondly, because I've committed some of my energies toward producing in recent years, and I detect the possibilities of the book being transmuted into a theatre or film experience. While I am not certain if you've already exercised your options in other media, I am greatly concerned that the usual producers in the flesh-markets of Hollywood and Broadway might secure the rights and not know what to do with it; or mount an effort which would destroy the delicate balance of folk wisdom and ritualistic style. In my best professional judgment (which is slightly better than shooting-craps-) THE SALT EATERS owns the potential of becoming an international classic film, i.e. BLACK ORPHEUS.

One foresees several obstacles to getting THE SALT EATERS onto the silver-screen through the usual manipulation of the commercial industry (though such a project would require the kind of multi-million dollar budgetary considerations afforded by a major film company). Firstly, many great novels never get to the screen because of subject matter or the demands of literary style (and it doesn't help that THE SALT EATERS is circumscribed by a black reality). ULYSSES took forever to reach the screen without too much success; and the same could be said for Malcolm Lowery's UNDER THE VOLCANO. Perhaps we will never see THE INVISIBLE MAN on screen.

Secondly, THE SALT EATERS requires a style commensurate with its vision. A simple folk-narrative such as HURRY UP SUNDOWN or ROOTS would simply be vitiating. A stylistic prototype might be CITIZEN CANE, though commercially unpromising; and certainly, BLACK ORPHEUS, which does have commercial appeal if one considers the exotic/erotic accessibility of THE SALT EATERS.

Thirdly, the question of who would be most adept at translating the vision/experience of THE SALT EATERS onto the screen. Clearly, the story reveals a woman's vision (which is good in the current film market). It should be directed by a woman. Ideally, the only woman I can think of that would be sensitive to the political/social and stylistic considerations of THE SALT EATERS is Lina Wertmeuller (SEVEN BEAUTIES) who is a prodigy of Felini (8½), and highly respected artistically/commercially in both Europe and the United States. She would be the ideal! After Wertmuller, one directs one's attention to "sensitive" black males with promise. Artistically (and with a common sense of the mythic), Bill Gunn (GANJA AND HESS) comes to mind; commercially, there is Michael Shultz (CAR WASH).

Certainly, I might add parenthetically, I would love to throw my name into the hopper of illustrious directors, but I'm sure that no one would bank several million on my fledgling experience. Thus, I'd be satisfied in developing the project as a producer/writer. At this point, I am not in a position to purchase the film-rights; but I certainly would like your permission to shop the idea so as to generate, not only money for the rights, but a realistic package for development. Obviously, I cannot ask you to turn down or restrain yourself from accepting other potential offers. However, I would like to have the first shot at developing the project for a limited period.

At the moment, I'm developing/producing a 2-hour Movie-of-the Week at CBS. I don't think, however, that television can realize the epic scale of THE SALT EATERS.

In any case, if you would like to pursue the notion of a film-project for THE SALT EATERS, I would appreciate hearing something from you straightaway. The question is, how does one catch-up with me (notice, there is no address on my stationary). I will be at my Chicago base (where I am functioning as Chairman of Theatre/Music at Columbia College) until the end of May. . . . It would be extremely expeditious, however, if you would send me your telephone number in Atlanta (or wherever you plan to be).

In the meantime, I trust that I have revealed more to you than my eagerness to exploit your masterful accomplishment. Once again, I want to thank you for providing such a generous and enlightening experience with THE SALT EATERS. I anxiously await your reply.

Sincerely,
Paul Carter Harrison[41]

Eager to pursue interest in *The Salt Eaters*, Bambara listed the screen opportunity among a list of projects that she hoped might attract the attention of Joan Daves, a high-powered international agent based in New York known for representing Pulitzer Prize winners.[42] Unlike some other political activist writers emerging from the 1960s who secured academic appointments, Bambara continued to relish her independence as a freelance writer-activist and wanted a literary agent who would be competitive in bringing her work into the publishing market. Hattie Gossett, her first agent, friend, and colleague, had been instrumental in encouraging Bambara to publish her short stories and was with Bambara in her first meeting with Toni Morrison at Random House. Now Bambara was interested in a professional agent who could devote time to the array of projects she was pursuing.

Because of the support, trust, and respect demonstrated by Toni Morrison for her work, Bambara did not fear the editing process of a mainstream publisher even as her work explored radical territory such as "creating a new language," one of her quests in writing *The Salt Eaters*.[43] Bambara was more alarmed by the restrictions she faced in academic settings than she was of having her independent spirit and inventive voice squashed or co-opted by the publishing industry. Kalamu ya Salaam pointed out that in the 1980s, black male writers who moved away from activist writing to secure academic appointments and gainful employment with government agencies were far more compromising than black women writers like Bambara who were exploring new cosmic thresholds in *The Salt Eaters*.[44] Women writers like Bambara were not being courted by established funders and academic institutions quite so fervently, according to Kalamu.

On August 8, seven months after the publication of *The Salt Eaters* and on the eve of taking off for several weeks of a rare vacation, Bambara wrote to Daves:

> Had thought I would have a moment, when I was last in New York, to drop in and explore with you your availability as my agent. Am on my way to Brazil for several weeks and did not want too much time to elapse before inquiring. Have several projects underway and could use a good agent. When I get back to the States, will call you.
>
> At present, I have a new collection of stories ready to go sometime in the fall. Random [House], of course, [you] would be the first to have a crack at it. I've been perfectly happy with Toni Morrison as my editor. I also have a chunk of the new novel shaped up, that can be typed by mid-September.
>
> In addition to the two books, am working on two scripts. Madison D. Lacy, Jr. of WGBH has offered me the job of screen writer for a project he's currently trying to get funded—a 90 minute biography of Zora Neale Hurston. Have checked union scales and that looks like $16,000, possibly more. In addition, am working on a script on Harper's Ferry: unlike Hollywood version(s), the drama is centered around the woman who blueprinted the campaign, Harriet Tubman; the woman who was bankrolling it, Marry Ellen Pleasants; and the people who engineered it, a number of runaways and Underground R.R. agents who had worked with Brown in Ohio and Kansas. Have no clear notion of where to send out feelers, but Woodie King of the New Federal Theater and Paul Carter Harrison, together with independent film makers Robert Gardner, Haile Gerima and others, have long expressed an interest in receiving a script from me. Ossie Davis and Ruby Dee, too, from time to time, have acquired [sic]. And I believe the subsidiary rights person at Random has rec'd inquiries on SALT. I would like to work on a film in '81, is the overriding impulse being expressed here (please pardon my machine which spells badly).[45]

At the end of her letter, Bambara also promised to contact Daves, who in fact became her agent, as soon as she returned from the trip to Brazil.[46]

Kambon Obayani had recently returned to the Americas after his teaching position in Libya and organized the Brazil vacation which he hoped would result in Bambara committing to leaving the United States to make a home with him in South America. While still living in Libya, Obayani had written

Bambara a letter that made his intentions clear: "Like you, I want to fly. I want to be able to disappear to transcend and to communicate with my spirit guides. I also want to heal, to be a healer medium and use the qualities through the word and sound to transform. There is much to do, but for some reason the way seems very bright and clear. I *LOVE* you. There are many levels we can and have to work through. Many webs to step from behind."[47]

The Brazil trip was productive for Bambara, as she was not only seeking opportunities to have *The Salt Eaters* translated into Portuguese, but also taking advantage of opportunities to meet with feminist Afrocentric Brazilian scholar Leila Gonzalez and consult with Yoruba practitioners.[48] Once back in the States, however, it soon became clear that Bambara never seriously considered relocating to Brazil. In September, Bambara's range of projects continued to widen, including new film projects and "assembling a collection of skits, articles, songs, graphics, how-to-manuals, annotated bibliography, journal entries, class action suit notes, etc. called *Organizing Women: Beyond Bread and Butter.*"[49] Another project Bambara aimed to complete was to assemble notes from 10 years of conducting writers' workshops. Bambara wrote:

> I thoroughly enjoy working with writers, developing writers, assisting writers. Like other Aries folks I know, I am not only a hard-head (we have a bad press) but a self-head; we Aries listen mainly to ourselves, the only teachers we have faith in. I get into a workshop and stay in open-bodied position. I can't wait to see what I'm going to teach/learn next. It's the best practice I know for mastering chords with the lid down.[50]

Years later, Obayani reflected on the end of their relationship as Bambara returned to her agenda of writing and community work. Obayani explained:

> No matter what, it was the work that came first for her. There was no line, no deviation between her life and the work. There was a difference between Toni and some other artists, however. I found Toni was very holistic and writing was not the end all. It was not everything to her. Working against the State, working for the people, working for the community was all a part of what she did whereas most artists I know it is the art and that's it.[51]

That same fall, a short piece of Bambara's fiction entitled "Story," part of a work-in-progress collection of short prose pieces called *SHE & HE*, was published in the September 29th issue of *Callaloo*, a journal of the African diaspora. "Story" is a love story that takes place in the South. It unfolds as a young shoemaker apprentice and his love serenade their love for one another as they ride double saddle on the "perfect stallion" into a scene of rich natural lushness.[52] The brief journey of romance and love ends at the foot of the "Good Old Folks Tree," where older women and younger children have placed pots of food and jugs of water on its branches, similar to rituals in honor of the ancestors that survived the tumultuous Middle Passage in *The Salt Eaters*. Like this story of romance, several of Bambara's intimate affairs tended to be warm and loving short stories rather than long-lasting relationships.

When alone, Bambara sometimes quietly chose to read her own writing which include short stories favorites such as "A Girl's Story," or a critical review such as her *New York Times* review of Gwendolyn Brooks's autobiography, *Report From Part One,* or even re-reading a *Redbook* magazine article like "The Children Who Got Cheated."[53] Bambara, however, rarely prioritized promoting her own work as famed authors often do. In fact, Bambara sometimes declined invitations to participate on panels that focused primarily on critical analysis of *The Salt Eaters.*

Nearly five years after *The Salt Eaters* was published, Charles Frye, a professor at Hampshire College, decided to address the frustration his undergraduate students with feminist leanings were having in accessing *The Salt Eaters* by organizing a seminar entitled "How to Think Black: A Symposium in Toni Cade Bambara's *The Salt Eaters.*"[54] Frye's earlier philosophical works explored the multiple meanings of "black" in biological, cultural, and metaphysical terms,[55] and he wanted to frame a similar discussion focused on *The Salt Eaters.* Charlyn Harper, Linda James Myers, and Eleanor W. Traylor joined Frye at the symposium and presented papers that included exploration of various African belief systems. Traylor turned to folk tales, the blues, and spirituals to illustrate "thinking black" in the context of *The Salt Eaters.*[56]

While deciphering *The Salt Eaters* for readers did not always capture Bambara's interests, promoting emerging black writers living in the south did. Two weeks before *The Salt Eaters* was released, Bambara immersed herself in planning a conference cosponsored by The Select Publishing Corporation and The Black Heritage Corporation, an organization which set aside an endowment to encourage publication of academic textbooks written by professors and staff of minority educational institutions. From March 21 to 23, 1980, editors and literary agents gathered at Pascal's Motor Inn, the infamous Atlanta black political hotspot, to review the manuscripts of writers interested in feedback and publishing possibilities.

In 1980, Bambara also collaborated with Sondra O'Neal, professor in the English Department at Emory University, to organize a massive black writers conference in Atlanta, a significant landmark conference for the southern Black Arts Movement. When Bambara moved to Atlanta in 1974, the writer was attracted to the cultural work already in motion. Bambara, however, made a significant contribution in growing a Black Arts Movement in the South that was much more inclusive of women than the historic 1960s' movement had been. Bambara's teaching, promotion of black publications, and development of writers' networks such as the Pamoja Writers Guild that met at her home were critical. Bambara is singularly significant as a champion of the Neo-Black Arts Movement in the South.

Cosponsors of the First Conference on Black South Literature and Art at Emory University, held from November 20 to 22, included SCAAW.[57] Other participating organizations to which Bambara had formal and informal ties included *Callaloo, First World,* and other theater and arts groups. Writers like Bambara who had sway on cultural arts councils and review panels, or held writers' positions at major academic institutions were well positioned to advise emerging writers at the conference. Opening speakers at the conference included culturally and politically conscious artists, activists, and international figures such as Andrew Young, long-time advocate for civil and human rights who also served as United States Ambassador to the United Nations and was elected mayor of Atlanta in 1982.

Undoubtedly, Bambara's continued organizing efforts in support of the black arts in Atlanta influenced friends and artists such as Reed, Sonia Sanchez, Ruby Dee, and Ossie Davis in seeing Atlanta as an important black arts mecca. Attracting thousands of artists, actors, writers, critics, and teachers interested in reflections on the black southern experience, the First Conference on Black South Literature hosted readings, workshops, and receptions at venues across Atlanta including the Atlanta University Center, the Phoenix Art Center, and the NAC. In addition to a focus on black literature, the Emory conference showcased visual arts, theater, and folklore. The Black Arts Movement in the 1960s had its base in cities such as New York, Detroit, Chicago, and Newark, but now new southern black voices were being heard in a southern black arts renaissance. Bambara viewed efforts such as building a black political union as key to development of the creative black arts movement in the South—just as key as they had been in earlier black arts movements. Bambara summed up her accomplishments in Atlanta as "instrumental in kicking doors open to some southern writers, actors, casting directors, etc. and it makes me feel good to have begun building a new constituency."[58]

Networking in Atlanta continued to take place in both formal and informal settings, and an intermingling with various art communities comprised a consistent part of Bambara's social life. Among the after-parties Bambara attended following various performances and conferences were the social gatherings hosted by William Jennings. Jennings, a member of the NAC staff who later headed the jazz program at Spelman College, remembered that Bambara was frequently accompanied by jazz musicians on such occasions:

> I remember a couple of times where she would show up with a musician friend. One time she came with bass player Dewey Sampson, who also was a Yoruba Priest. Another time she arrived with Earl Turbinton, a New Orleans saxophone player. That night an animated conversation ensued late into the night about improvisation being primarily a science, or was it intuition. I just remember her dates being musicians.[59]

In Bambara's fiction, male characters were often musicians or artists as well. In the short story "Medley," for example—adapted into a one-woman show where Ruby Dee performed as Sweet Pea, a manicurist—the protagonist's romantic adventures included a sometimes half-hearted romance with

Larry Landers, a bass player.[60] About Larry, Bambara writes: "couldn't play for nuthin . . . but was baad in the shower, though."[61] It was at those times that Landers provided "the most intricate weaving, walking, bopping, strutting bottom to my singing I ever heard." Sweet Pea is so inspired by her musician boyfriend that she herself belts out songs by artists including Jelly Roll Morton, Bessie Smith, Billie, Nat King Cole, and King Pleasure. In Sweet Pea's voice, Bambara writes: "And I was Yma Sumac for one minute there, up there breathing some rare air and losing my mind, I was so high on just sheer music."[62] Yma Sumac, the Peruvian singer, was known for cascading through octaves of music and frequently boasted of her lineage, which included indigenous warriors who had waged warfare against the Spanish imperialists.

As Jennings' recollections of conversations with Bambara reveal, Bambara sustained a strong interest in the potential of Spelman College to influence the arts in progressive ways. Jennings remembered an extended discussion with Bambara at one of the parties he hosted, where Bambara urged him to promote a jazz scholarship fund for Spelman students. Bambara also offered to write liner notes for future recordings of the Spelman Jazz Ensemble because she was so disappointed in the notes for their early 1980s' album, *Fearless Warrior*, which she believed to be deserving of more enthusiastic praise. Bambara was very excited about the album and the cover art designed by John Riddle, who also was affiliated with the NAC, Jennings recalled decades later. Jennings told Bambara at the party, "I was hesitant about approaching you with no money—someone as well-known as you are. It doesn't seem right to ask you to write liner notes for free." Bambara responded simply, "Don't hesitate."[63] A future opportunity, however, never came.

At the beginning of the new year, in a letter dated January 1, 1981, Reed, then chair of the newly established Columbus Foundation which recognized cutting-edge multicultural works, wrote Bambara to inform her that she would be recognized in its second award ceremony at the Public Theater in New York that spring.[64] At the book award ceremony, Joseph Papp along with Reed and her editor and friend Toni Morrison, would host the awards in a program that included music from Hugh Masekela and a cultural arts performance by the Asian Arts Repertory Company, reinforcing the Foundation's interest in promoting multiculturalism in literature and the arts. A year later, Morrison received the American Book Award for *Beloved,* which later won the Pulitzer Prize. Also in 1981, City College added to Bambara's growing accolades when awarding Toni Cade Bambara, along with Paule Marshall and Toni Morrison, the City College Langston Hughes Award for Lifetime Contributions to African American Arts & Letters. Additionally that year, the *New York Times* listed *The Salt Eaters* in its short listing of New and Noteworthy Paperbacks. Seeing the novel quickly produced in paperback may have pleased Bambara as much as the *New York Times* listing. Bambara remained eager for her books to be printed in more affordable paperback editions in order for them to more readily reach those who might find the purchase of a hardback to be a luxury.

In spite of the acclaim *The Salt Eaters* had received, there was disappointment about the quick drop-off of book sales after its first year of publication. Morrison pointed out that the problems Bambara faced as a first-time novelist were shared by other black writers. At a Columbia University forum where Morrison joined James Baldwin and Amiri Baraka on a panel, Morrison explained, "First novel, poetry, combined forms and experimental forms are not forthcoming from established publishers. They don't earn out—meaning the break-even point is never met. It's not profitable. . . . That situation is devastating to all writers, so you can imagine its practical annihilation of third world writers."[65]

The short-lived interest of mainstream booksellers occurred despite the *New York Times* accolades. Morrison pointed out that "there was a great deal of optimism here, even among the salesmen, because her previous collection of short stories had sold so well. . . . But booksellers wanted something hot, something that would move quickly. We had a very difficult time getting that book into the stores. No matter how enthusiastic we are, we can't put a gun to the bookseller's head. First novels suffer, and so do minority novelists."[66]

The drop in *The Salt Eaters'* sales may have confirmed for Bambara that there was no better time to invest more of her energy in writing scripts. Once Bambara explained that "writing is like sewing—you're more likely to get at it if you don't have to haul the machine out of the closet, clean off the table, and search around for the bobbin box."[67] To create what Bambara considered appropriate space for developing the Zora Neale Hurston script, Bambara chose to sometimes work outdoors in the sun. Bambara wrote:

> In preparation for the upcoming ninety-minute TV film on the life and work of Zora Neale Hurston I set up a four-by-eight foot slab of Sheet-rock on the- yard atop three sawhorses. I unrolled a yard or two of butcher paper, and with a fistful of pens worked barefoot, standing up moving back and forth acting out the scenes. It seemed the most appropriate way to get started. Zora is too big, too bold, too outdoors, too down-home, to capture and release at a desk with a notebook.[68]

But the Zora scriptwriting project would end abruptly for a number of reasons. Bambara wrote WGBH, the public television station in Boston who contracted her to write the script:

> I am sorry all around—great project, fine group to have worked with—but a series of unforeseen emergencies took me out of action for a month. Had thought I could rally and recoup. But I'm not that fast and not that good . . . yet. I apologize for the delay and confusion I may have caused. I know what a big drag it is, depending on others to deliver so one can maintain one's own sense of timing and balance.[69]

Bambara later provided more details on her failure to produce the deliverable within the expected timeframe, citing as factors the escalation of events surrounding the murdered and missing children's case in Atlanta, as well as complications resulting from the inexperienced team, whereby unseasoned individuals were testing their filmmaking skills for the first time. Bambara also had casting disagreements with the team's perceptions of Zora as a character. In a letter to June Jordan about the project, Bambara revealed: "Am keeping a journal of the Zora film project, including all the bullshit arguments like— 'Toni, your treatment very much lifts up the woman-work relationship and advances an essay about the nature of perception (how Z[ora] learned to perceive folk stuff as valuable subject matter, novels as a cultural maintenance tool, etc. and how she worked in spite of weird visions others held of her) but what about the men?'"[70]

Fortunately, through her published writing, Bambara's perceptions of Zora have not been totally lost. In her introduction for the "Sanctified Church," Bambara described Zora in a holistic way that also mirrored some of Bambara's multiple interests and had attributes of characters that appeared in some of Bambara's short stories and novels. About Zora, "scandalized for wearing pants," Toni recalled: "Waitress, manicurist, librettist, secretary/companion, producer, scenarist, domestic, novelist, drama coach, file clerk, storyist, traveloguist, playwright, cook. The woman, quite simply, did not play."[71]

Bambara also had a mission. At the time of the release of *The Salt Eaters,* Bambara balanced as many identities as she had claimed for Zora Neale Hurston; she was busy as lecturer, researcher, storyteller, dancer, and essayist. Bambara also kept her commitments to organizing and providing supports for writers, filmmakers, across the diaspora, and women. Although the extent of recognition that Bambara received for *The Salt Eaters* was short-lived, it would turn out to be a once in a lifetime experience.

NOTES

1. Toni Cade Bambara, "Working at It in Four Parts," Spelman Archives, Atlanta.

2. John Leonard, "Books of the Times," *New York Times*, November 27, 1981.

3. Ibid.

4. Monica Walker, Interview by author, October 2011.

5. Ibid.

6. Ibid.

7. Ibid.

8. Ibid.

9. Furaha Saba, "Toni Cade Bambara Interprets the Health and Sexuality of Women," *Southern Rural Women's Network Newsletter*, January 1983.

10. Ibid.

11. Ibid.

12. Ibid.

13. Ishmael Reed, *Airing Dirty Laundry* (New York: Addison-Wesley Publishing Co., 1993), 168.

14. Billie Jean Young, Interview by author, April 2010.

15. Billie Jean Young, "Fannie Lou Hamer," in *Wild Women in the Whirlwind: Afra-American Culture and the Literary Renaissance* (Westport, CT: Praeger, 1989), 134.

16. Sey Chassler, Letter to Toni Cade Bambara, March 25, 1980, Spelman Archives, Atlanta.

17. Lucille Clifton, "The Magic Mama," *Redbook,* November 1969.

18. Toni Cade Bambara, "The Mama Load," *Redbook,* 182.

19. Ibid., 190.

20. Ibid.

21. Ibid., 188.

22. Ibid., 190.

23. Ibid., 188.

24. Toni Cade Bambara, *The Salt Eaters,* 51.

25. Leila Bronson, Letter to the editors of *Redbook,* 1980, Spelman Archives, Atlanta.

26. National Council of Magazines, Letter to Toni Cade Bambara, April 1, 1908, Spelman Archives, Atlanta.

27. Toni Cade Bambara, Itinerary, Week of April 20, 1980, Spelman Archives, Atlanta.

28. 1980 Fine Arts Festival Flier, Talladega College, Spelman Archives, Atlanta.

29. Toni Cade Bambara, Itinerary, Week of April 20, 1980. Author's Personal Collection.

30. Harold Kaminesky, M.D., Interview by author, 1977.

31. Kalamu ya Salaam, "Searching for the Mother Tongue: An Interview with Toni Cade Bambara," in *Savoring the Salt* (Philadelphia: Temple University Press, 2008), 63.

32. Toni Cade Bambara, "Dedication of Nelson Stevens Mural, Centennial Address," in *The Tuskegee Centennial* (Tuskegee: Tuskegee University Press, 1981).

33. Ibid.

34. Ibid.

35. Ibid.

36. Ibid.

37. Toni Cade Bambara, "The War of the Wall," in *Deep Sightings and Rescue Missions* (New York: Vintage Books, 1996), 57–59.

38. Ibid., 63.

39. For a discussion of the significance of Oscar Micheaux, see Pearl Bowser and Louise Spence, *Writing Himself into History: Oscar Micheaux, His Silent Films, and His Audience* (New Brunswick: Rutgers University Press, 2000).

40. Julie Dash, Interview by author, March 2012.

41. Paul Carter Harrison, Letter to Toni Cade Bambara, May 1, 1980, Spelman Archives, Atlanta.

42. Toni Cade Bambara, Letter to Joan Daves, August 8, 1980, Spelman Archives, Atlanta.

43. Kalamu ya Salaam, "Searching for the Mother Tongue," 20.

44. Kalamu ya Salaam, "If the Hat Don't Fit, How Come We're Wearing It?" In *What Is Life? Reclaiming the Black Blues Self* (Chicago: Third World Press, 1994), 125.

45. Toni Cade Bambara, Letter to Joan Daves, August 8, 1980, Spelman Archives, Atlanta.

46. Ibid.

47. Kambon Obayani, Interview by author, October 2011.

48. Ibid.

49. Bambara, "Working at It in Four Parts."

50. Ibid.

51. Obayani, Interview by author.

52. Toni Cade Bambara, "Story," *Callalloo,* October 7, 1979, 31–36.

53. Bambara, "Working at It in Four Parts."

54. Charles A. Frye, Charlyn Harper, Linda James Myers, and Eleanor W. Traylor, "How to Think Black: A Symposium in Toni Cade Bambara's The Salt Eaters," *Contributions in Black Studies* 6, no. 1 (The Blues Vision): Article 4, 1983.

55. Charles A. Frye, *Towards a Philosophy of Black Studies* (San Francisco: R & E Research Associates, 1978).

56. Frye et al., "How to Think Black."

57. "Literature and Art Featured at Conference," *Campus Report* 33, no. 5 (1980), 3.

58. Bambara, "Working at It in Four Parts."

59. William Jennings, Interview by author, May 2011.

60. Ruby Dee, Letter to Toni Cade Bambara, August 7, 1980, Spelman Archives, Atlanta.

61. Toni Cade Bambara, "Medley," in *The Sea Birds Are Still Alive* (New York: Vintage Books, 1982), 105.

62. Ibid., 123.

63. Jennings interview.

64. Ishmael Reed, Letter to Toni Cade Bambara, January 1, 1981.

65. Mel Watkins, "Hard Times for Black Writers," *New York Times,* February 22, 1981.

66. Ibid.

67. Bambara, "Working at It in Four Parts."

68. Toni Cade Bambara, "Salvation Is the Issue," in *Black Women Writers (1950–1980),* edited by Mari Evans (New York: Anchor Books, 1984), 45.

69. Toni Cade Bambara, Letter to Dian Miller, September 10, 1981.

70. Toni Cade Bambara, Letter to June Jordan, undated. June Jordan Papers, Schlesinger Library, Box 28, Folder 12.

71. Toni Cade Bambara, "Some Forward Remarks," in *The Sanctified Church,* ed. Zora Neale Hurston (New York: Marlowe and Company, 1981), 9–13.

EIGHT

Moving the Global Movement

They used to tell her in Sunday school that five verses a day would help solve problems. Told her in junior high that algebra sharpened that ability too. Was told at home that the community that named her, claimed her, sustained her, held the answers, she had only to listen.[1]

In 1980, Bambara was at the midpoint of the 10 years she would spend living in Atlanta. Bambara's first five years there had been devoted to writing fiction and finding new ways to recognize the work of emerging writers, particularly in the South. Now her writing in the second five years yielded work on a second novel, which Bambara at one point titled *If Blessing Comes*. That book would be published posthumously as *Those Bones Are Not My Child*, as a result of her friend and editor Toni Morrison's commitment to edit the work. Between 1980 and 1985, in addition to the grueling investigative work needed to write the book on the cases of Atlanta's missing and murdered children, Bambara also began to pursue film work. In 1983, Bambara received a Hollywood contract to write the screenplay for *Tar Baby,* Toni Morrison's most recent novel. *Tar Baby* addressed themes that Bambara also honored in her own writing, but just as had happened to her Zora Neale Hurston film project with public television, Bambara lost the *Tar Baby* contract. In Bambara's last years in Atlanta, what did continue to flow—in a mighty stream—was her work as a grassroots activist and writer.

As soon as Bambara completed writing the prologue for *If Blessing Comes* in the fall of 1981, for example, she began to read aloud from it frequently, aiming

Bambara, an organizer of SCAAW (Southern Collective of African American Writers), speaking on a panel at the National Black Arts Festival, Robert W. Woodruff Library, Atlanta University Center, 1988. Copyright Susan Ross.

to awaken communities to myths perpetuated by official reports and investigations surrounding the missing and murdered Atlanta children cases. Bambara also linked concerns about the disappeared in Atlanta with struggles across the nation and around the globe that focused on disappeared populations. Seven years after Bambara began writing about the Atlanta tragedy, she told students at Hampshire College how her involvement with a global movement began:

> I was at the time—seven years ago—obsessed with disappearances: disappearances of children in Trenton, New Jersey; [the disappearances] of men, women, and children in Atlanta; the disappearances of civil rights workers in Birmingham, Alabama who were being unearthed and pulled out of the rivers; the disappearances of families; the disappearances in Central and South America of trade unionists, students, Jews, Indians; the disappearances from Atlanta and elsewhere of families who might have been in Jonestown, Guyana during the massacre but whose bodies were not sent home. So that when the children, men, and women began systematically disappearing in Atlanta, it caught everybody's attention—most especially began to catch my attention—because I work in the street. I'm a street organizer primarily and as I say I began to jot down observations.[2]

Bambara also explained in her talk how the book she was writing was a call to respond to the emergency of disappearances encircling the globe:

> I started working on the book as a novel attempting to document the community's version of what happened—what it means to live under siege—and to watch

agency after agency, institution after institution lie and betray you; and to watch leader after leader become compromised and betray you and to continue going on buying further and further into the official version of things until you discover you are part and parcel of the politics of invisibility and silence, meaning essentially that you have given up your right to think clearly. You have given up your history. You have given up your faculty for reasoning in the hopes that the official version will be simple and easy and allow you to sleep at night and allow you to avert your eyes so you will not have to look at what you know because if you look at what you know you may have to take responsibility for your eyes.[3]

While Bambara initially aimed to use the 1980s as a time to primarily concentrate on film projects, living in a community—and accepting her own self-designation as a community scribe and street organizer—began to mean abandoning her immediate agenda for making films in order to commit herself to what became a painful search for truth in the Atlanta cases. The investigative work was sometimes grueling and so was the writing. Even though Bambara had several opportunities for international travel which provided welcomed opportunities to build international alliances, Bambara could not escape reminders of the weight of her unpublished epic novel. Bambara viewed it as her responsibility to bring the voices of the community into discussions of the Atlanta crisis through her fiction. It also mattered that from the time she first moved to Atlanta until a decade later, Bambara sometimes found Atlanta to be stifling to her independent thinking and creative spirit. It is not surprising that in 1985, Bambara decided to leave Atlanta.

Beginning in 1979, Bambara, who often spoke of the importance of journal-writing in her workshops, started keeping informal notebook entries about the unfolding Atlanta tragedy. In her journal Bambara recorded how her postman first captured her attention when asking her questions about what she knew about the missing children's cases. Bambara was to have similar conversations with neighbors, the community's psychic reader, and women she'd meet in the laundromat—where Bambara liked to write because of the bright lighting—as well as perform impromptu readings that were prone to happen in the laundromat setting simply because one of the women had asked her what she was writing in her notebooks.[4]

Initially conceived as a nonfiction work, *If Blessing Comes* eventually developed into a novel. As Bambara explained later, this provided her with an opportunity to explore differences between "the documentary and the fictional impulse."[5] In *If Blessing Comes*, Bambara aimed for a blend of the genre of investigative journalism with the spirit of thriller drama found in film. Years after she started work on *If Blessing Comes*, Bambara said her decision to abandon a journalistic approach in favor of fiction was partially out of a concern for her safety and to protect herself against possible libel suits.[6] In the midst of writing the novel she emphasized that she was not interested in exploring the guilt charges against Wayne Williams, the man arrested as the primary suspect in the case; Bambara wanted the tragedy to be seen in the larger context of the greater physical, social, and economic injustices that allowed the cases to be ignored. In her writing and talks, the author criticized the city's failure to al-locate needed resources to uncover the facts underlying the cases.[7]

While documenting events unfolding in Atlanta through extensive factual details, using real names, places, and events, the novel centers on a fictional-ized family, the Spencer's, who are swept into the Atlanta tragedy when their 12-year-old son Sundiata ("Sonny") fails to return home from a camping trip. Zala, Sonny's mother, is similar to many other central female characters in Bambara's short stories: she wears her hair in a towering Afro, works at the neighborhood arts center, and is a manicurist who stays in touch with the heartbeat of the community through conversations at the barber shop where Zala has a manicure table. Like the women in her novel, *The Salt Eaters,* who use working their crafts as a self-healing art, Zala brings her paintbrushes home from a fictional Neighbor Arts Center and uses her craft as a kind of medita-tion. Along with everything else she does, Zala, who is separated from her husband Spence—a Vietnam veteran—hopes to find time to design T-shirts for the upcoming Third World Film Festival and makes halters, macramé hang-ings, tapestries, and weavings for the African Village in Atlanta's Piedmont Park.[8] Similar to Bambara, Zala is a cultural worker.

Bambara projects through the character of Zala her own outrage regard-ing officials who classified missing and murdered children as runaways and even accused parents of murdering their own children. In the midst of the strain of failed efforts to find her son, Zala does not become the superwoman who keeps her pain within; she explodes.[9] At one point, Bambara described irrationality as the collective state of mind of the Atlanta community living in the midst of terrorism. Bambara argued that irrational behavior could be expected when surrounded by terrorism. And in the prologue to the Atlanta novel, Bambara described her own disoriented state of mind when she believed her own daughter was missing. Nevertheless, Bambara argued that justified outrage and even moments of irrationality made more sense than succumb-ing to amnesia: "You are running down the streets of southwest Atlanta like a crazy woman. . . . Maybe you are a crazy woman, but you'd rather embrace madness than amnesia."[10]

At one point, Zala, at the peak of her anguish as though speaking in tongues, began to speak as a woman who believed she had the power to stand on equal ground with the most powerful source in the universe. In doing so, Zala finds clarity, independence, and strength as she frees her voice and liberates her spirit.

About Zala, Bambara wrote: "She'd come out of the garden and learned to speak up. Forget you, she said, feeling wild and free and crazy fine. Enjoying the sweet, crooked pleasure of hearing her voice so strong and defiant. . . . She laughed and the streak of lightning turned milky. Heahhhh. I've been here, Lord, but where the hell were you?"[11]

Although Zala is frustrated and drained by her search for her missing son, she never gives up hope. After nearly a year of tracking down false leads, Zala receives a phone call from a Florida hospital pediatric nurse who describes a mutilated child wasting away in the children's ward. The nurse explains that the boy was found wandering in a daze on the highway nearly naked and barefoot. At first the child was thought to be one of the boat children from Cuba or Haiti, but information the hospital received about the missing children's cases in Atlanta led the nurse to contact families there.

This child is indeed Zala's missing child, but Sonny has been so brutalized his mother does not recognize him. Devastated by the trauma, Zala realized that her recovery would depend on her ability "to hem up the dragging flesh of her life with careful, tiny stitches."[12] But, Zala also knew she needed help. And Zala's family found a healing space not in Atlanta, but in Epps, Alabama, where Zala's mother—known as Mama Loveyetta or Lovey to the community—lived. Known for talking to plants, keeping bees, and working with the Federation of Southern Cooperatives, Mama Loveyetta is one of Bambara's long line of women characters who heal. In Epps, Zala finds the familiar in the clothes her mother has placed on the bushes to dry, breathes in the scent of her mother's freshly laundered sheets, and finds the Bible on her bed opened to the book of Daniel, the book of dreams, divine revelations, and interpretations. And Zala finally dreams. She sees "her children running across a wide savannah, a baobab silhouetted against the red sun, the legs of the gazelles a blur."[13]

At the close of the novel, when the community gathers at the Seven Hills Congregational Church, Zala stands in the pulpit, wearing a T-shirt and jeans instead of a pastoral robe. For inspiration for the message, Zala does not read Bible verses, but offers the poems of Maya Angelou, Gwendolyn Brooks, and Alexis De Veaux. The pastor signals the progressive tone of the church when his invocation recognizes the power of female in the spirit as well as male, calling on the Father and the Mother in prayer. Zala takes her cue to begin her message from a woman in the audience who sees her own beauty in a hand-held mirror before clicking her compact shut, a signal Zala interprets as one for her to begin speaking. In the here and now community message that Zala delivers, Zala warns that "coerced silence is terrorism,"[14] an issue that Bambara similarly addressed in her public talks and lectures.

It would be years before Bambara would complete the writing of this novel, but when the prologue was completed in the fall of 1981, Wayne Williams had been arrested and charged with 2 of the 27 Atlanta child murders. As Bambara continued to work on the novel, she repeatedly returned to the question of possible government cover-ups in the case.[15]

Meanwhile, Bambara increased her calls for action around the cases and engaged the community as an organizer. On February 5, 1981, a recent visit to Atlanta by her friend June Jordan provided an opportunity for Bambara to talk about the shattering events surrounding the murdered and missing children's cases. A symposium hosted by Spelman College on "The Black Aesthetic and the Writer" included Bambara, Jordan, and Mary Helen Washington.[16]

Bambara also seized any opportunity she could to organize as an activist. Taking advantage of a short taxi ride home from the airport after a flight from

Chicago, Bambara told the cab driver, "Let's set up a self-defense studio and gather up all the vets and martial arts folks and folks with heart to spare." [17] Bambara suggested that the cabdriver stop for coffee, where they exchanged phone numbers. The cab driver later called to let Bambara know he had invited some vets to his house for dinner to discuss strategies. In a letter to Jordan, Bambara described the cab driver that she aligned forces with as "one of them real old timey young brothers raised by daddy and uncle and older men who hunt and have gold teeth and know how to swing a hammer and take pride in planing a door so it travels smoothly over carpet." [18] Indeed, Bambara brought as much creative energy to her community organizing as she did to her writing.

In the spring of 1981, Bambara was able to pause and seek some diversion through travel to St. Croix, Virgin Islands, as a participant in a Women Writers Symposium. The symposium, the first of its kind in the Virgin Islands, was organized by Gloria I. Joseph, a literary writer and intellectual with years of academic teaching experience in the United States and abroad. Initially Bambara hoped to provide an opportunity for a group of children from Atlanta to travel with her to the Caribbean island, but was unable to find sources of support for the children's travel; but Karma, her daughter, did join her in the getaway. The event was held at the College of the Virgin Islands (now the University of the V.I.), and featured four internationally known feminist writers and poets: Michelle Cliff, Toni Cade Bambara, Audre Lorde, and Adrienne Rich. While in St. Croix, Bambara, as she frequently did, visited local schools. The author read excerpts from her work in progress, *If Blessing Comes*, and she engaged students with her creative and political version of "Little Red Riding Hood." Again Bambara aimed to heighten children's awareness of the misguided beliefs and inequitable relationships that the stories presented in mainstream literature often perpetuate.

Staying at Joseph's home, Bambara learned how Joseph managed her thriving honey business, and offered to promote the business in the United States. "Toni was always telling me there was a market, but we could hardly keep up with orders in St. Croix," Joseph added. "Toni truly loved the honey and I regularly sent bottles to her. In her inimitable way, she described how she had to hide the honey from her mother, who also loved it." The honey even carries Bambara's nickname for Joseph. Bambara showed her love for humor again when she fondly nicknamed Joseph "doc locs" because she had a doctorate and wore her hair in dreadlocks. And that is how the business was known, and all labels the name, "Doc Locs' Honey." [19]

Joseph and Bambara knew each other well from previous visits. About the writer's ability to interpret dreams, Joseph explained, "Bambara analyzed and broke the dream down in terms of the orishas and the ancestors and the time zones. It was incredible. That's what impressed me about Toni, you drop one little pebble in the water and she can elaborate on each ripple that ascended out from that pebble." In St. Croix, the writer relaxed as they also remembered Bambara's visit to Amherst, Massachusetts. Bambara had been invited along with a number of other notable figures, including Mari Evans, Audre Lorde, Betty Shabazz, and Adrienne Rich as guest lecturers in Joseph's course, "The Significant Role of Black Women in Women's Studies" at Hampshire College. Joseph recalled how Bambara not only addressed the role of black women in her discussions, but also how "every bit of Toni's energy—no matter how it came forth—emanated from a principle, certainly a revolutionary principle which included doing whatever you can to bring about in a compassionate way or through other meaningful ways equity in the world."[20] After the class, Bambara was moved by the enthusiastic welcome she received from the students who included presenting her with a cake trimmed in red, black, and green, the colors of the black liberation flag. A decade later in St. Croix, Joseph could see Bambara's revolutionary character was still alive in spite of the difficulties she was facing in Atlanta.

While in St. Croix, again Bambara demonstrated her resilient political spirit as she resonated with the formation of new activist women's groups. The Women's Coalition of St. Croix, an organization that promoted equality for women through strategies that addressed racism and sexism, was an outgrowth of the women writers' conference she attended there. There were also discussions about the organization that Joseph founded to increase ties with women in South Africa during the anti-apartheid struggle.[21] Bambara served on the Advisory Board of Sisters in Support of Sisters in South Africa (SISA), along with an array of other international activists and cultural workers, including James Baldwin, Angela Davis, Woody King, Max Roach, Ida Lewis, Acklyn Lynch, and Loretta Ross.[22] Through leadership provided by Joseph and the sister board members, SISA worked to awaken the U.S. public to the ongoing resistance in South Africa through supporting women's self-help groups such as the Zamani Soweto Sisters and the Maggie Magaba Trust. Undoubtedly, Bambara welcomed opportunities to link her organizing efforts in Atlanta surrounding the murdered and missing children cases with the growing anti-apartheid movement.

But, even with these diversions from the Atlanta trauma, Bambara and her daughter now had to face the agony of going home. When they first arrived in Atlanta, memories of the state of panic which Bambara and her daughter felt when they first arrived in St. Croix were palpable. Bambara later remembered: "And my daughter and I got down there and we did not let go of each other's hand. We noticed that people were reacting to us strongly. We thought we were cool. We were crazy—we were stark raving mad. We could not sleep; we could not let go of each other. I could not allow her out of my sight and that was in February of '81."[23]

Joseph also remembered the challenges Bambara had to face in Atlanta as threatening and difficult: "It was typical of Toni to be out there burning and blazing, but yet you knew it had to be eating her—she's only human. Atlanta took its toll. It had an effect on her, enough for her to leave Atlanta."[24] Joseph stated that it seemed as though the closer Bambara came to revealing truthful information about the murders, the more threatened her life became.

Once she returned to Atlanta, Bambara continued to support SISA, but Bambara again prioritized work on the murdered and missing children. Bambara was so immersed in the writing of *If Blessing Comes* that she told a reporter from *The Drum,* "I'm working on that book now and would rather not dissipate my energy blabbering. I prefer to invest that energy in getting the story out, the community's story, the story that never got told, the story whose edges were so distorted or eclipsed by the media and the cops' version of things that people throughout the rest of the country are asking all the wrong questions."[25] Bambara also told *The Drum* that she expected the Atlanta book to be in bookstores within the next several months.[26]

As the Atlanta crisis continued to unfold Bambara had opportunities for lighter moments as audiences continued to flock to hear her speak, loyal followers of the politically radical and woman-centered points of view in her works. In April 1981, the Jomandi Productions, directed by Pearl Cleage, staged Bambara's short story "Witchbird." Bambara appreciated viewing the production in a community theater converted from a gym, a venue accessible to all. In a positive review entitled "Witchbird's Warning: To Thine Own Self Be True," the city's daily black newspaper, the *Atlanta Daily News,* described the core theme of the play as centering on a woman's determination to explore the dreams "that have been begging her attention for years."[27] A four-person dance troupe in a performance "that unfolded like dreams" was a dominating force in the play.[28] The female narrator in "Witchbird," an independent and free-spirited actor, who demanded scripts that promoted free expression also claimed her right for time to explore some of her "new sheet music gathering dust on the piano,"[29] a reminder of Bambara's own interest in collecting sheet music and finding solace in her own piano renditions. In the midst of writing about the Atlanta tragedy, Jomandi's production of "Witchbird" was a welcomed diversion.

Unfortunately, a month later, Bambara's life and the lives of countless others were jolted by the news of another tragedy, this time a personal one: Hoyt Fuller's death caused by a heart attack on May 11, 1981. Having only recently moved to Atlanta to establish the black scholarly journal *First World,* Fuller, an internationally recognized intellectual giant, had been Bambara's cherished friend and a long-time supporter of her work, since the publication of her short stories in the *Negro Digest* decades earlier—a popular literary magazine that Fuller edited. The mutuality of their respect was reflected a year earlier when Bambara worked to secure a grant from the Literary Magazine Council to support *First World* and lobbied for a teaching position for him at Atlanta University. Once again, Bambara was disappointed when she received news from the University that while it respected Hoyt's work, the $17,000 yearly that Bambara recommended as a salary for Fuller was out of the question.[30] A year earlier, Bambara forwarded Fuller the news that external sources of funding would be needed to secure a position for him at Clark College. In an ominous closing note, Bambara wrote: "You're looking fine and sound fine. I shall assume then that you are fine and will not be scaring the hell out of us any time soon."[31]

The range of artists and activists who gathered in Atlanta on May 16 for the memorial honoring Fuller, a long-time preeminent voice in the Pan-African movement, spoke volumes to the range of his influence. Bambara joined "Witnesses" James Baldwin, Gwendolyn Brooks, Howard Dodson, Jan Douglass, Mari Evans, Richard Long, Haki Madhubuti, Sondra O'Neal, Dudley Randall, Kalamu ya Salaam, Sonia Sanchez, James Turner, Joyce Winters, and others in celebrating Fuller's life and work.[32]

Bambara wrote to Jordan shortly after the loss of her friend with hopes that *First World* would continue to be published. It was also a moment where Bambara remembered how much she valued her own freedom of movement.

> And then Hoyt. What a loss. I feel this gaping hole widening already. Was a fine memorial. We did a few TV spots and got an item or two in local papers here but damn. Am about to empty out some boxes (boxes have to be my very best favorite item; my husband used to court me by bringing me empty boxes; my neighbors bring them by and leave'm on the porch like bouquets or pots of greens. I adore throwing out things is what it's about). Anyway, about to take some boxes over to Hoyt's. Several of the folks from Chicago and other parts have hung over to catalogue and inventory and pack. The general feeling is we've got to fund raise and keep magazine going. Family says to keep house going too.[33]

In the letter's handwritten postscript, Bambara revealed more of her agony about the loss of another friend as she wrote Jordan:

> Last time I saw Hoyt, he was strolling along with that cane he no longer had to lean on. Had taken to hitting and poking people with it, which he loooooved to do. Had on his oatmeal slacks and rich deep turquoise velour shirt. I quite naturally hailed him: "Ain't you fine," cause I love to mess with him. We talked about I don't-remember-what. The lack of rage in ATL [about] the children. I remember that. And he told me to take care of myself. Which was funny coming from him. I was fussing about his losing weight. Food bored Hoyt. We badmouthed AU for not giving him a job. Talked about Cornell and that grueling trip. I'm not sure what else, but what I remember is his saying that Larry Neale was too damn young to die, too damn young and valuable. (there'd just been another memorial and Larry's play was being adv/mounted). And then he goes. At 57. Too much.[34]

In 1982, as Bambara continued with work on the murdered and missing children novel, she received an invitation that would require her to leave the country for a year-long position as writer-in-residence in the Department of English at the University of Ibadan in Nigeria.[35] Esi Kinney, her friend and colleague from Livingston College, was a member of the Theater Arts Department at the University of Ibadan. Bambara's interest in traditional African culture was long-standing, and an opportunity to not only escape the day-to-day disappointments in Atlanta, but to deepen her understanding of Yoruba traditions in the cradle of Yoruba culture which the Nigerian stint offered must have been inviting. Andrea Benton Rushing, who received a Fulbright that supported her teaching in Nigeria in the 1980s, recalled Bambara's long-standing interest in

Yoruba culture and their extended correspondence on the language of women's clothing in southwest Nigeria. Rushing remembered Bambara talking about her divinations, solstice celebrations, and a neighborhood root person dropping by her house, and more than one divination where her orisha was revealed.

About Bambara's personal explorations of diverse spiritual traditions, Rushing reflected:

> Unlike most people in her generation which is my generation too, she didn't grow up in a religious home so religion to her did not mean the Baptist Church or the Methodist Church. Religions like the Yoruba religion have women deities woven into them and for someone who is so imbued with a woman's power so refreshingly motivated in women escaping victimization, she [Bambara] did not see being a roots woman like Minnie Ransom in *Salt Eaters* being shameful or a sign of ignorance.[36]

Perhaps an array of factors such as the uncompleted novel, opportunities for film work, concern about child care, or lack of resources prevented Bambara from accepting the writer-in residence position at the University of Ibadan. There is no question, however, that Bambara's knowledge base regarding ancient African religions continued to influence her writing and activism. Bambara called on African American communities to tap into rituals that evoke memory of their African heritage, and she unabashedly celebrated filmmakers, writers, and dancers whose cultural works reflected African traditions.

Bambara's unflagging commitment to support and encourage writers across the African diaspora would continue whether in the United States or abroad. Although Bambara was far more apt to invest energy in new writers than seasoned ones, Bambara also positioned herself to support publication of works by recognized writers that mainstream presses failed to support. Prior to the death of her friend Hoyt Fuller, Bambara, who was on the Advisory Board of the Georgia University Press, worked along with Fuller to encourage Georgia University Press to publish John Oliver Killens's book *Youngblood*. Having known Killens from her early writing days when Killens organized the Harlem Writers Guild, Bambara also championed Killens's novel on the black Russian, *Pushkin*. In a November 1982 letter addressed to "Her Excellency, Toni Cade Bambara," Killens warmly saluted Bambara and expressed "profound appreciation" to her and "our late brother Hoyt Fuller, for the part you played in calling YOUNGBLOOD to the attention of the University of Georgia Press."[37] Killens added, "Thank you also, my Queen, for dubbing me the 'father of the Neo black arts.' I humbly accept the designation, and I accept and understand the responsibility it poses for me. And now to PUSHKIN, THE GREAT BLACK RUSSIAN."[38] Bambara must have smiled as Killens signed his letter, "Your loyal and humble subject," and wished her "the best of health and fighting spirit."[39] At the time, Bambara was increasingly seeing work in film along with writing as a vehicle for expressing her "fighting spirit."

In July 1982, Bambara welcomed another opportunity to leave Atlanta. This time Bambara would have a chance to strengthen her skills in film as she participated in a screenplay conference at the University of London. In a letter that began with a personalized note to her daughter and was followed by a letter to her mother, Bambara expressed excitement about progress being made in her writing and seemed jubilant about the growing list of new project ideas. Bambara seemed light-hearted and free of the agony of Bambara's prolonged focus on the Atlanta missing and murdered cases.

In this letter, addressed to "Bambara and Brehon," Bambara again demonstrated that she didn't censor subject matter when writing to her daughter; her letter included sections that could have easily been written to a peer:

> Hello, Sweetheart, I'm having the bestest time. Been looking all morning for an envelope to mail you some books I think you would enjoy. Will probably get them off first thing Monday morning. . . . Anyway. I'm having a smashing time as I said in the previous letter. Have been writing like 6 people—stories, plays, teleplays, film scripts. Lots of ideas, lots of energy, time, a room of my own near the kitchen where I keep the kettle on for great cups of tea while I work so I don't smoke myself to death // have been meeting such wonderful people. Sistuhs who have lived here all their lives and talk in the most unexpected and colorful way with a lot of "blimey" and "life, deaf, and all of it," and "bloody well will do it, mate, ah don mind tellinya." Here, the Indians call themselves Black and live together with folks from the Caribbean, Africa, and those who were born here or have lived here, grew up here. Met a sister you'd adore, a little woman, name Pratihba, from Calcutta. Very pretty and bright and tough and very funny. A sense of humour like yours. We sat up last night with one of the sistuhs who keeps me in stitches with her "blimey" and drank wine, ate cherries, spit pits into a bowl and exchanged news of how colored folks are faring on this and that side of the Atlantic. She has eyes like yours and laughs like you. So needless to say I love her and find her beautiful. But also she plays jacks and loves to swim.[40]

Bambara continued her letter with a Part II where she told her mother how she was organizing among women writers of color. At last, the author is finding the renewal she was seeking after being so deeply immersed in the Atlanta trauma.

> Hi Mommy, thought of you this morning as I passed an elder in the park doing a lite trot around the tennis court, stopping from time to time to stretch, bend and swing her arms about. Have found at last how to eat here. The Greek bakeries. The Italian fruit stands, the curry shops and Chinese restaurants. And the Dutch have the best coffee. What a busy city. Lots of "lunch theatres" little hole-in-the-wall places that put on 45 minute plays in the afternoon and then again in the evenings. Tonight Mr. Abdul . . . and I are going to see a play that's supposed to be quite good, the music especially. . . . The minute my head hits the pillow, I'm gone. Perhaps because I take hot baths and read as the water seeps out (the woman across hall who shares bath bathes in A.M. after a run so we've been working things out). And at first light—even with curtains drawn (we moved to new quarters y'day so I'm right in front on the street across from Cartwright Gardens and tennis court)—I'm up bright eyed and raring to go. I have never, I mean NEVAH been so ON—writing, walking, running, poking about, visiting, dining, writing, organizing

meetings, writing, sleeping soundly and waking refreshed after 6 hours and ready to write, write. The course goes well. I've got a whole folio of ideas for plays and stories as well as a number of drafts of nearly complete things. . . . Mama, thank you so much for support and well wishes and enthusiasm, not to mention making it possible to come here. I realllllllly appreciate it. Tomorrow I think I'll take a walk through flea markets on Portobello Road. There's Sunday market I hear which can be marvelous. Been eyeing the feet of several folk around here and they say the shoes are from Portobello. Good enough. I'll check it out. Tell Karma thanks for her sandals. The brown ones she outgrew. They're absolutely perfect. Been wearing them ever since I got here except when out in my yellow little heels being cute. Spent the afternoon with the pub/ed of Salt (it's doing well, I'll do some readings and things the last week in July) and that was an eye-opener. I asked about Black writers here. Blank. Any interest in having sistuhs here do an anthology. Mute. Any contact with Black women's groups for readings for me. Blank. I went off, I mean I really went off. So. Publish a writer—safe. At a distance; safe, already with a rep & major pub behind her—like me and that's supposed to get all the writers here off their backs. Been plotting with the Afr/Asian group all morning about pulling writers to do an anthology. Have it pub by small Blk press and really push it. Then when Wom Press come round to reprint or pick up for their book club, sistuhs raise the prices and laugh. I'm having a good time. Making trouble, creating great stuff I didn't know I had in me. Life is so good. Take great care of yourself, Mother. Warm regards to all. // Ta, Toni

This letter to her mother once again demonstrated how fulfilled Bambara felt when championing the works of women writers of color. And soon after returning to Atlanta, Bambara took a rare moment to celebrate her own success. Now, Bambara appeared to be entering a new season in her life. In a letter from the National Endowment for the Arts, Bambara learned that she would be awarded a $12,500 grant from the Endowment's Literature Program in support of her professional writing career.[41] At the end of 1982, Bambara was ecstatic as she wrote to her cousin Carole Brown:

Hey Cuz, your letter sure was traveling in a delicious bunch of mail. Rec'd notification today that I won an NEA grant for literature. Whoooeee. Gonna run right out and buy a car. I cried, Karma hugged me and jumped up and down. We been sooo broke right in through here. Usually are in Fall and Winter cause I refuse to work in summer time, and do like burrowing in for the winter instead of romping around lecturing etc. in all that cold. I'm sooo pleased with myself, Carole Ann, cause I've managed to get grants for other people, for organizations, groups, but never for me. Ain't never been eligible for unemployment either. Ya know what I mean. So this is sweet. Tooo sweet since all I did was submit 50 pages of the manuscript I'm working on. Enclosing the current issue of Race and Class, a radical journal from Third World folks in England. I think it's in bookstores around your way. Do call Ish Reed's attention to it and Barbara C should you be seeing them any time soon.[42]

Bambara's letter continued with reference to her avoidance of commercialized mainstream holidays. For her, holidays meant more time for writing. Bambara continued in her letter:

No, I won't be in New York for holidays. I generally try to ignore holidays. They depress me. And for past 12 years have made it a habit to send Helen and Karma to the Islands or someplace hip so I can work undisturbed. Working at the moment on a book about Atlanta. It's kicking my ass. Such energy to fight off despair, to not wallow in cloying sentimentality, grief, etc, anger, no rage, producing, instead of a useable document, an absolute chill out. Book should be on the stands in Nov 83; that is, if I can finish up in next 8 weeeeeks and get it out of my hair. Then I begin work on the movie script—"Tar Baby"—based on Toni Morrison's novel, starring Howard Ellsworth Rollins from "Ragtime." Heh Heh. I plan to be all up in the production. So have kept my calendar clear from now till next winter. Which means, working on the Atlanta bk and doing a few scribbly notes now and then on the movie, I keep the phone unplugged most of the time. . . . Anyhow. Have no plans to interrupt schedule for travel as much as I'd looove to get away from this typewriter, death, corpses, bullshit and all the rest that's entailed trying to document the community's story before amnesia sets utterly in . . .[43]

In this letter, Bambara's excitement continued to mount in the way of a get-happy dance performed by a member of a sanctified church:

Time out, Cuz, while I look at the National Endowment for the Arts letter and scream a little bit. I've submitted work to Ford, Guggenheim etc and to NEA in years past. No go. But last year I was on the review committee and had to wade through several thousand fiction manuscripts. I learned a lot. Have learned, for [instance], how to edit mercilessly—mostly cut—cause I'm inclined to be loooong winded and to clutter up the prose with dense shit. Getting lean. Getting Hooray. The two house cats are lookin up at me from their curled-sleep positions on the heat registers wondering what is wrong with the crazy bitch today. Will probably be hollering for days now. Do me good. Been so quiet up here with this machine (finally got sensible and invested in an IBM electric, so I don't dread having to type anymore . . . in a year or so will be able to think on the machine and then will move on to the word processor which Miz Karma says I should master as soon as possible and quit being a primitive. . . . I shall miss black BIC pens and long yellow pads. Alas.)
    And now I must shower and shampoo and do my nails. My girlfriend Jane [Poindexter] and I are stepping out on the town tonight. We keep saying we will and then it rains or something's on the TV or we're broke. Old fogeys our daughters say. But I'm raring to go tonight.[44]

Over the next several months, Bambara's commitment to write would be interrupted by travel, activism, and her passion for work in film. In a contract dated February 7, 1983, Bambara was asked to provide the script for Morrison's novel *Tar Baby* within the timeframe of a little more than seven months.[45] Although Bambara completed the script, it was rejected by the production team.

Despite disappointment in the aborted *Tar Baby* contract, Bambara did not challenge the two pages of criticism of her script, which pointed out as problematic such elements as the draft's overuse of movable graphics, the length of time spent on particular characters rather than others, sparse dialogue in certain sections, and use of flashbacks.[46] In her letter accepting the rejection of her script, Bambara wrote that she believed that having spent more time in Atlanta working on the script would not have prevented an inevitable rejection of her work based on the criticism she received.[47] Bambara may have put the screenplay aside when joining 95 other artists who spent July 25 to August 25 at the Djerasi Ranch in California. During that month, Bambara worked on her novel, *If Blessing Comes*.[48] In discussing some of the criticisms of Bambara's draft screenplay, Morrison surmised:

> If you do a screen play, I have since learned, you have to leave space for the director. Also actors in film don't talk for long periods of time, so you can't have 250 words in a row the way you would in a novel or short story, because they generally have 3 or 4 sentences back and forth. There are few monologues. Anyway, the movie was never made and her screenplay was not suitable and she agreed that it wasn't when we were talking about it, but she was paid $30,000.[49]

The film project was a loss and the Atlanta book stalled. Bambara also missed the collegiality of an artistic community that throbbed with "the kind of crazed obsessive intensity that characterizes for me the life of most artists I know."[50] It certainly seemed to be the rhythm with which Bambara wanted to live her life. And, New York was where she could hear Yiddish, Spanish, Chinese, Greek, and English from around the world.[51]

While writers like Chinua Achebe and filmmaker Ousmane Sembene were instructive in print and on screen in providing new ways to explore language, Bambara also longed to hear a diversity of the spoken word on a far more regular and casual basis; it was how she said she continued to train her ear. It was also a skill that Bambara's friend Sanchez attributed to being born in New York. Sanchez said, "When you grow up in New York, you learn how to maneuver and manipulate your way through the world. After living in New York, there is no place you can't live from a small town to a big city. As a New Yorker, you develop listening skills that contribute to an ability to speak with all kinds of people where ever you happen to be. Both Toni and I mastered the international language of 'New Yorkese.'"[52]

About Atlanta, Bambara sadly noted even a lack of cross-cultural interest within the African community in informal settings. Bambara wrote, "It is not often, even, that Nigerians, Ethiopians and Africans of the Americas break bread together."[53] Maybe Bambara longed for more opportunities to move in and out of settings where her "New Yorkese" would be useful and welcomed. As long as Bambara lived in Atlanta, she was constantly reassessing her decision to move there.

Other signs signaled a hunger for change. In 1983, the roof in Bambara's former home where her mother now lived on Mayflower Street collapsed.[54] The Mayflower House was also her daughter's second home, as her mother often took care of Karma when she was traveling. Again, Bambara stopped work to talk with insurance agents and to relocate her mother to a safer environment.

In 1984, Bambara again found solace through travel, making yet another trip to London, this time to read from her work at The First International Feminist Book Fair in London and to network with other feminist writers from the United States, Europe, India, Australia, the Caribbean, and Africa.[55] At The Factory in North Paddington on June 12, 1984, writer Sam Greenlee remembered Bambara arriving late that night and joking about two white women jumping up to give her their seats as Bambara suggested that they might have thought it was a political act.[56] Greenlee told the audience in the introduction, "Toni is an activist and a writer and springs from the time when there was no distinction between the two."[57]

That night once again, Bambara began her talk with her call and response version of the yellow-haired bandit named Goldilocks and raised the question with the audience of how to expand the Third World cinema movement through increased support and distribution of films, such as *Awake From Mourning, South Africa Belongs To Us,* or *When You Strike A Woman You Strike A Rock.* Bambara also wanted the audience to consider the need for a movement to counter U.S. domination in the production of movies, television programs, and text books that are distributed worldwide.[58] In general, Bambara wanted to see works like Senegalese filmmaker Ombene Sembene's *Ceddo,* produced in 1976, more widely distributed. Bambara viewed Sembene's *Ceddo* as significant in its use of dream imagery and in its creative presentation of an African sense of nonlinear time—moving forward, backward, and into the present without boundaries; Sembene also honored African rituals and traditions. His work called for cultural resistance as his characters speak Wolof, not the colonial language. In the film, Sembene used the camera to zoom in for close-ups of the intricate designs and array of colors in the brilliant African natural landscape, and its parallels in the design of the traditional dress and adornment worn by the characters in the film, standing firm in the robes of their own culture.

When speaking in London, Bambara, as tended to be the case elsewhere, preferred to facilitate a discussion rather than to lecture. That night at the workshop, Bambara cautioned the audience to be mindful that her enthusiasm to suggest courses of action for those gathered at the workshop would be a less troubling form of cultural imperialism, but cultural imperialism, nevertheless, if it failed to include a collaborative process.[59]

The series of international travel Bambara pursued to communities that more closely shared her political perspectives continued into the new year with a second trip to Cuba. While in Cuba, Bambara had an opportunity to reaffirm her commitment as a self-identified cultural worker who repeatedly linked the political with the cultural. In January 1985, Bambara was part of a delegation of black women writers to Cuba sponsored by the Black Scholar Press. This delegation to Cuba included Jayne Cortez, Audre Lorde, Gloria I. Joseph, Verta Mae Grosvenor, Mari Evans, Mildred Pitts Walker, Alexis De Veaux, and Mel Edwards, a close male friend of Jayne Cortez who organized many of the travel details.[60] These writers were part of a historical stream of black artists dating back through Langston Hughes, to include Amiri Baraka and jazz greats like Dizzy Gillespie—artists who united cultural and political interests in the two countries. While in Cuba, Bambara had an opportunity to visit cultural institutions, talk with workers, and meet with the producer of a Cuban film she had long promoted, *Lucia*. Joseph also recalled relaxing moments in Cuba where she and Bambara comfortably walked the streets and debated roof-top massages at their hotel. "As for massages, Toni made it perfectly clear that she did not like, nor would she have any of those bone crushing massages,—the kind that they call deep muscle massages. I want my body to feel relaxed after a massage, not like I've been beaten up. I opted for a routine massage; Toni declined getting one." Joseph said that experiences with her friend in Cuba were enjoyable as usual with Bambara offering her unique combination of artistic genius, humor, and huge body of ancestral and historical knowledge, in easy conversational tones.[61]

Nancy Morejon, an internationally acclaimed poet and now Cuba's poet laureate, recalled her initial impression of Bambara when she welcomed the writers at the airport for the 10-day visit. More than two decades later, Morejon said, "Bambara stood out from the group because of her laughter, upbeat nature and frequent fun-filled jokes."[62] Although Morejon was meeting Bambara in person for the first time, she was familiar with Bambara's writing. Morejon explained that even prior to Bambara's visits to the island, her work, along with the work of Gwendolyn Brooks, was some of the most widely known black American women's writing in Cuba. Hers and Brooks's works had been translated into Spanish and included in the popular anthology edited by foremost Cuban editor José Rodriguez Feo, *Antologia de cuentos norteamericanos*, in the 1960s. The anthology was widely read not only in Cuba, but also across the Spanish-speaking world. "Both the styles of Gwendolyn Brooks and Bambara were linked by their abilities in guiding the experience of discovery of who we are as they pulled apart the self-hatred that sometimes is in our minds and heart," Morejon said.[63]

Reading Bambara's open style of writing provided a bridge for Morejon and other women writers to use their insights to explore relationships within the black family and to challenge the traditional roles ascribed to women. The Afrocentric perspective in Bambara's fiction which included references to ancestral spirits and African deities deepened ties with Cuban writers familiar with Yoruba traditions. In 1970, Bambara's widely read edited volume, *The Black Woman*, and Morejon's later well-known poem, "*Mujernegra*" ("Black Woman") both call attention to the need for a self-liberation among black women.[64]

For Bambara, her second visit to Cuba also held significance because it fed her belief regarding the importance of writers establishing relationships within the community without having to sacrifice their writing. "Our country strives to provide a special space for poets, writers, and all artists not just in the academy, but in the society as a whole. Writers are expected to have an understanding of Cubans in the provinces, Cubans in the capital, Cubans across classes. This is a duty," Morejon said. "At the same time, there is recognition that space and time are needed to work on the quality of your craft. If you don't do that, you're lost."[65]

About the significance of the exchange with Bambara and the other black women writers, Morejon concluded:

> We tasted our common experience. The visit was like a gift to me. It kept the gulf stream of culture flowing between us just as the best jazz men in Cuba and in the United States have done in so many of their great relationships. They opened windows. They opened up horizons. I can't say that one visit opened gates, but the visit certainly opened human windows in terms of the political and social experiences that grew out of it. I kept in touch with Toni after that.[66]

Bambara returned to Atlanta strengthened by the same sense that she had on her first visit to Cuba that writing remained an important way to contribute to struggle. Meeting with Cuban filmmakers must have had a similar impact. But, there were other realities such as her still unfinished manuscript and perhaps, an encroaching weariness with unfinished film projects. Even the ground beneath her was beginning to shift as members of the longstanding writing group Pomaja Guild started to scatter seeking new opportunities. In an unmailed postcard to a former Pamoja member, Sara Wanambwa, recently elected mayor of Shorter, Alabama, Bambara provided news that the accomplished poet Nikky Finney[67] had moved to Lexington to teach at the University of Kentucky and her friend Malaika Adero, who had also assisted her tirelessly in research on the Atlanta children's cases, was now in New York working as a prominent editor at a New York publishing company. Bambara remained optimistic about the future as she wrote: "I'm up to my neck finishing Atlanta novel. The Third World Film Festival is going on now. Wonderful. My daughter will be 15 next month. Funny, gorgeous and very tall. I'm giving serious thought to moving to Philly, seem to be falling asleep here."[68]

As usual Bambara encouraged writing: "But do snatch a few minutes each day to log stuff in a journal to document all this. Hump, um, humph. And yeah you really must keep working on the Uganda book. Nothing much to report from this end. Workshop continues. All's well."[69]

As summer approached Bambara gave greater attention to an exodus from Atlanta and maybe an exit from so many reminders of the Atlanta case. Bambara clearly wanted to focus on work driven by her passion for work in film.

The move and its aftermath presented more than the usual set of challenges. Bambara turned to her journal to not simply chronicle events but to find answers within herself. That July, Bambara wrote about managing a major relocation including selling her home and belief in her ability to move forward through mantras such as the one she wrote in her journal: "Everything is in divine order. I entered the world with abundance, all the responses I need. I have only to . . . see and claim."[70] Bambara now searched for the interconnections within herself that previous characters in her fiction had hoped to find.

Richard Long, the first to hire Bambara at Atlanta University a decade earlier, remembered his thoughts on hearing about Bambara's decision to leave
the South:

> My perception of Toni was primarily as a writer in Atlanta. She was always very
> very pleasant and had a delightful sense of humor . . . I was a little surprised when
> I learned that she would be leaving Atlanta. I am not at all sure that I knew it
> was about the murder thing, until subsequently I learned she was writing a book
> about it. And the book originally was intended to be an analysis and it changed
> its character and form later on and became a fictionalized work. . . . In my view
> she had reacted in what I considered to be a somewhat of an illogical fashion to
> what happened here. And indeed here in Atlanta there was not a great deal of total
> unity on what happened particularly when the young man who [allegedly com-
> mitted the crimes] was finally indicted for it came forth. Many people said nobody
> like that could have done it. People wanted it to be some highly racial or even like
> a Ku Klux Klan kind of thing. . . . Of course during the period, I did have a direct
> encounter with James Baldwin who came here to do his work on it and I actually
> traveled around with James Baldwin who was my house guest . . .
>
> But, I was surprised when she left. I just felt she was functioning in Atlanta in
> a very wonderful sense.[71]

In Bambara's short story "The Survivor," published in 1972, Bambara describes Jewel, the story's narrator, as an actor who dreams of being a filmmaker. Jewel travels to the home of her grandmother, M'dear, a midwife with
training in elocution, to have her baby. Through flashbacks, the reader learns
about Jewel's troubled state of mind during her pregnancy: laundry undone,
house unkempt, and hair in need of a shampoo. While dumping ashes from the
ashtray and rearranging pillows, Cathy, her niece, tells Jewel a story she heard
in childhood that begins:

> Somebody makes a pot of coffee or maybe it was a stew, and no matter. And they
> put in salt instead of sugar. So they don't know what to do . . . .
>
> So some bright person suggests they dump some cracked eggshells in to ab-
> sorb the salt. But then the eggshells turn to a funny color. Like inedible-looking.
> So some other Einstein decides on some kerosene to change the color . . .
>
> So they wind up with this terrible mess of eggshells and car tires and bicycle
> chains and whatnot and they're tearing their hair out as to how to turn this into
> a good stew or pot of coffee or whatever it was supposed to be, I forget. So some-
> one with half a brain says they should call in the lady from Philadelphia. Or the
> lady from Mali in some versions, depending on what folks are printing the book.
> And the lady strolls in with her umbrella and Red Cross shoes and dumps the
> shit out the back door and sets a fresh pot of water on to boil.
>
> "And you are the lady from Philadelphia?"
>
> And I'm here to tell you that you are losing your mind and have to get out of
> here.[72]

Andrea Rushing, who corresponded with Bambara and hosted her readings
at Amherst College, remembered the period preceding Bambara's departure

from Atlanta as a challenging time. Rushing said about her friend: "When you see her on stage or you see her holding forth at a dinner table she seems in complete command of what's going on, but there's another Toni who writes you about the house being disheveled, her hair in a wreck, she can't find anything, and she has deadlines."[73] Rushing valued a similar candor in Bambara's short stories, which reflected a black female reality that other black women writers chose to keep hidden behind the image of the iconic "strong black woman."[74]

Rushing said about the black women characters typically found in the fiction of black women writers: "Nobody goes crazy. If you are black women you are strong you can come through anything and you have come through everything and nothing touches you. . . . But in real life people are having nervous breakdowns. . . . In real life people are too depressed to get out of the bed. In real life people's houses do look like the 2nd World War was fought in it and their hair is standing up on the top of their heads." Rushing discussed the personal significance and healing qualities of Bambara's writing and letters to her saying, "I felt Toni's writing gave me permission to be falling apart at the seams. It didn't make falling apart at the seams feel better, but it was like not only had she written about this but she was confiding in me this was happening in real life." Rushing remembered a photograph on one of the dust jackets of Toni's books where Toni is wearing a wonderful head tie. "And I remember asking her about it and she said it was a man's shirt. That she had nothing else to tie her head up with and she couldn't go out anywhere looking like her hair looked. And the contrast between how the head tie looked and that it was really a man's shirt, it was the way she allowed her life to unfold."[75]

At this point, some of Bambara's Atlanta friends also noticed signs of disarray in Bambara's life. Her long-standing friend Cheryl Chisholm who frequently visited Bambara in Atlanta after visits with her grandmother, Marie Graves Nash, who lived across the street from Bambara on Simpson Street. Before leaving Atlanta there were conversations, some at Bambara's home, where Bambara suggested that she and Chisholm collaborate in making a film. At the time, Chisholm viewed the disarray that she found in Bambara's home as she was about to move to Philadelphia as an expression of Bambara's adventurous nonconforming lifestyle. "I simply thought that this is the way she likes to live," Chisholm remembered. Later, Chisholm would see the disorder as a possible sign of depression. Chisholm recalled:

> When she got ready to move to Philadelphia, she packed up a very few boxes of things and she left all that stuff in her house. She left old precious pieces of furniture that had belonged to her family for years. She left collections of important black magazines and journals. As far as I know she did not leave her writing on the Atlanta children's cases, but she might have left the rest. As far as I know, what she packed up and took with her were some clothes and the book she was working on at the time. She left the pots, the pans and the dishes. It was too much. She [Toni] couldn't deal with it and she picked up and left it.[76]

Another friend, Ama Saran, who assisted Bambara in packing, had similar memories of the house, including a nonworking stove and unwanted toys piled up in a corner at the time Bambara moved.[77] At times, Bambara's commitment to be a constant resource to others may have meant that critical matters in her personal life did not receive needed attention. Maybe, that was a choice she made.

bell hooks also recalled Bambara's devotion to supporting the work of others as she wrote: "Days and nights spent in her company engaged in fierce intellectual dialectical debate and dialogue were inspiring. An avid reader of periodicals and books, Toni's down-home manner often deflected attention away from the scope of her intellectual insights. I had never met a black woman writer as generous with her time and ideas as Toni Cade Bambara."[78]

Before finally leaving Atlanta, Bambara received the good news that Julie Dash, her husband AJ [Arthur Jafa, cinematographer], and their baby had recently moved there from Los Angeles, in order to begin making what would become the film *Daughters of the Dust*. Typical of Bambara, she wanted Dash to know how much she supported the project. Nearly 30 years later, Dash vividly remembered first meeting Bambara and the influence it had when Bambara arrived at their home unannounced. Dash recalled the surprise meeting and its impact: "I was sitting in the dining room area holding my daughter in my arms when Toni walked in the door. I was impressed, inspired and stunned."[79]

In Bambara's last days in Atlanta, her friends Chisholm and Guy-Sheftall hosted a farewell party for Bambara at Guy-Sheftall's home.[80] Both Chisholm and Guy-Sheftall were among the original circle of women who valued Bambara's intellectual depth and commitment to community work as *sui generis* just as colleagues and friends at Queens College, City College, and Livingston College did before them. During the gathering, Bambara did not disturb that long-held image.

The only written description that Bambara provided about her departure from Atlanta in 1985 appeared in the later published Epilogue to *Those Bones Are Not My Child*. As tended to be the case, there are no hints of despair found in this description. Instead, Bambara chose to place the moment of her departure from Atlanta with Karma in an historical context as she often advised others to do. On July 8, 1987, Bambara wrote: "Storage box packed, letter finished, you look around at the TV in time to get a final glimpse of the man being turned into a matinee idol. In addition to arming the thug Savimbi to topple Angola, Oliver North also organized the invasion of Grenada. You lick the envelope closed and dump your bag on the floor for your keys. It's 1981 all over again until you two reach the sidewalk heading for the post office. People are shooting off guns still and flinging firecrackers all over the street. They must have foreseen that you two would need an extension of the Independence Day celebrations."[81] Once again, Bambara found solace in the community that she said named and claimed her.

NOTES

1. Toni Cade Bambara, *Those Bones Are Not My Child* (New York: Pantheon, 1999), 213.

2. Toni Cade Bambara, "Contending Forces: Exploring Afro-American Women's Fiction," Lecture at Hampshire College, April 1987.

3. Ibid.

4. Toni Cade Bambara, "Excerpt from the Atlanta Notebooks 80/81," Spelman Archives, Atlanta.

5. Toni Cade Bambara, Lecture and Reading, "Contending Forces: Exploring Afro-American Women's Fiction." Hampshire College, April 2, 1987. *Weekly Bulletin* March 27 to April 3, 1987.

6. Ibid.

7. Ibid.

8. Bambara, *Those Bones Are Not My Child*, 166.

9. Ibid., 236.

10. Ibid., 8.

11. Ibid., 236.

12. Ibid., 519.

13. Ibid., 553.

14. Ibid., 661.

15. Bambara Lecture, Hampshire College.

16. "Spelman Slates Symposium on the Black Aesthetic," *Atlanta Daily World,* February 5, 1981.

17. Toni Cade Bambara, Letter to June Jordan, February 25, 1981, June Jordan Papers, Schlesinger Library, Box 28, Folder 12.

18. Ibid.

19. Gloria I. Joseph, Interview by author, March 2011.

20. Ibid.

21. Ibid.

22. Advisory Board List, Sisters in Support of Sisters in South Africa (SISA), Spelman Archives, Atlanta.

23. Akasha (Gloria) Hull, "A Conversation with Toni Cade Bambara," in *Conversations with Toni Cade Bambara,* ed. Thabiti Lewis (Jackson: University Press of Mississippi, 2012), 103.

24. Interview with Gloria I. Joseph.

25. "Interview with Toni Cade Bambara," *The Drum* 12, no. 1 (1982): 43–44.

26. Ibid.

27. Deric Gilliard, "Witchbird's Warning: To Thine Own Self Be True," *Atlanta Daily World,* April 28, 1981.

28. Ibid.

29. Toni Cade Bambara, "Witchbird," in *The Sea Birds Are Still Alive* (New York: Random House), 169.

30. Gloria P. Walker, Letter to Toni Cade Bambara, May 5, 1980, Archives Research Center, Atlanta University Center, Robert W. Woodruff Library, Atlanta.

31. Toni Cade Bambara, Letter to Hoyt Fuller, May 5, 1980, Archives Research Center, Atlanta University Center, Robert W. Woodruff Library, Atlanta.

32. "Remembering Hoyt: In the Words of Some of His Friends," May 16, 1981, Archives Research Center, Atlanta University Center, Robert W. Woodruff Library, Atlanta.

33. Toni Cade Bambara, Letter to June Jordan, Undated, June Jordan Papers, Schlesinger Library, Box 28, Folder 12.

34. Ibid.

35. University of Ibadan, Letter to Toni Cade Bambara, February 17, 1982, Spelman Archives, Atlanta.

36. Andrea Benton Rushing, Interview by author.

37. John Oliver Killens, Letter, Spelman Archives, Atlanta.

38. Ibid.

39. Ibid.

40. Toni Cade Bambara, Letter to Bambara and Brehon, Courtesy of Walter Cade III.

41. Frank Hodsoll, Letter to Toni Cade Bambara, December 7, 1982, Spelman Archives, Atlanta.

42. Toni Cade Bambara, Letter to Carole Brown, December 11, 1982, Courtesy of Carole Brown.

43. Ibid.

44. Ibid.

45. Joncar Productions, Contract Award, February 7, 1983, Spelman Archives, Atlanta.

46. Jonathan Sanger, Letter to Toni Cade Bambara, July 14, 1983, Spelman Archives, Atlanta.

47. Toni Cade Bambara, Letter to Jonathan Sanger, August 3, 1983, Spelman Archives, Atlanta.

48. Michelle Finch, Interview by author, August 2011.

49. Toni Morrison, Interview by author, March 2012.

50. Toni Cade Bambara, "Working at It in Four Parts," Spelman Archives, Atlanta.

51. Ibid.

52. Sonia Sanchez, Interview by author, November 2012.

53. Ibid.

54. Toni Cade Bambara, Letter to State Insurance Commission Office, September 1983, Spelman Archives, Atlanta.

55. Ibid.

56. Sam Greenlee, Interview by author.

57. Bambara, Panelist, The Factory.

58. Ibid.

59. Ibid.

60. Gloria Joseph, Interview by author.

61. Ibid.

62. Nancy Morejon, Interview by author, October 2010.

63. Ibid.

64. Nancy Morejon, "Black Woman," in Where the Island Sleeps Like A Wing (San Francisco: The Black Scholar Press, 1985), 87.

65. Morejon, Interview.

66. Ibid.

67. In Nikki Finney, Head Off & Split (Evanston: Tri Quarterly Books/Northwestern University Press, 2011), the epigraph written to Finney comes from a postcard to Finney written from her hospice bed in 1995. It reads: "Do not leave the arena to the fools." Head Off & Split won an American Book Award.

68. Toni Cade Bambara, postcard to Sara, undated, Spelman Archives, Atlanta.

69. Ibid.

70. Toni Cade Bambara, Journal entry, July 15, 1983.

71. Richard Long, Interview by author, April 2011.

72. Toni Cade Bambara, "The Survivor," *Gorilla, My Love* (New York: Random House, 1972), 113.

73. Andrea Benton Rushing, Interview by author, September 2011.

74. Ibid.

75. Ibid.

76. Cheryl Chisholm, Interview by author.

77. Ama Saran, Interview by author, June 2010.

78. bell hooks, "Remembering Toni Cade Bambara," in *Remembered Rapture: The Writer at Work* (New York: Henry, Holt and Company, 1999), 231–37.

79. Julie Dash, Interview by author, March 2012.

80. Beverly Guy-Sheftall, Interview by author.

81. Bambara, *Those Bones Are Not My Child*, 669.

NINE

New Life in Film

The literatures of the U.S.A. that emerge from the commercial industry, from the independent press community, from the university press community are now beginning to reflect a racial, ethnic, religious, class, sexual and political diversity that begins to reflect the actuality of life in the U.S. And this movement going on in literature is buttressed by an emerging independent multi-cultural cinema and video movement that, in turn is reinforced by the multi-culture curriculum movement taking place in the schools and universities.[1]

Bambara returned to the northeast in 1985, to make Philadelphia, Pennsylvania, her home. Once in Philadelphia, Bambara found a community that inspired her work in video and film in similar ways that community influenced her work in Atlanta. Even after Bambara left Atlanta, her house remained a symbol of community for those who had gathered there over the years. About the house that Bambara left at 992 Simpson Street in Atlanta, photographer Susan Ross recalled that several people showed interest in resources to buy the house after Bambara left. Ross remembered,

We wanted to keep that house as a cultural center after she left. The house also symbolized some of the intersections in Bambara's life as it towered over downtown Atlanta and stood at the edges of both a middle class neighborhood and a working class black community. . . . You had an incredible view of the city. It was just gorgeous seeing the city from up there, but you're right in the heart of the Vine City neighborhood. You're right in the heart of the hood and the edge of a middle class area; so it's a people's house in many ways. People were there all the time, all kinds of people from all kinds of backgrounds.[2]

Now in Philadelphia, the city resonated with Bambara in many ways and offered practical reasons for settling in the city. After a year of living on Upsal Street in Philadelphia's Mount Airy section in a house plagued with structural problems, Bambara moved into the Valley Green Co-op on Wissahickon Avenue in Philadelphia's historic Germantown community. There she combined two apartments and had ample room for the weaving loom left behind by the former owner's wife—and for her many bookshelves. For her daughter Karma, Bambara decided on Philadelphia's all girls' public high school, which boasted a positive academic reputation. Friends in Philadelphia included poet Sonia Sanchez, who lived in walking distance from Bambara, and Jane Poindexter, a long-time friend who had left Atlanta for Philadelphia with her own daughter about the same time as Bambara. The company of sister-friends helped to make the city an inviting one.

Bambara, coordinating writer for the documentary, *W.E.B. Du Bois: Four Voices*, greets Herbert Ross, Atlanta University scholar, who was later interviewed for the documentary, National Black Arts Festival, 1990. Copyright Susan Ross.

More than any place else in Philadelphia, however, the Scribe Video Center, headed by Louis Massiah, became home base for Bambara's cultural work. As director, Massiah aimed to build Scribe as a center for community-based video projects, screening cutting-edge documentaries, and developing other video production skills among emerging filmmakers. For Bambara, Scribe was what the Neighborhood Arts Center (NAC) had initially been for her in Atlanta: a place where she could apply her creativity, intellectual depth, and passion for community work. Although she had remained a part of the full-time staff for only a year at the NAC, Bambara remained at Scribe for nine years, longer than any place she had ever worked in her life.

In her collaboration with Scribe, Bambara finally found a base from which to pursue her passion in film. In Philadelphia, Bambara partnered with Massiah in the production of three documentaries: *The Bombing of Osage Avenue,* on the Philadelphia police attack against MOVE, killing 11 people and destroying 51 homes in an African American neighborhood; *Cecil B. Moore: Master Tactician of Direct Action (1987),* on the black Philadelphian civil rights activist; and *W.E.B. Du Bois: A Biography in Four Voices,* on the international cultural and political giant. In Atlanta, Bambara had been a force in supporting emerging black writers. The Philadelphia years similarly were marked by Bambara's efforts to support a new wave of women and other Afrocentric filmmakers across the African diaspora. And, Bambara continued to write. Essays focusing on activism through filmmaking along with short stories appeared in *Deep Sightings and Rescue Missions,* a collection also edited by Toni Morrison and published posthumously.

Bambara moved to Philadelphia just months after the police bombing and the fire that ensued, destroying a series of homes in the predominantly black neighborhood in West Philadelphia where MOVE, the radical black organization that espoused a natural lifestyle and self-defense, had its base. On May 16, three days after the tragic event, Bambara introduced her friend and writer John O. Killens, a speaker at the "Literary Roots" symposium sponsored by *The Georgia Review* at the University of Georgia. Bambara's introduction included an arousing condemnation of media and government reports that attempted to justify the assault. (See Appendix: "A Call to Action.") *The Bombing of Osage Avenue,* a film that Bambara worked on with Massiah and one she also narrated, provided the first Afrocentric documentary perspective on the tragedy. In making a commitment to work on the film, Bambara immersed herself in the heartbreaking realities of yet another violent injustice, while still reeling from the Atlanta murdered and missing children's cases.

As she had in the writing of *Those Bones Are Not My Child,* Bambara approached the subject as an integral part of the community whose story she was telling, serving in the role of community scribe. She eschewed the third-person authoritarian, uninvolved voice that was standard for documentaries of the period. In the first-person preface to her Atlanta novel, Bambara assumed a similar voice: that of a mother and neighbor living in the community under siege.

Later, Bambara told a reporter how Philadelphians received the documentary. Describing the crowd who marched to the local television station when the film was first screened in Philadelphia, Bambara explained that the community praised the documentary because it was the first film that covered the tragedy from an "Afrocentric perspective, and it privileged the black voice."[3]

In her narration of *The Bombing of Osage Avenue,* Bambara returned to themes that are prominent in her writing: memory, community, and respect for elders as storytellers. For example, Bambara wanted viewers of the film to know that Cobbs Creek, the community bombed by the city of Philadelphia, was originally Lenape land. Again Bambara wanted to link the struggles of people of color, this time through remembrance of the stories of Native Americans. Bambara also turns to elders for some of the most compelling interviews in the film. And, at the close of the film, the community is seeking to find ways to return to wholeness, a quest that is also central in Bambara's later fiction.

Bambara brought assets like her listening ear to making documentaries. Her unique style of narration rang with musicality and poetry without sacrificing the hard-hitting commentary that the subject required. Earlier Bambara's profound understanding of jazz influenced her writing. From the beginning, Bambara's keen interest and sense of responsibility regarding the importance of listening to voices in working-class communities including women, children, and elders influenced her writing. Voices that mainstream media often ignored, or forgot, or simply did not respect mattered to the writer. Identifying herself as a community scribe from childhood, Bambara brings to film in the last decade of her life, the values and perspectives gained from a lifetime of listening in communities and aligning with community activists around the world.

Massiah observed how creative and pioneering Bambara's style of narration was in documentary film, and reflected on the care she took in making certain her tone, cadence, and resonance reflected the images being viewed on the screen. Massiah explained how Bambara's role as writer was different from the way writers typically function when working on a documentary:

> Film, ultimately, is not chiefly about the writer's words, it is about images. The writer's task in an interview-based documentary is a structural exercise. It is finding the story. Typically you might engage a writer to create a treatment when you begin a documentary, but not to work interactively as you produce and edit a work. The idea of a writer of Toni's genius simply writing a treatment is obscene because so much of her gift is finding narrative structure from the way interview subjects talk, understanding the power and choice of words, and using narration as counterpoint.[4]

Indeed, the ideas and principles that shaped Bambara's personal life bore fruit in her work.

The Bombing of Osage Avenue film credits identify Bambara as the narrator. For Bambara what mattered was being engaged in a collaborative process. Meanwhile, the narration provided by Bambara in the documentary was viewed as groundbreaking. Internationally recognized social documentary filmmaker John Akomfrah, who later collaborated with Bambara in the film he directed, *Seven Songs for Malcolm X,* commented on the new standard Bambara was setting by breaking the mode of the established documentary voice. Akomfrah explained, "Because it was Toni, a widely respected writer of stature, we immediately paid attention to what she was bringing in 'Osage' as different from the standard voice of documentary. Because the voice was Toni's, the film's new narrative style was more readily accepted as a model than it might have been if Toni were lesser known."[5] Akomfrah continued, "Before seeing *The Bombing of Osage Avenue,* I had not questioned the standard type of narration, where the narrator serves to describe the visual and tells you through their eyes what is being viewed. Toni's narration provided space for the viewer to walk with Toni and see people and events with their own eyes." About Bambara's narration style, Akomfrah found her film narration to be similar to her writing: "poetic and personal as well as political without being preachy." About the writer, Akomfrah concluded, "She comes to the film as a narrator with the profound sense of black intimacy which is the tone of her life."[6]

Scholar and prolific Guyanese writer Jan Carew agreed with Akomfrah about the significance of Bambara's narration. Carew wrote:

> When I heard of that brilliant documentary film about MOVE, *The Bombing of Osage Avenue,* and heard her voice in the narration of that movie, it literally tore the heart out of me. Toni entered so deeply into the psyche of the people who had suffered during that atrocious bombing and had a kind of Nazi final solution inflicted on them. All too few had raised their voices against this atrocity, and of the few who did none were more eloquent than Toni Cade as she spoke the truth to power with fearlessness.[7]

The completion of the film and its immediate success as a compelling documentary confirmed for Bambara that her decision to move to Philadelphia had been a wise one. The film aired nationally on public broadcast stations in 1986 and was screened widely at film festivals. *The Bombing of Osage Avenue* won awards from the Pennsylvania Association of Broadcasters and the National Black Programming Consortium for the work.[8]

Throughout the making of *The Bombing of Osage Avenue,* Bambara continued working at Scribe in other capacities, where she conducted scriptwriting workshops and later headed Scribe's Community Vision Program. The Community Vision Program encouraged and equipped community-based organizations committed to social change to use video as an instrument to recruit, raise funds, inform, educate, and mobilize. In the workshops, Bambara warned community organizations that they might be surprised to find how dysfunctional hierarchies in their organizations are once they began using a community eye to document these organizations through video. Bambara urged workshop participants to look in-depth at the organizations they targeted as subjects. In reflecting on her work at Scribe, Bambara explained, "It was surprising to some that the process of understanding their community organization could be long and producing a 10 minute video could take a year. The video process helped them to uncover surprising truths about the power bases within their organization which sometimes rested outside of the community."[9] So clearly in her approach to teaching workshops, Bambara continued to be a community organizer in her unique way as she challenged students to use the video lens as a tool for transforming institutions rather than merely documenting them.

As might be expected, Bambara's scriptwriting workshops were unconventional. Take-home assignments for the students—blue-color workers, feminists, activists and youth—included screening dramas and documentaries, inviting another workshop participant for a chat about a movie over coffee, reading at least two versions of "Little Red Riding Hood" (Perrault's and Grimm's), and recording their dreams that often held powerful images for the storyteller.[10]

Just as she had always done in her previous workshops, Bambara also encouraged the workshop participants to challenge the status quo. She now used conversations in filmmaking workshops to challenge standard habits of framing, lighting, use of color, kinds of narratives, and editing practices she viewed as problematic. Instead, Bambara encouraged workshop participants to consider the best technical means of accommodating their own points of view, visions, perspectives, and cultural modalities.[11] For Bambara as always, it was politically informed cultural work that mattered.

Not all of Bambara's and Massiah's collaborative projects at Scribe were completed. In 1987, Bambara again was engaged as a cultural worker in a film project entitled *Come As You Are,* a feature film that intended to focus on the takeover of a luxury apartment building by homeless squatters. After completing work on the award-winning documentary, Bambara believed she had the skills to finally tackle a script for a feature film. At the time, Bambara revealed in an interview, "Now I feel competent and bold and arrogant to do what I want to do, which are feature films."[12]

In October 1987, the UN Year of the Homeless, Bambara campaigned with Philadelphia's Homeless Union, where squatters hoped to bring media attention to their plight "as they slide from crisis into varying states of marginality."[13]

Bambara wrote several proposals to obtain funding for what would have been her first feature film. Focused on the growing insurgency of the homeless movement, the writer wanted to include stories emanating from the homeless that included ceremonies narrated in Spanish, Haitian Creole, Lakota, and Greek. In a proposal for funding, Bambara wrote, "The stories have to do with the development of tent cities, squatters' camps, and sweat group houses; with individual coming-of-age and quest-for-community dramas; and with the growing solidarity between self-help projects in Reaganvilles' and those in Sanctuary Movement safe houses, battered women shelters, tenants' associations, welfare rights organizations, farm cooperatives and native American reservations."[14] Bambara indicated that the diversity of stories would require the use of some English subtitles. Similar to the rallying cry issued in the Atlanta novel, Bambara's homeless film plot included community members who would rise up "to challenge the politics of silence, invisibility, and difference."[15] At Scribe, Bambara continued to employ her style of organizing, which was to open doors for members of diverse grassroots communities to tell their own stories. The funding needed for the feature film project, however, never materialized.

In her journal on October 3, 1987, Bambara reflected: "I am determined to keep plugging away, keeping on top of the work: meetings, banners for squatters."[16] Her journal note that day also mentioned "dream presence and a troubling knee."[17] As the writer and organizer sometimes walked with a cane, Bambara would explain the limp in her knee as a problem related to rheumatism, arthritis, or sciatica.[18] Using humor to divert attention from her health challenges, the writer once joked that her limp was the price she paid for her love of high heels and short skirts. Bambara often found ways to escape conversations focusing on her health issues.

In her journal, she also remembered going to New York for the funeral of James Baldwin where the black literati, political activists, and an array of artists gathered at the Cathedral of St. John the Divine on December 8 in a jubilant celebration of Baldwin's life. The ceremony included drumming from Babatunde Olatunji's Ensemble, singing from Odetta, and Amiri Baraka provided the eulogy. Familiar faces in the crowd and on the podium included speakers like her friends Verta Mae Grosvenor, Toni Morrison, and Maya Angelou. From a distance, Bambara saw her former husband Tony Batten, "white haired and balding up in the stand," who was there taping the memorial for CCNY [City College of New York] and 250 community radio stations.[19] Interestingly, Bambara's entry reads almost as a roster of who she saw that day, offering no hint of her own sentiments.

Bambara found herself at home in Philadelphia on March 25, 1988. In other years she'd often found herself on the road at the time of her birthday; Women's History Month and Black History Month continued to be times that academic institutions most often reached out to her for the guest lectures that provided her with some income. But in 1988, Bambara quietly celebrated her 48th birthday at home. She noted in her journal: "Didn't comb my hair. Or do anything Special. Got some mail out. Bought myself mud cloth . . . L. Holmes, Francese [Janet Francendese, Temple University Press] dropped by."[20]

A month later, Rudolph Byrd called Bambara to tell her that his recommendation that she come to Carleton College for the month of May as Writer in Residence there had been accepted. Bambara agreed on the condition that "she would not have to attend departmental meetings or issue blue book exams for her to read and grade." Bambara flew to Minnesota wearing "a hip leather pantsuit ensemble," topped by her "somewhat crumpled Afro." She carried no baggage even though her stay was a month long. Byrd also noted that Bambara walked with "a very confident gait which had a strange up and down motion, this the result of something like a deformity in her right leg."[21]

At Carlton College, texts for Bambara's fiction workshop included Zora Neal Hurston's *Their Eyes Were Watching God,* Toni Morrison's *The Bluest Eye,* and her own novel *The Salt Eaters.* Bambara also facilitated a workshop with a community activism orientation, intended to develop narrative, aural, or visual strategies as part of communication work and to integrate ideas about how cultural workers could equip communities for political action and transformation. Bambara argued that the mission of the cultural worker needed to be far more holistic than the activist who frequently focused on single issues. In contrast, the cultural worker aimed to address the integrity of the total community including women, children, and elders. As an activist, Bambara's passion for organizing among women began in the 1970s and continued throughout her life.

Another opportunity for organizing among women came in 1988, when Bambara appeared on a panel at the Women Against Racism women's conference, where she made time for unscheduled meetings and lengthy one-on-one conversations. At the conference, the writer networked and bonded with Native American activist Lakota Harden, who grew up with family members who were strong leaders in the Indian movement at Wounded Knee. Years later, Harden recalled, "When I saw Toni, I saw my aunt—always tough never showing her emotions—a warrior soldier who never showed her own vulnerability. When I met Toni, I felt I already knew her and loved her." But later that day, Harden said the unexpected happened in the "Unlearning Racism" workshop that Harden was facilitating: "A miracle occurred. She had her head in my lap and she was crying. She was so strong and her humanity was based on that strength and vision. In that workshop, she simply let go."[22] Because Bambara seldom cried publicly, this was an extraordinary occasion. Perhaps the writer sensed that the circle of women in the workshop offered a safe place for her to release her emotions. Not surprisingly, however, she did not reveal the source of her pain.

At the conference, Harden also joined Angela Davis and other nationally known activists on a panel where Harden cautioned the gathering of woman activists against draining their energies by taking care of nation and community while forgetting to take care of themselves. Harden also recalled how inadvertently she said that at the time she was on the verge of homelessness, unable to pay the rent for the campus housing where she and her children lived. "I didn't know what I was going to do and right before the conference I remember I started searching the homeless shelters," Harden said. "At the conference sitting next to Angela, I was feeling inadequate, sometimes reaching in my pocket to simply hold the sage I had put there."[23] Harden continued:

> When the final panel ended we were on a raised platform in this huge room of at least a 1,000 women. Next thing you know people lined up right away in three different lines with their questions and most of them were for Angela. So I was kind of sitting there and chilling and glad that I was done, relaxed. And, then Toni got up and she said she noticed that I had said earlier we need to do more

than revere our leaders. We need to care about them, and even ask, "Did you take your vitamins today?" That was significant to her. She said, "This isn't a question, this is a comment." She also said "Go through your notes and you'll notice what I am saying." That's when she repeated what I said. I had been speaking from my heart, and I was talking about the hardships faced by leaders who go down. And, all of a sudden out of my mouth popped I'm about to become homeless. That's all Toni said and the conference participants began coming up and handing me money/checks. A long line formed around the conference room as each woman gave what she could. Hugs and tears all around . . . Toni could be bold and strong yet she had a humility that was so beautiful.[24]

Tapping into the spirit of sisterhood that encircled the conference, Bambara's reminder about Harden's financial challenges prompted conference participants to donate money to help Harden pay her rent.

During the conference, Bambara also encouraged Harden to begin work on the book she'd been talking about writing and to do it soon, so that she could read it. On March 3, following Bambara's call to action to support Harden, Bambara received a gift from Harden with an attached note: "My cousin Marcy (who you met tonight) made these earrings right after the Wounded Knee occupation. They are the . . . liberation colors of [The American Indian Movement]. We'd like you to have them."[25]

Throughout her life, Bambara continued to be interested in the cultural works of others and created community among cultural workers, even when it lessened time for her writing. In conversations with cultural workers, Bambara tended to focus on the work to be done rather than her personal experiences. Conversations with Morrison included private life. Morrison confirmed the mutuality in their friendship when she said, "There were moments when she revealed in conversations things that I would never repeat because she really was a very public person in her teaching, in her political activity, and organizing. But there was this other very, very private person."[26] Morrison added:

> I do remember her openness and mine about guys, but it was all couched in hilarity—all of it. She came here to my house where I live now a couple of times, maybe three. I remember she was here when I moved in. I live on a river, very close to the river; you can walk into it. We were trying to take the boxes and unload them and put books up. My sister was here too and we would do one or two boxes and then we'd sit outside for an hour and look at the water. (laughter) It took forever to get moved.[27]

That day Bambara may have recalled a letter more than a decade ago from Morrison where she described the gifts of the river: music, colors, a place for surrender. In her letter Morrison wrote, "Actually I'd like to just sit on the river bank for a while, or at least that's what I tell myself."[28] In Morrison's award-winning novel, *Beloved*, the river is a place for birthing and rebirthing of the spirit. It is also a place of healing and remembrance.[29]

Recalling another of their memorable times, Morrison again spoke of their friendship, with laughter and joy. "I took her to SUNY Albany once. I was teaching up there. I had a sponsored chair and she came. I made her drive part of the way. She was annoyed, but she was very stimulating to the class."[30]

When Bambara traveled to the State University of New York at Albany (SUNY) to participate in the Birth of Black Cinema Project, which had grown out of earlier conversations between Bambara and Morrison, Morrison was then teaching as the Schweitzer Chair at SUNY. At the Conference in November 1988, Bambara's talk focused on Haile Gerima's film *Ashes and Embers*.[31] The conference provided Bambara another venue to further explore her vision for political and cultural movement through film.

Haile Gerima, Ousmane Sembene, and Manthia Diawara were at the forefront in creating films that challenged European cultural colonialism, and that championed cultural resistance among women, families, and children of the diaspora in ways that Bambara found aligned with her writing and work as an internationalist. Morrison provided an opportunity for Bambara to discuss her growing knowledge about significant contributions to film being made by filmmakers across the African diaspora when she invited her to the State University of New York in Albany.

During this time, Bambara also continued to champion another filmmaker whom she met earlier in Atlanta, Julie Dash. From the beginning of the making of the groundbreaking film *Daughters of the Dust,* Bambara celebrated its creator Dash as a woman filmmaker whose feature film offered a perspective that validated women through characters that they could see themselves reflected in. When a trailer for *Daughters of The Dust* was finally shown at a retreat for women of color filmmakers at Sundance Institute (http://www.sundance.org/about/history/), sponsored by the Public Broadcasting Company in 1988, Bambara was in the audience cheering the accomplished work.[32] Bambara and Dash shared a special kind of sisterhood as Bambara, a self-identified Afrafemcentrist, hailed *Daughters of the Dust* because "it fulfills the promise of Afrafemcentrists who choose film as their instrument for self-expression."[33]

Bambara and Dash also shared similar interests in the themes they chose to mine in their creative works. For example, both *The Salt Eaters* and *Daughters of the Dust* are free of the standard linear sense of time, moving forward and backward in circular fashion and escaping standard tracking by calendars or clocks. Although both stories unfold within a day, the extent to which the story meanders inside and outside of standard measurement creates a sense of biblical time—resonant of how days are measured in the creation story found in Genesis.

Seeing limitations in working within the confines of the vocabulary and structure of the English language, both Bambara and Dash wanted to explore new ways to give cultural meaning to the language found in their works. Bambara's concern for dignifying black language is evident in her early short stories where she rejected slang, using her acute listening ear to capture pronunciation and meaning. Bambara used a structure that had been lost in the more common and frequently denigrating use of slang, sometimes called pidgin English. About *Daughters of the Dust,* Bambara wrote: "The storytelling mode is *indabe* my children and crik-crak, the African-derived communal, purposeful, handing down of group lore and group values in a call-and-response circle."[34]

Using music and dance to trigger remembrances reflects Bambara's understanding of how critical the institution of music is in African culture. In *The Salt Eaters,* women dance to the chant "remember." Similarly, the soundtrack of *Daughters of The Dust* opens with Ibo chanting and the first word that is clearly spoken in English is "remember." In *Daughters of the Dust,* there is music emanating from the steady pounding of rice husking, which has the power of the drum to flash their minds back to visions of remembrance such as women making indigo-dyed cloth, an African cultural tradition like so many others that survived the Middle Passage. The film is set in a place called Ibo Landing, the name a reminder of the bloodied slave trade, but also a blessing in the name's remembrance of home and the culture that lives in the "bridge culture" found in the music, the language, the mural painting that "constitutes a praise song to the will and imagination of a diasporized and besieged people to forge a culture that can be sustained."[35]

Most importantly, in writing about *Daughters of the Dust,* Bambara described a force she identifies as "Nommo," as being at the core of the film. Bambara defines "Nommo" as a "harmonizing energy that connects body/mind/spirit/self/community with the universe."[36] This is the wholeness as wellness that Bambara described in *The Salt Eaters,* her novel of healing and recovery: individuals and communities who create wholeness within themselves, family, and community rendering them in harmony with the universe and manifesting health.

It is not surprising that when Dash completed work on *Daughters of the Dust* and years later wrote a book about it, Dash asked Bambara to write the introduction. "When someone suggested I ask Toni to write the forward for *The Making of An African American Woman's Film: Daughters of the Dust,* I was terrified. I shouldn't have been. She responded with a vehement, 'Yeah!'" Dash noted that in writing that introduction Bambara demonstrated an incredible ability to place the project in its historical context.[37]

In 1987, Bambara called for another kind of remembrance. Speaking at the Black Storyteller's Conference at Medgar Evers College in Brooklyn, the author again turned her attention to the loss of Africans during the Middle Passage. The writer suggested that rituals, ceremonies, underwater plaques, and monuments could begin to honor the spirits of African ancestors who dared to jump ship rather than be enslaved. Hoping to deliver a wake-up call, the writer often said, "We willingly embrace amnesia and willingly self-administer knockout drops. More horrendous is the fact that we have all that power that we don't tap; we don't tap into the ancestral presence in those waters."[38]

Once again Bambara demonstrated her commitment to community organizing and inspired others to do the same. Her agenda continued to be filled with even new aspirations. In the 1980s, Bambara decided to pursue a doctorate in American Studies at the State University of New York, Buffalo. Having declined previous opportunities to pursue doctoral work, it is not clear why Bambara made the decision at this point in her life. With her daughter now at Howard University, the writer may have been seeking the financial stability that a future teaching position in a university could provide. The program also offered an opportunity for Bambara to focus on creative autobiographic writing. Bambara ultimately left the program without completing the doctorate, but later received two honorary doctorates: one from the State University of New York at Albany in 1990 and another from Denison University in Ohio several years later in 1993. Once again, Bambara welcomed a relationship with the academy from the outskirts rather than from within.

Commuting from Philadelphia to upstate New York when required, Bambara spent nights at the home of Endesha Holland, playwright and member of the SUNY faculty.[39] There, her circle of sister friends included Kamau-Harris, whom Bambara had hosted more than a decade ago at her home in Atlanta. Years later, Kamau-Harris remembered how the women's collective meeting at Holland's home was similar to women's circles in Atlanta that Bambara also joined. In Buffalo, in the midst of lively conversations, the women always made certain that there was a pot of greens cooking on the stove; Bambara fixed cornbread. Bambara whose late-night habits included coffee and cigarettes, sometimes stayed up later than others, chatting about the Atlanta days with Kamau-Harris.[40] After a long night of conversation, Bambara would sometimes walk upstairs to the room Holland had renamed the Alice Childress room, where any member of the group could find quiet moments for meditation. The times with Bambara in Buffalo reminded Kamau-Harris of earlier times in Atlanta when Bambara had initiated a women's group with a meeting in her backyard in the attempt to develop a communal investment system that would support emerging writers and other artists with their projects.

At SUNY, Bambara was involved with developing The International Women's Playwright Conference. Bambara's work with emerging playwrights resonated with Bambara's mission of building global networks. The idea for the conference was conceived in Holland's kitchen in a conversation with Bambara, Holland, and Kamau-Harris. Bambara's long-time friend Kamau-Harris, who later became the first president of this international group of playwrights, said, "I remember Toni wanted the conference to be an international one from the moment the idea came up and insisted that we could make it happen."[41]

In October 1988, Tess Onwueme, a young Nigerian playwright, was among the more than 100 women gathered from countries around the world including China, Cuba, and South Africa. Visiting the United States for the first time to showcase their work in venues on campus and in the community, Onwueme's play, *The Desert Encroaching*, was among the theatrical works in a first-time production in the United States.[42] "All of the black women playwrights including Alice Childress, were housed at Endesha's home and I was the youngest among them,"[43] Onwueme recalled years later. Onwueme, who remembered Bambara as being the cultural equivalent of the fiery Angela Davis, said that Bambara and Childress, more than others, made an impression on her that not only influenced her work as a playwright, but also as a poet and scholar. Bambara's concern for her personal well-being also made an impression. In a conversation with Onwueme in Holland's kitchen, Bambara learned that the playwright, then a nursing mother of twin babies and visiting from Nigeria, one night developed cramps and needed urgent care. Wanting to be certain that Onwueme was not compromised in any way on the opening night of her play, Bambara quickly arranged for the young playwright to get the needed medical care.[44] While there were countless women at the playwrights conference, Onwueme, who later rose in the American academy to become University Professor of Global Letters at the University of Wisconsin, remembered Bambara being singularly significant in how she encouraged her to be an artist who had the power to question the political and social status quo.[45]

At the end of the 1980s, not only was Bambara travelling across states to pursue academic work, but she also managed to find time for the international travel that she cherished most. Cuba had become a place of return for her, because it hosted a circle of cultural workers who helped her in the mid-1970s to accept writing as a meaningful way to contribute to revolutionary work. It also was a nation that continued producing film works of interest to Bambara. In March 1989, Bambara made her third visit to Cuba, following her previous visits in 1973 and 1986. During her Cuban visit, Bambara met with Assata Shakur and her daughter, as well as with Chilean and Argentinean artists who aimed to produce Amiri Baraka's play The Dutchman.[46] During this trip sponsored by the Writers Guild of America East, Assata asked Bambara to extend special greetings to Sonia Sanchez. When Bambara asked Assata what other visitors from the states might bring her such as "tapes of music, books, ball point pens, mason jars of pot liquor, pan of peach cobbler, film, typing paper, cassettes of independent Black films, etc.," Assata's requests probably made Bambara smile. Assata simply responded: "Spices . . . I need everything of course but I'd appreciate some spices . . . and lots of hugs . . . I don't need anything . . . just tell them to get here."[47]

While in Cuba dancing at Mt. Lugar to the music of accomplished jazz trumpeter Arturo Sandoval, Bambara entered her activist mode when she called what she labeled a "bathroom conference" with a few of the Cuban women she'd met. Bambara made notes that the women who wore wigs, extensions, and face powder to camouflage their natural skin color wanted to increase Bambara's understanding of the impact of Euro-centered standards of beauty. They also asked if women of color faced similar problems of skin color bias in the United States. Bambara wrote in her notes: "Sisters in the bathroom conference met me later and I gave them the SAGE journal, [A Scholarly Journal on Black Woman], issue with Angela on the cover (whom of course they know and love) and they wished to know who was dark here (mostly wanted to know if I had any dark people in my family and if I had more social privileges than my dark siblings)."[48] The image of Angela Davis that Bambara chose to share with the Cuban club dancers reminded them that this revolutionary icon chose to not only reject capitalism, but also refused to conform to European influenced standards of beauty. The Cuban women may have surmised that Davis's light complexion and education would have made it easy for Davis to assume a middle-class lifestyle, but Davis chose not to become a part of the bourgeoisie. The author's gift to the Cuban dancers was to encourage them to recognize their beauty rather than to be ashamed of their darker skin which they attempted to camouflage with cosmetics. Bambara again demonstrated that any place where women gathered, from the kitchen to the lady's room, could be claimed as a space for progressive organizing and rethinking their self-image as women of color.

Back from Cuba on March 19, Bambara began to prepare for travel to Atlanta where she and Louis Massiah would screen and discuss the film, *The Bombing of Osage Avenue,* their first collaborative documentary work. The night before Bambara's 50th birthday celebration, the African Film Society sponsored a community viewing of the film at Zembezi's International Night Club in Atlanta.[49]

The following night at the historic Hammond House, not far from where Bambara previously lived when she first moved to Atlanta, more than 100 people responded to an invitation from Susan Ross to join Beverly Guy-Sheftall, Billye Avery, Cheryl Chisholm, and a host of other family members and friends for an evening of reminiscing.[50] Later writing about the gathering, writer Pearl Cleage recalled that she "stood in a crowded room and cheered the triumphant genius of sister writer Toni Cade Bambara." Not the least bit distracted by the conservative politics of the newly elected George Bush and Dan Quayle, "sisters served fried potatoes and caviar," and danced in their hip outfits, comfortable being "funny and outrageous and silly and stylish and absolutely free."[51]

When Bambara turned 50, Bambara again announced her writing on the Atlanta missing children's book was done. In a letter that might not have been mailed to her friend, the writer bell hooks, Bambara once again believed that she had finished work on the novel, maintained her usual high pace of activity, and charted out work for the future:

> I've FINALLY gotten the Atlanta mss. Out of my house/out of my hair/off my back . . .
>
> Things not too bad at this end. Miss Girl is off to Howard next week. I have JAMMED CRAMMED my Fall schedule so I won't have time to call her up and remind her to brush her teeth or other foolishness. I'll be teaching 2 days a week at U of Delaware, doing a once a month seminar in Jersey, a 6 week video course in Philly, a 10 week writing workshop down the block, working on two film scripts, two short story collections, and helping the homeless union plot how to take over a luxury building that's . . . tied up in litigation.
>
> . . . What I plan to do now is follow a bunch of senior citizens out to Atlantic City in those buses that pay you back what you spent on fare in quarters so you can play the slot machines. . . . The old folks gamble and sit on the benches. I interview the kitchen help. . . .[52]

Bambara had returned to her urban pace and her lifetime passion of listening to stories which began decades ago in Harlem.

When Bambara moved to Philadelphia, Sanchez remembered how Bambara found the location ideal for catching a bus to Atlantic City where Bambara could use her well-honed listening skills to absorb the array of stories she heard about relationships, romance, and work. On the bus to Atlantic City, Bambara could hear the stories of workers and elders headed to the casinos or the beach. More than likely, the rhythms of Harlem and the sounds of the black rural south or an amalgamation of the two were music to her ears—a concert that included blues, rap, jazz, and gospel.

Years later, Sanchez vividly recalled walking to the corner of Wayne Avenue to make her usual purchase of *The New York Times* when suddenly hearing Bambara's familiar voice cry out:

> "Hey, what you doing? Get on the bus going to Atlantic City. Come on. You won't believe the stories you'll hear . . . "
>
> "I've got kids at home and only enough money for the newspaper in my pocket."
>
> "They give you all the money you need on the bus just for going."
>
> "I can't just leave the kids without telling them where I am going."

In Philadelphia, Bambara made time for an array of activities that satisfied her hunger for stories and making films, but her novel on the murdered and missing children remained unpublished. It can only be speculated as to what blocked the publication of the novel for so many years. Even though editors wanted to see the book shortened, the manuscript remained a lengthy one. As Bambara must have wrestled with concerns from the publisher, Bambara also had conflicting demands on her time. Morrison pointed out that another contributing factor to the delay in publishing the book was its length. Morrison said, "The manuscript that I got was 1500 pages and so that was not publishable unless I wanted to do it in two volumes." Recalling the process of editing *Those Bones Are Not My Child,* Morrison explained another set of complications:

> She kept changing the ending. She had more information. There was another situation. There was another conversation. It [the data] just never left. And she had more to say on it. She had several endings and when she finally decided on not the Ku Klux Klan or the racists as the killers, she ended up with the boy who was missing—the way in which he came back and couldn't talk because he probably had been molested and so on. I thought it [the ending] was really elegant actually—much better.[53]

The book was finally published posthumously. Morrison's commitment to see that *Those Bones Are Not My Child* was published was a culmination of decades of work as editor and advocate of Bambara's writing.[54]

Bambara often extolled the important role that circles of women had served in her life, providing support mechanisms for the development of their own creative works and the works of others. Together, Morrison and Bambara instituted something they called "Black Women Walk on Water Achievement Awards." Morrison or Bambara would mail each other an "awardee" letter providing evidence as to why the writer deserved "Walk on Water" recognition, sometimes including a small check in the envelope.[55]

References to circles—storytelling circles, prayer circles, call and response circles—figured prominently in Bambara's writing and film work. Circles were dominant in the entire worldview she lived by. Bambara's ideas about the significance of the circle can be traced to the African diaspora including the cosmology of the Bambara people of Mali, whose name she had embraced. Bambara-land cosmology also provides a framework for the importance of seeing the past in the present, another idea that dominates Bambara's work. In writing about Souleman Cisse's film *Yeelen,* Manthia Diawara, born in Mali and a friend of the writer, could easily be describing Bambara's sense that time is always returning to the beginning when he described how Cisse depicted time in his classic film. Diawara wrote: "Like all of Cisse's films Yeelen ends as it begins. The globe of the sun rises on a new day and a child finds his way into the world. This reflects the Bambara's sense of time as circular, not linear. In the West, clock time proceeds inexorably forward towards an undefined future. Bambara time starts and stops, at different speeds for different people, ultimately to reencounter its own beginning."[56] Similar to those who adhere to an African philosophy that recognizes the future in seeing the past, Bambara's writing endlessly mines this idea as she calls for awakenings from amnesia and finds a true sense of collective brightness, the source of creation, in reuniting past, future, and present through memory.

In the early 1990s, Bambara's work and the work she influenced in film did see the light of day. In her film work, Bambara reencountered her own beginnings as she now pursued a passion that began in her early growing years and was apparent in the frequent references she made to film in her first short stories. In her activism, Bambara continued to return to creating circles through workshops as she did following the publication of her first book, *The Black Woman.*

When Bambara moved to Philadelphia, she prioritized contributing to the development of new films and organizing among filmmakers—particularly creating networks and identifying resources to promote women filmmakers and filmmakers across the African diaspora. Bambara also continued to teach on campuses and facilitate workshops at the Scribe Video Center. Now as an activist focusing on film as an instrument for change, Bambara carried her activist voice into the narration of award-winning documentaries, used workshop formats to encourage new scriptwriters, wrote essays that supported filmmakers who challenged the status quo, and organized networks within the community among the homeless and other disenfranchised groups. Similar to earlier work with emerging black writers, Bambara mentored and encouraged new filmmakers. Now, however, her own film projects through support from Scribe made it to the screen. Beginning with her role in the production of *The Bombing of Osage Avenue*, Bambara's political vision guided the documentary projects that included storytelling circles, collectives, and numerous salutes to cultural workers. Bambara was finding joy in film.

NOTES

1. Toni Cade Bambara, "State of the Arts I: Contemporary American Fiction Panel," Poetry Center of the 92nd Street Y, January 6, 1992.

2. Susan Ross, Interview by author, September, 2012.

3. Valerie Boyd, "'Osage Avenue' Docu Shoots for Truths of Bombing in City of Brotherly Love," *The Atlanta Journal and Constitution*, March 24, 1989.

4. Louis Massiah, Interview by author, November 2012.

5. John Akomfrah, Interview by author, April 2011.

6. Ibid.

7. Jan Carew, "A Timeless Truthteller," *Savoring the Salt: The Legacy of Toni Cade Bambara,* ed. Linda Janet Holmes and Cheryl Wall (Philadelphia: Temple University Press, 2008), 162.

8. Toni Cade Bambara, Curriculum Vitae, Spelman Archives.

9. Toni Cade Bambara, panelist, "Books and Other Acts: Contemporary Women Writers and Social Change," Dartmouth College, weekend of May 5, 1995.

10. Toni Cade Bambara: Script Writing Workshop Notes, Scribe Video Center, Spelman Archives, Atlanta.

11. Toni Cade Bambara, Scriptwriting Workshop Notes, August, 8, 15, 22, 29, 1987, Spelman Archives, Atlanta.

12. Akasha (Gloria) Hull, "A Conversation with Akasha Hull," in *Conversations with Toni Cade Bambara*, edited by Thabiti Lewis (Jackson: University of Mississippi Press, 2012) 108.

13. Toni Cade Bambara, Letter to Volker Schlondorff, undated.

14. Toni Cade Bambara and Louis Massiah, "From the Margin to the Center: Voices of the Homeless Movement," Proposal, 1987.

15. Ibid.

16. Toni Cade Bambara, Journal note, October 3, 1987, Spelman Archives, Atlanta.

17. Ibid.

18. Jane Kerina, Interview by author, September 2010.

19. Bambara, "Jimmy Baldwin's Funeral Tuesday 12:00."

20. Toni Cade Bambara, Journal note, March 25, 1988, Spelman Archives, Atlanta.

21. Rudolph Byrd, "The Feeling of Transport," in *Savoring the Salt*, ed. Linda Holmes and Cheryl Wall (Philadelphia: Temple University Press, 2007), 175.

22. Lakota Harden, Interview by author, June 2010.

23. Ibid.

24. Ibid.

25. Lakota Harden, Note to Toni Cade Bambara, March 3, 1988, Atlanta Archives, Atlanta.

26. Toni Morrison, Interview by author, March 2012.

27. Ibid.

28. Toni Morrison, Letter to Toni, December 9, 1974. Courtesy of Karma Bambara Smith.

29. For a discussion of memory and ancestral presence associated with water in *Beloved,* see K. Zauditu-Selassie, *African Spiritual Traditions in the Novels of Toni Morrison* (Gainesville: University Press of Florida, 2009), 157.

30. Toni Morrison, Interview by author, March 2012.

31. Suzanne Lance, Letter to Toni Cade Bambara, June 16, 1988, Spelman Archives, Atlanta.

32. Michelle Parkerson, Interview by author, March 2012.

33. Toni Cade Bambara, "Reading the Signs," in *Deep Sightings and Rescue Missions* (New York: Vintage Books, 1996), 97.

34. Ibid., 100.

35. Ibid., 106.

36. Ibid., 113.

37. Julie Dash, Interview by author, March 2012.

38. Zala Chandler, Interview with "Toni Cade Bambara and Sonia Sanchez," in *Wild Women in the Whirlwind,* ed. Joanne M. Braxton and Andree Nicola McLaughlin (New Brunswick: Rutger University Press, 1990), 348.

39. Akua Kamau-Harris, Interview by author, July 2, 2010.

40. Ibid.

41. Ibid.

42. Tess Onuwemi, Interview by author, September 2011.

43. Ibid.

44. Ibid.

45. Ibid.

46. Toni Cade Bambara, Memo to "Tayari Ya Salaam and Fulanni Ali of the July Trip Group, and other Interested Folks," March 19, 1989, Spelman Archives, Atlanta.

47. Ibid.

48. Toni Cade Bambara, Personal observations in Cuba, undated, Spelman Archives, Atlanta.

49. Valery Boyd, "Osage Avenue Docu Shoots for Truths of Bombing in City of Brotherly Love," *The Atlanta Journal and Constitution,* March 24, 1989.

50. Susan Ross, "Sprinkle Your Fancy," Birthday Party Invitation, Spelman Archives, Atlanta.

51. Pearl Cleage, "Beverly's Boots," in *Deals with the Devil and Other Reasons to Riot* (New York: Ballantine Books, 1987), 88–91.

52. Toni Cade Bambara, Unmailed letter to Gloria Watkins (known by her pen name as bell hooks), August 12, 1989.

53. Toni Morrison, Interview by author, March 2012.

54. Reviews of *Those Bone Are Not My Child* that later appeared in leading American newspapers were mostly positive. For selected examples, see Sven Birketts, "Death in Atlanta," *The New York Times,* January 2, 2000; James Miller, "Search for the Lost," *Boston Globe,* October 17, 1999; Randall Keenan, "Toni Cade Bambara's Posthumous Novel Is a Wise, Tough and Knowledgeable Look at the World of Atlanta Child Murders," *Chicago Tribune,* October 17, 1999.

55. Toni Morrison, "Tribute to Toni Cade Bambara," Memorial Service, December 17, 1995.

56. Manthia Diawara, "Seeking Brightness," *Yeelen,* California Newsreel Brochure.

TEN

The Struggle Continues

Like we were saying at dinner that time talking about making out wills and having a funeral. I think I'd like to be cremated and have my ashes scattered as they do in a favorite place, that'd be the seals' pool in Central Park. But I don't suppose the zoo people would appreciate it, not to mention the seals.[1]

In the final five years of her life, Bambara's health presented challenges as she also wanted to keep commitments made for film work, writing, and conducting workshops. Bambara drew lessons from her own writing, particularly those ideas found in *The Salt Eaters,* which call for creating wholeness within one's self and in the community by interconnecting sometimes competing forces emanating from still-divided political and spiritual camps. During this period in her life, Bambara faced intense medical treatments and expressed concern that a writing block affected her health.[2] Even so, Bambara continued to work as activist and writer. Like a dancer possessed in a ring shout, Bambara released her spirit in ways that appeared endless. Nevertheless, on December 9, 1995, the writer lost her battle with cancer at the age of 56.

Between 1990 and 1995, many areas of Bambara's life moved toward a sense of completion. Bambara visited and corresponded with friends whom she met during her high school and college years. In 1990, Bambara returned to Simpson College where her Queens College friend Melvin Wilk continued to teach. A little more than a decade before, she had been the sixth recipient of the George Washington Carver Award and delivered the Carver lecture. This time she read as part of the Poets and Writers Series.[3]

Spelman College students honor Bambara at her 50th birthday party held at Atlanta's Hammonds House and Museum, March 25, 1989. Copyright Susan Ross.

Bambara's hands as she speaks on an Audre Lorde panel focusing on spirituality and healing, National Black Arts Festival, July 1994. Copyright Susan Ross.

Also in 1990, Bambara spent time with Mary Helen Washington, a colleague who repeatedly included Bambara's short stories in her anthologies. Through this colleague, Bambara learned of a collective of Boston-area black writers called the Dark Room Collective and responded positively to an invitation to attend one of its readings. In subsequent decades, members of the Dark Room Collective went on to become some of the most influential poets in the United States, including Pulitzer Prize winner Natasha Tretheway, who was appointed U.S. Poet Laureate in 2012. Pulitzer Prize winner Tracy K. Smith, Kevin Young, and Thomas Sayers Ellis are among the other recognized writers with roots in the collective.[4] The Dark Room Collective founding member Sharan Strange remembered:

> We considered Mary Helen to be a sort of guardian angel; she was one of our most enthusiastic supporters, and she had also sent Alice Walker to us, when Ms. Walker asked if she could "come by" while she was in town to visit the series she had heard so much about. No doubt it was Mary Helen who had recommended us to Alice Walker!
>
> And she also contacted us to let us know that Toni Cade Bambara would be in Cambridge, and asked us if we wanted to meet her—which, of course, we did! As with Ms. Walker, we organized a special reading for Ms. Bambara on March 3, 1990 in our living room at 31 Inman Street in Central Square. Our agenda of readings was scheduled a season at a time, but we insisted on being organic and flexible—so when the gift of such an unexpected engagement was offered, we welcomed it, and made room. I don't recall exactly what Toni Cade read—whether a short story or novel excerpt or essay—but I do recall that she talked about her life as an activist, and especially the important film documentary work that she was doing with Louis Massiah's Scribe Media Center in Philadelphia. She was serious and fierce, and we were certainly in awe of her; but she was also generous in her time with us, and expressed genuine appreciation and support of our efforts at attempting to build a literary community and champion Black literary voices in a town where they weren't heard often enough—your mode of activism.[5]

Building community among black writers and students certainly resonated with Bambara as this more than anything else continued to be the fruit of her activism.

At the beginning of 1991, Bambara had another opportunity to briefly interact with black students and to enjoy yet another reunion. Bell Chevigny and Bambara welcomed a surprise meeting at the University of California, Santa Cruz, where the author was a visiting artist-scholar and Chevigny was also a visiting professor at University of California, Santa Cruz. Years later Chevigny remembered the charming Santa Cruz campus: "like an enchanted forest, eucalyptus trees, tall pines, and bridges over ravines"—prompting a conversation about Bambara considering a move to California to live.[6]

"Toni, how do you like it here? Would you stay here if you had a chance?"

"No. There's no community here."

"What do you mean?"

"Too few black folks."[7]

Chevigny, who is white, recalled, "That's probably why whenever she encountered black students, she would strike up a conversation . . . When she caught up with them or waylaid them, she urged them to get together in solidarity. And probably she did encourage that to happen to some degree."[8] Bambara never wanted to miss an opportunity to organize political activity among students on campus.

That fall, Bambara was part of an invited delegation of internationally recognized American writers invited by PEN and the Italian Cultural Institute to attend the Internationale Premio Mondello ceremonies in Sicily where Kurt Vonnegut, the American novelist, and Andrea Zonzotto, the Italian poet, received awards that year.[9] A delegation of writers from China and Russia also attended the week-long event at the Grande Mondello Hotel on the Tyrrhenian Sea in Sicily. When she returned to Philadelphia, Bambara told some of her closest friends including Chisholm about her new relationship with Anthony Valerio, a New York writer, whom she met at the conference. "'I'm in love,' she told me in a sonorous voice," Chisholm recalled, dropping her voice several octaves to imitate the sensual sound of Bambara's voice.[10]

As the relationship deepened, Valerio moved from Greenwich Village to an apartment in Philadelphia as he became more enthralled in the new romance. In the time Valerio spent with Bambara, Chisholm remembered Bambara being excited about how Valerio organized the papers strewn across her bed and scattered throughout her bedroom, encouraging her to return to writing on her manuscript.[11] At the peak of their relationship, Valerio even established a day-time writing schedule for the two of them to follow. Chisholm explained, "At the end of the day of writing at exactly 4 P.M., Anthony, who prepared wonderful Italian meals, would knock on her door with a basket in hand for them to go shopping for groceries. The reward at the end of the day was shop, cook, eat and play," Bambara told Chisholm.[12]

In February 1992, Bambara wrote Chevigny about plans for coming into New York. In a quick postcard to Chevigny, Bambara mentioned *Daughters of the Dust* and reminisced about their time in California earlier: whale watching, supping, and dancing to a record Bambara carried with her of Cuban singer Celia Cruz.[13] On the postcard Bambara also wrote about being in New York at Symphony Space for the popular "Selected Shorts" program on March 18th. Bambara wrote Chevigny and her husband, "We'll give you two a holler." Bambara's postcard ends: "All's well at this end. New book contract. 2 film projects granted. And lovely man-luv etc. Trust much hilarity at that end, eh? Love, Toni."[14]

"I remember we found her at Symphony Space with a white man beside her," Chevigny said. Bambara, who participated in the selection of short stories read that evening, was on stage introducing some of the readers. Chevigny remembered a pleasant evening as she learned how much Bambara appreciated her new friend. During dinner, Bambara talked about how grateful she was for Valerio's support.

Even with the excitement of new romance in the air, Chevigny noted feeling a twinge of sadness as Bambara appeared a bit more frail than she did just months ago when in California. Regarding Bambara's relationship with Valerio, Chisholm observed, "In the beginning Toni was grateful to be writing again and thought it was all kind of nice. Later she resented the scheduling. Toni frequently wrote late at night and wanted no interruptions, not even a plate of food could be put in front of her. Valerio's rigid writing schedule became oppressive to her."[15] Bambara soon reclaimed her free and independent lifestyle.

In January 1993, Bambara travelled again, this time to London to narrate the film *Seven Songs for Malcolm*; Bambara expressed some health concerns to her hosts, but her illness failed to dampen her creativity or energetic spirit. The film's director John Akomfrah and producer Lina Gopaul wanted to be certain to find the type of luxurious accommodations that would assure her comfort. When working on the film, Bambara was housed at the Cumberland Hotel, opposite London's Hyde Park.[16]

Gopaul said that in many ways the production of the film expressed the Pan-African spirit of Malcolm X. Describing *Seven Songs for Malcolm X* as a singular favorite, Gopaul explained, "African Americans were on the crew as the project included individuals across the African Diaspora. . . . One of the reasons we wanted Toni to do the voice over is that she did not project a typical journalistic voice. Her voice was unquestionably subjective. We chose Toni because we loved the way she projects that same kind of uniqueness into her writing."[17]

Akomfrah recalled that from their first meeting with Bambara in London, she insisted upon a profoundly democratic process in their collaboration. Akomfrah said:

> She listened to the intentions of those developing the documentary and rather than offering a critique of the project as some in consulting roles do, Bambara became part of the process, raising narrative questions as the film was being made. She did not come with an agenda. She would always listen first to our ambitions or intentions, then she would start to suggest how to approach them. She always had deep respect for our opinions. She wanted to be part of the process. She rejected the idea of coming in to critique a product—being brought into the process at its end. She raised narrative questions as the film was being made. And Toni helped shape how the story would emerge. As a novelist she understood storytelling structure and principles . . . understood how voice worked in general. Similar to her short stories, always in the mix was the political, the allegorical, the serious and the comedic. She wanted to be in your zone and once there stayed in that zone with you.[18]

For Bambara, work on the project also provided a space for reflecting on the concentric circles found in her own activism from the 1960s to the present moment.

In the 1990s, Bambara involved herself in another film project. In this work, Bambara shared her encyclopedic film knowledge on black giants in silent filmmaking when featured in *Midnight Ramble: The Story of the Black Film Industry,* a documentary produced by Pearl Bowser, Clyde Taylor, and Bestor Cram that aired on public television as part of "The American Experience."[19] The documentary focused on the success of Oscar Micheaux, a pioneering African American filmmaker, in bringing to the American screen dignified and authentic images of blacks at a time when Hollywood films such as *Birth of a Nation* portrayed blacks in demeaning stereotypic roles. On September 22, 1993, Bambara's friend Massiah wrote Bambara about her significant role as a resource and narrator for the documentary *Midnight Ramble:*

> You of course, are the star and voice of the film. Your analysis and narrative make the film very accessible . . .
>
> I hope you realize what an inspiration and resource you are to the international independent film community: Seven Songs for Malcolm, Midnight Ramble, Bricando Charco [*Bricando el charco: Portrait of a Puerto Rican*] . . . Du Bois, More Than Property—1993 is the year of Bambara in film.[20]

During this time, Bambara also began writing a treatment for another film she wanted to develop that was sparked by learning that the National Association of Black Scuba divers had retrieved artifacts from the ship *Henrietta Marie* off the coast of Florida. The ship carried enslaved Africans including infants in the tiny shackles that the black divers found. In 1993 she proposed a film that would open with visual sensations created by falling items like a "paint brush, sketchbook, journal, TV aerial, pillow leaves, seashells, fish . . . a piece of African cloth, an amulet."[21] Some of these falling sensations may have been images streaming from another part of her unconsciousness, for in November 1993, Bambara was hospitalized and diagnosed with cancer.

It is not known if Bambara may have known or suspected illness before then. Bambara's short story "Going Critical," which is set in the 1980s on a beach, a setting that Bambara also personally enjoyed whenever she could, is primarily a conversation between Clara and her daughter, Honey, about Clara's impending death. Bambara called the time period in which the story is set "The time of the Emptying Vessel." When Clara speaks with her daughter, she has exhausted her list of healers and has endured chemotherapy.[22]

Cancer, Clara imagines, is "the disease of new beginnings" or the "result of a few cells trying to start things up again."[23] Clara explains to her daughter her view that cancer is "characteristic of these times, Honey. It signals the beginning of the new age. There'll be epidemics. And folks, you know it, are not prepared."[24] Honey is at times annoyed with her mother's outlook. She has spent her entire lifetime with a mother who was marked by others in the community as different, beginning in her childhood, when there were complaints from a neighbor about "their incense, candles, and 'strange ways.'"[25] Even though

Clara is concerned that Honey is not using her gifts, she makes certain that her daughter recognizes them: reading auras and being clairvoyant.[26]

In "Going Critical," it appears that what Clara calls her "precious work" may have taken a toll on her physical health. Clara is an activist who organizes to raise awareness of nuclear test programs and the impact of pollution on fish and other environmental dangers. The geographic scope of her work is widespread: "Dog River, Alabama; Santa Barbara Harbor, California; Anacostia River, D.C.; Radar Creek, Ohio; San Jancinto River, Texas; Snake River, Washington."[27] While sitting on the beach, Honey suggests to her mother that she rest. The rest suggested would be long enough for Honey to load the car, but her mother finds even the suggestion of a brief rest not to her liking. Honey's mother replies in a way that captures Bambara's attitude about continuing with "precious work" even when faced with challenges: "Girl, don't you know my sitting days are over? And there's work to do and we need to talk."[28] Not only is Bambara's character Clara devoted to "the work," so is Velma in *The Salt Eaters* as are many of the women in Bambara's short stories. And, so is Bambara.

Indeed, for Bambara, being confined or putting work aside was never an option. The choice Bambara made was to continue with the work. Despite her health challenges, Bambara's interest in film remained ebullient. Like the young feisty female narrator in her popular early short story "Gorilla, My Love," Bambara remained passionate about seeing the films she wanted to see on screen. Bambara also continued to read from her writing and to talk about organizing possibilities as the writer wanted to keep the flame of local organizing efforts burning wherever she went. On February 20, 1994, for example, Bambara traveled to Alabama, the home of women of the Epps cooperative that she met when she'd first moved to Atlanta years ago. While in Alabama, Bambara spoke and signed books at Roots & Wings, an independent, black-owned cultural bookstore.[29] During her visit, the writer also learned about efforts to organize a black organic farmers' network, received updates from her friend, Georgette Norman, about progress she was making in developing a local black arts cultural center, and met with Gwen Patton, a veteran civil rights activist, who contributed to her book *The Black Woman*.

In May 1994, Bambara received a letter from Leah Wise, a friend whom she collaborated with years earlier when coediting a special edition of *Southern Exposure* in the mid-1970s in Atlanta. Now executive director of the Southeast Regional Economic Justice Network, Wise asked Bambara about writing a book review. As a longtime friend, Wise knew that writing was the work Bambara was compelled to do and probably thought the task might be therapeutic. Wise wrote:

I hope this note finds you well. I had heard you were ill and tried to leave a message on your answering machine to express my concern (and to confirm the rumor) awhile back. Don't know if you ever got it. Someone else told me they saw you recently and that you were in your "fine" form (expressed with

emphasis, so I took it to mean, physical, mental, emotional, spiritual). I hope
their assessment is true and that you are free of the pain and agony of illness.

I have not a clue what you are up to these days. Nonetheless I am writing
with a request, one that promises at least some enjoyment for you. I am sending
you this wonderful book which I hope you will read eagerly and want to write
a review of. If this is not possible, I am hoping you will recommend it to some
national publications with whom you have contact: NY Times (?), NY Review of
Books (?), Essence (?), Emerge (?), Washington Post (?), etc. etc. that it be reviewed. Secondly can you help set up a reading for Mab [Segrest] in the Philadelphia area or recommend whom we could contact, especially at universities, who
might be interested? I think you will find Memoirs of A Race Traitor a thought-
provoking account, and an unusual bit of story-telling for a white Alabaman.
Anyway, I am anxious to learn your response.

. . . I am going through a bit of transition myself. For one thing, fatigue has
caught up with me. Actually, I am at one of those places where I wish I could
catch you on the phone and mull over a few thoughts/experiences. I always gain
a sense of context from talking with you, besides being inspired and humored
immensely, and only regret we see each other so infrequently.

Many thanks for taking a look at this. I hope it is a request of joy and not a
burden.[30]

The months that followed included more medical treatments, but in the fall
Bambara is hopeful that her integrative approach to health and well-being will
work. In a journal entry marked "Autumn Sat. Oct 5, 1994," Bambara wrote:
"Chemo. cat scans next week. Then restorative surgery. Hurrah to reclaim my
body! Am sure for what—. . . to swim, mvmnt class, 4x a wkexer. Regimen."[31]
The next weekend Bambara headed to New York for historic reflections on
her life.

In a taped interview for the Hatch-Billops series on artists, Bambara was
interviewed by Massiah who drove her to New York from Philadelphia on
Sunday, October 9, for the series funded by the National Endowment for the
Arts and the New York Council of the Arts. Through hundreds of interviews,
John Hatch and Camille Billops have documented the lives of a wide range of
artists. Bambara and Massiah met earlier at a Philadelphia coffee shop a couple
of blocks away from Scribe to brainstorm about possible questions for the interview and for Bambara to reflect on responses to them. About their meeting,
Massiah recalled, "It definitely helped me in shaping the interview and preparing me for Toni's responses."[32]

In the conversation in the downtown loft of her long-time friend Billops,
Bambara was introspective and revealed more about her family life, growing
up years, and how the community shaped who she became than she had in
previously published essays. For the interview, her mother as well as a host of
friends joined the author for the taping. The interview provided a rare event
where Bambara allowed herself to speak freely about herself. When asked
about her present life phase, Bambara's answers were typically optimistic and
upbeat as she indicated that she had tapped into the healing power found in

dance and meditation rather than dwelling on the prognosis of medical doctors.[33] Then Bambara explained:

> In reclaiming the body from the biomedical syndicate as well as from the naturo-pathic types I have been dealing with, the best way I know of recovering the body is movement. It is only when I am dancing that I inhabit all of my body. When I was in academia, that life would drive me up into my mouth, and all of me would be huddled behind my teeth, and I would have to remind myself that I have this space to stretch out in. When I am totally in my body, I know it, be-cause when I run into people, all of me remembers them. My thigh remembers them, my mind is everywhere, and I also feel gigantic. When I walk down the street, I feel very large, physically as well as spiritually. I feel like everybody is a friend of mine and everybody is just wonderful. . . .[34]

Bambara also said she witnessed "spirit guides all around her," but quickly translated it into a more familiar word for her audience, "angels."[35] Bambara also explained: "I'm trying to write things I have never written before, again writing beyond myself."[36]

For a time, the writer's work went on with only some interruptions and her published short stories continued to draw worldwide attention. On November 21, 1994, the BBC wrote Bambara a letter with hopes that she could write a short story to be transmitted on air a year later.[37] They had recently aired three of the writer's stories, including "The Hammer Man," which the BBC reported to have been highly successful.[38]

When Bambara wrote Trina Robbins, a friend with whom she first shared her writing interests in high school, Bambara connected with someone she saw no more than twice since leaving Queens. Robbins who now lived in California was a prominent feminist cartoonist. The two friends had recently seen each other again for the first time in decades. On January 28, 1995, Bambara began her lively and information-filled letter:

> Hello ole friend. Somewhere in this house under the various geological layers is a letter I started to you some years ago when your first package caught up with me in England, having followed me all over the place. It was probably in the fall of 93 that I started composing to you cuz shortly after that I was on my ass on the operating table and am only just now reclaiming my body, my life, from the medical syndicate. Phew! Got a letter in mail recently from the Amer Cancer Soc asking for a donation, and flipped right out, inasmuchas, now that I've added health activist to wardrobe of hats, am all too aware of how many $billions the AMA and gang spend yearly running out of town whomsoever with inexpensive nontoxic regimens. Anyway, All that to say, been out of it for a while, Now have an assistant helping me find a path to my scripts and other manuscripts. And am glad to be writing to you at last, Trina.
>
> How great it was to see you that time in Oakland—thought I had caught the name change years prior—how? Lemme tax my brain, a movie credit I think. Some late sci fi movie that had me pressed to the glass trying to discern whether actress was Trina Perlso or not and then scrutinized the credits.

Anyway, what I'm doing these days is building a media-access facility in Philly so that community orgs and indiv and co-ops can produce videos and create alternative distrib ntwks and screening venues while at same time challenging the kept media to open up and get democratic. Its called the Scribe Video Center. And I must say the best docus, experimentals, and short dramas I've seen at festivals and on PBS around the country bear the Scribe imprimatur (or whatever the hell that word is). One of the most glorious things about being at Scribe, a garage and overhead apt arrangement, is that it's one of the few thangs I've been engaged in over the years that I didn't have to start from scratch. What a luxury, to come to a city and find a base of operation already operating. So I conduct script writing workshops and act as production facilitator to community based orgs who elect to use video as a tool for social change (which strikes me as weird in that I barely know how to turn a camera on, BUT BOY DO I KNOW ABOUT COMMUNITY GROUPS AND HOW TO FASHION NEW FILM PRACTICES TO DO THEIR VISIONS JUSTICE). Starting in Spring doing production on my own scripts. First out is a piece about the goddess, which I started at Toni Morrison's atelier program at Princeton—gathered together women from Wom Studies, Comp lit, and Theatre Depts. and we are building a garden of goddesses, which is an installation and an extended performance. . . . I seem to be fixated, so putting pieces together (umpteenprose pieces called GODDESS SIGHTINGS . . .

Thanks for the package stuff. What a nice visit, Trina. Re adult comics in France—when last there coupla years ago (scheduled to retrn now that my French editions are doing so well) was knocked out by an illustrated Celine— refused to buy it cuz I don't like Celine but ohhhh the art work. Must make the rounds of Philly bookstores now and make sure they're carrying you.

Still writing as well. Yes, ain't it the best!

Bambara concluded this lengthy letter to her high school friend with a humorous reference to playing the numbers and extended abundant good wishes for starting the new year. She wrote:

. . . I get up to NY rarely but that's likely to change as I keep being offered a writers wkshp at NYU, lately a film and writing wkshop (something I call Storying— a workshop for readers, writers, filmmakers, and spectators.)

My typing's getting as erratic as my handwriting, a sure sign I need to take a nap. Ahhh HAH, I note to near-same zip codes. Time to play a number.

I wish us both a hilarious, productive, safe, prosperous, healthy, sexy, and generally resplendent 1995.[39]

The week after writing her reflective letter, Bambara packed her suitcases and headed for a film conference in Washington, DC. Bambara carried with her the works of emerging filmmakers, young women of color, from the Scribe Video Center. Aishah Shahidah-Simmons recalled Bambara's extensive influence on up and coming filmmakers and other women filmmakers of color. Years later, Shahidah-Simmons vividly remembered her response when Bambara first invited her to Scribe to take a four-week scriptwriting course over

20 years ago. Then Shahidah-Simmons was unaware of the success of other black women filmmakers in using the medium to produce activist works. Bambara became an immediate mentor, providing extensive feedback on her early treatments for film and introducing her to other activist filmmakers of color. Shahidah-Simmons explained: "Toni gave permission to claim an identity as a filmmaker before I was able to claim it. She opened up a world. She affirmed."[40] Shahidah-Simmons also recalled Bambara's influence as a feminist who challenged accepted norms that shaped language and behaviors which marginalized and oppressed women. Shahidah-Simmon's film *Silence Broken,* an eight-minute short film about an African American lesbian who refuses to be silent about racism, sexism, and homophobia, was the first film Shahidah-Simmons produced after enrolling in Bambara's scriptwriting class. Later, in 1994, a writing assignment from Bambara emanating from one of the last workshops Bambara taught at Scribe became the roadmap for Shahidah-Simmons to develop her documentary, *NO!,* an award-winning film calling for increased activism to end rampant sexual violence in the black community.[41]

Remembering that 1995 was also the 25th anniversary of Bambara's monumental work, *The Black Woman,* Shahidah-Simmons said: "By now Toni was also a mentor, sister, teacher friend to yet another generation—a generation of women my age who are film makers beginning to use their camera lens as activist tools."[42] In January, Bambara joined Donald Bogle, Clyde Taylor, and Manthia Diawara as panelists at a conference sponsored by the National Museum of American History: *100 Years of Black Film.* At the conference, Bambara acted as an ambassador of Image Weavers, an emerging group of women of color filmmakers including Shahidah-Simmons and several members who first met Bambara when taking her scriptwriting class at the Scribe Video Center. The group formed because women of color recognized that they were not receiving grants and their works were not being viewed seriously. As a result the women of color filmmaking collective began hosting independent screening events that showcased their own work. Bambara carried the message of Image Weavers to the conference that more needed to be done to provide screening and promotion opportunities for a new generation of women of color film filmmakers.[43] Later that month on January 27, 1995, Bambara attended a showcase of Image Weavers work at the Education Center's Feminist Film and Video Series in Philadelphia. Bambara braved inclement weather and battled her own failing health to join the standing room only crowd that night.

In a loving letter to her mother on March 9, 1995, Bambara continued to look to the future. Although having recently written a review on Dorothy West's novel *The Wedding* for *The Philadelphia Enquirer,* the author mentioned a writing block and the ongoing difficulties with the Atlanta novel. In the letter Bambara confessed to feeling a pattern of dryness, which may have referred to her stalled writing projects. On the other hand, Bambara looked forward to launching a new workshop for college students. Bambara wrote:

Now if I can just get a story or two out, maybe I can break this block I've been suffering lo these many moons (which has affected my health so profoundly). Would be nice to get this Atlanta novel out into the world, the two or more collections of stories cluttering up the joint, the nine or more short scripts for video. Then, I'd have the $ and the streamlined psyche to find myself a lovely new home and begin a nice clean chapter of living. Ahhhhh . . .

Nothing much to report from this end . . . except that I've been designing a terrific workshop for writers and filmmakers and creative types who keep track of themselves via journals. It's called STORYING. And what we do is read Tales, Fables, Myths and extract the archetype pattern (or write a monologue from one character's point of view, for example, the wolf sez "She was hot. He had on a jaunty hood. It was red. Everything she had on was red. Oh, you couldn't very well miss her. She was asking for it.") such as the hero's journey trying to get home (Ulysses, for ex) or the youth trying to move out into the world as an independent (almost any fairy tale, such as Jack and Beanstalk or 3 Little Pigs).

In a nutshell, what we discover is—most novels, plays, movies are based on one of 15 or so patterns. Also, if we can discern a given pattern in own life at moment, perhaps reading tales of that type (for ex, I've been DRY for months, so began reading desert stories—Moses in the desert, Christ in the desert, Deborah in the desert, Simon Styilites in the desert, etc) for whatever insight it might offer. Had done a small version of this in script writing class last year and am still getting mail and phone feedback about it and urging to do a major workshop on just that one exercise (since so few of the script writing participants see the same movies or read the same books, I found myself one day resorting to Little Red Riding Hood, not that everyone read it, the generation under 30 have barely heard of European (much less anybody else's) fairy tales, but have heard something, enough for a discussion to illustrate whatever point I was making that day about drama, narrative, character development.) Got really interesting when I started assigning the reading of tales, parables, myths to assist us in scripting.

Anyway—I think/feel/intuit/am convinced that I am on to something useful/therapeutic/interesting so am writing a lot on it each day. One day it seems to mostly be about how to write. Next day seems more about how to plumb one's psyche. Next day how to read ancient texts for the purpose of connecting with the universe (re-ligious, as they say). . . . I dream about it as well, get up and write, then in morning type. I don't doubt that the epiphanies are part of my recovery regime. But also think that regime is sharable with, transferrable to, and transformative for others.[44]

A few months later, Bambara traveled to Dartmouth for the May 5 weekend to join writers Dorothy Allison, Cherríe Moraga, and others at a conference, "Books and Other Acts: Contemporary Women Writers and Social Change." Organized for working-class women writers and activists by Grace Paley, this time Bambara would read from her own work and talk about her work at Scribe with Community Visions. Bambara also read excerpts from the sketches she was developing from a work-in-progress tentatively titled *Goddess Sightings*.[45]

Two and a half years earlier, Allison met Bambara at the National Book Awards when Allison had a chance to speak to Ralph Ellison and be introduced to Bambara who sat at the same table with Ellison that night. Allison had only recently read *The Salt Eaters*. About that evening Allison wrote: "Later as I was headed out a doorway, Toni Cade Bambara came up to me again and put her hand on my sleeve. 'We should talk sometime,' she said."[46]

At the gathering of women activist writers at Dartmouth College, Bambara and Allison finally talked—briefly. A reflection on freedom and Bambara that Allison later wrote includes their conversation while walking toward the Dartmouth Inn and mentions their first meeting:

> The nod she gave me then was welcoming, the smile open and trustworthy. Still, it was two and a half years before we saw each other again—at a small college in New Hampshire for a gathering of women writers that Grace Paley had assembled. We wound up on two panels and did a reading together. She read from a story about some of the characters who had been in *The Salt Eaters*. I read a story pulled out of the first draft of *Cavedweller*, a prose poem about a mother's enormous sense of guilt and shame. After reading when the conference was winding down, I met up with Toni Cade Bambara walking toward the Dartmouth Inn and we finally had a minute to talk.
>
> We started out on the subject of faith and the church, an embattled sense of faith on both our parts, a difficult relationship with any church. But we had both grown up to it, and she teased me about my preacher's cadences. I quoted back to her a few lines from the piece she had read earlier. The rhythms of language were the same.
>
> "We know who we are," she said with a laugh.
>
> We did, I thought. But I cannot say now how we got onto the subject of political activism, other than it was so much a part of both our lives. It had been what we had all been talking about over the two days of that gathering. Was there any way to be a woman writer in 1995 and not be an activist? Well, of course there was. But was there any way we ourselves could write and not be activists? Of course there was not. It was a select group, one constructed by the very astute Grace Paley. All of us believed that what we wrote challenged every notion this culture had of who and what we were supposed to be. That was inherently political even if we did not use the usual language of rhetoric. Black feminist, lesbian feminist, community activist, cultural warrior—sometimes the language for these categories seems grandiose, but not as large as what is meant by these labels.

It is not surprising that their conversation included a reference to the novel on the Atlanta children's cases. In this writer-to-writer conversation, Bambara opened up about her challenges and even mentioned struggling with her health. Allison continued:

> Toni Cade Bambara told me she had been editing a videotape, and she didn't know when she was going to finish the book she had been writing for at least a decade. She hadn't been well this winter, she said. I nodded. I knew how that felt. I had been traveling little college to little college, trying to write on airplanes and in hotels, always exhausted and guilty about not being home with my partner and son. Worse, I was pretty sure that the book I had started out

to write was gone, and a completely different one was coming onto the page. I wasn't sure how I felt about that fact, could barely articulate it to myself, much less my editor or agent. I was able to say it to Toni Cade Bambara. We were talking as writers together and my uncertainties were not so exceptional in that context.

In their late evening conversations, the writers turned to a brief discussion about the writing craft. Allison recalled in her reflection:

> It was storytelling we got onto—the drive toward storytelling, the feeling that the particular stories we had to tell no one else would tell if we didn't. "There isn't," she said at one point. "Not like we do it," I agreed. "Not at all," she said. She did not smile when she said that.
>
> For me the moment was wonderful—coda and completion to all the discussions of the weekend. The women who had read and argued and explained their own work had been passionately engaged in a way I believed writers should be engaged. It had seemed we were united in purpose and conviction, with work to do that pulled us toward the future. There was permission in that context to make mistakes, to be wrong and to go on anyway. I thought about the fragment that Toni Cade Bambara had read earlier that evening, the draft of a story she said she had not yet gotten quite right, the way she said she would get it right. She knew she would. That was a luxurious concept for me, the sense that the work was ongoing and would find its own rhythm. I wanted to believe that more strongly for myself. But it was late, and we were both tired. We would talk again, I said. Toni nodded and went on up the steps. This time I believed it. I looked forward to it.[47]

But, there would be no next time.

In the sketches that Bambara increasingly read from in the last year of her life, Bambara returned to the ideas found in *The Salt Eaters,* whose characters included the Seven Sisters, an alliance that included women of the corn, rice, plantain, and yam. These sketches are set in Sistren Place, house of the Seven Sisters Coop where "the sisters gathered for the Spring equinox."[48] One of the characters Bambara explored is a woman named Gurin, someone who could "turn dirt to plant coriander, ginger root, lemon grass, thyme, Swiss chard, rhubarb, 5 kinds of squash. And gourds, lots of gourds—flat bottomed, goose neck, fat on the vine."[49] Gurin had "freed herself from men who snipped and twisted and wrenched to what he prized."[50] In returning to talking and writing about the Seven Sisters, Bambara continued to place her hope for seeing the future in women who could map out their lives through collective work.

In the circle of returning or the idea of Sankofa—"go back and fetch it"— Bambara also returned to many of the concepts of transformation, creating wholeness, and claiming wellness that she wrote about in her healing work, *The Salt Eaters.* This time not just for others or the planet, but for herself. Now, increasingly, Bambara did demand time to retreat to her own space for personal healing. Bambara wrote in her journal earlier that spring on April 21, 1995: "work in water color-got me a paint box for $11. Gray raining muggy day but pleasant. A bit wonderful though people generally nuts all week—maybe a full moon. . . . I feel good actually. Enjoying, drawing and painting & day dreaming. . . . Also shiatsu classes 4 weeks, voice lessons."[51]

In the summer months that followed in 1995, there were more requests—the kind that Bambara probably found to be of interest. The Commonwealth of Kentucky's Division of Assessment requested permission to use as a reading passage an excerpt from "Raymond's Run." Bambara learned that 53,000 students might read the passage as part of the reading portion of the assessment.[52] There was also a possibility that the excerpt might be selected as part of an informational booklet that included examples of the type of material used in the test.

After meeting Bambara in August 1995, at Howard University, Daryl Cumber Dance told the writer that she wanted to include one of Bambara's short stories in her anthology on styles of humor found in writing in the black community. Dance wrote the author to say she was having difficulty in deciding between "The Lesson," "Medley," and "My Man Bovanne" for inclusion as the selected humorous short story in the collection. In her assessment of Bambara's work, Dance concluded, "Yours is certainly the unequaled, essential, nonpareil voice without which this work will not be complete."[53] When Dance's collection of African American women's humor was published it included several selections by Bambara: "The Lesson," "The Johnson Girls," and "A Sort of Preface."[54]

Near the end of November, Bambara accepted Morrison's invitation to spend a few days at her downtown New York apartment which she rarely used. Malaika Adero, Cheryl Chisholm, Louis Massiah, Manthia Diawara, and Clyde Taylor were among the many people who visited and whose conversation enlivened Bambara as they drank wine and sang praises to the terimisu that was served. Meanwhile, Bambara gave honor to the late jazz vocalist Sarah Vaughn, choosing to fill the room with her music at one point. No nurse or medical assistant accompanied Bambara and there was no visible medical equipment in the room. A recent book of essays by her friend Ishmael Reed lay on the coffee table, the only book in sight. Bambara demanded cheerfulness at what could be described as a kind of farewell party.

When Bambara returned to Philadelphia, a taxi drove her to Louis Massiah's brownstone in North Philadelphia for yet another party. This time it was to celebrate the showing of the rough cut of the film which she narrated along with Thulani Davis, Amiri Baraka, and Wesley Brown: *W. E. B. Du Bois: A Biography in Four Voices.* That same day Bambara watched the film, back straight, eyes glued to the screen. At the end of the gathering, Bambara would reiterate her idea for another party. This time the request was for a tea party with sterling silver tea ware. That party never happened. Bambara lost her battle with cancer on December 9, 1995.

The day after Bambara passed away, friends and family gathered at the home of Jane Poindexter to begin planning for a memorial and to remember Bambara with stories that sometimes evoked needed laughter. Over the next several days, Bambara's friend Sanchez recalled making phone calls to local churches hoping to secure a place for the memorial service. After calling several churches that all had fees, Sanchez contacted the Painted Bride Art Center in Philadelphia where the staff welcomed hosting the memorial service. "Although I called churches, a religious setting just didn't seem right for Toni," Sanchez said. Remembering that Bambara attended numerous cultural events at the Painted Bride during the years she lived in Philadelphia, Sanchez said, "Her spirit was definitely there."[55] Indeed, music, dance, poetry, and laughter filled the memorial held in Philadelphia. In a memorial organized by Adero at the Schomburg Research Center in Black Culture in New York, and at the memorial in Oakland, California, organized by Joyce Carol Thomas, a writer who Bambara also influenced, the Bambara parties continued with a spirit of remembrance and joy in countless tributes.

At Bambara's memorial service at the Painted Bride in Philadelphia, Morrison announced a gift of a different kind in her tribute to her friend: Morrison said that she would do whatever she could to make certain that *Those Bones Are Not My Child* was published. And she kept her commitment.

Years later, Morrison explained,

> I was very busy doing something of my own and I stopped for three months and just did it. Then I had the good fortune of getting a copy editor that I knew was as good a line editor as I was and she helped enormously. Every time I recommended a cut it would hurt and every time she recommended a cut it would hurt because all of it was so fascinating, so interesting. But I had to shape it and pull it back to something publishable and manageable. As you know, she had several titles, but I liked the first one . . .[56]

Morrison's commitment to see that *Those Bones Are Not My Child* was published was the culmination of decades of work as editor and advocate of Bambara's writing.

Morrison also wrote about the novel in an essay entitled "Massacre of the Innocents," which was the cover story on London's *The Independent on Sunday*.[57] In *The Sunday Review*, Morrison began her article by describing the significance of Bambara's long-awaited novel: "The publication of no book (including my own) has made me happier than this one: Toni Cade Bambara's novel, *Those Bones Are Not My Child* . . . I believed the story it told was absolutely critical to 20th-century literature and its absence was too melancholy to contemplate. It was the work of one of the most brilliant writers I have personally ever known."[58]

Fifteen years after the passing of her friend, Morrison said, "I felt I knew her in a way that nobody else did. Only in the way that editors know about writers— twists and turns, how they think. It's a very linguistically intimate place. If you have a truly positive relationship with your editor, there's nothing to rival it."[59]

About *The Salt Eaters*, Morrison reiterated that Bambara's first novel "was a canvass of Toni's emotional and intellectual life and that made reading it difficult."[60] What matters, however, Morrison explained is the genius in the work. Morrison said:

> There's this other thing that a lot of writers don't have, which is the confidence and the clarity. It's not ego-bound confidence. It's just confidence in the ability and the material . . . I can't think of any writers who are better then she is at all. The closest may be some of the works I have read by Edwidge Dandicat, that sort of hit that note. There's a process of selection that goes on in writing that is found in the structure, the selection of what to write, what sentences to cut; it's a constant refining of the original idea.[61]

About why Bambara's collective body of published writing has yet to receive the literary accolades it deserves, Morrison concluded, "She was first-rate and I really think that she is in a category that is pretty much hers. More attention should be given not just to the pleasure of reading her work and its resonance with our culture, but to the detailed analysis of her writing—and only scholars can provide that. You're not going to get that in the newspaper."[62]

What Bambara did receive during her lifetime was appreciation from fellow cultural workers who were inspired by her work. And that acknowledgment of her influence continues today. College students, poets, and filmmakers who once gathered at Bambara's kitchen table in Atlanta have dedicated works to her. Poets have honored her with poems that carry her name. Black women health activists have made reading *The Black Woman* (re-issued in 2005) and *The Salt Eaters* central to their movements. Students of color on college campuses see power in student organizations that this activist-writer helped to create. And Bambara's impact on filmmakers who enrolled in the writer's scriptwriting workshops at the Scribe Video Center can be seen in documentaries that cry out for social justice and honor cultural traditions.

Bambara was an historic black woman activist and writer. The author's writings provide many examples of creating wholeness through introspection, political acts, and cultural work. Bambara lived a life free of boundaries. And that is a joyous revolt.

NOTES

1. Toni Cade Bambara, Letter to Helen Brehon, July 12, 1982.
2. Toni Cade Bambara, Letter to Helen Brehon, March 9, 1995.
3. Stephen G. Jennings, Letter to Family of Toni Cade Bambara, December 12, 1985, Spelman Archives, Atlanta.
4. Sharan Strange, Interview by Chantal James, April 2012.
5. Ibid.
6. Bell Gale Chevigny, Interview by author, March 2012.
7. Ibid.
8. Ibid.
9. Silvio Marchetti, Letter to Ms. Bambara, October 2, 1981, Spelman Archives, Atlanta.
10. Cheryl Chisholm, Interview by author, October 2012.

11. Ibid.

12. Ibid.

13. Ibid.

14. Ibid.

15. Ibid.

16. Black Audio Film Collective letter to Bambara, undated, Spelman Archives, Atlanta.

17. Lina Gopaul, Interview by author, November 2012.

18. John Akomfrah, Interview by author, April 2011.

19. *Midnight Ramble,* directed by Peal Bowser (Boston, 1994), film.

20. Louis Massiah, Letter to Bambara, September 22, 1993, Spelman archives, Atlanta.

21. Toni Cade Bambara, Film Notes, Spelman Archives, Atlanta.

22. Toni Cade Bambara, "Going Critical," in *Deep Sightings and Rescue Missions* (New York: Vintage Books, 1996), 5–26.

23. Ibid., 16.

24. Ibid.

25. Ibid., 10.

26. Ibid., 12.

27. Ibid., 15.

28. Ibid.

29. Roots and Wings Flyer, Spelman Archives, Atlanta.

30. Leah Wise, Letter to Toni Cade Bambara, May 5, 1994.

31. Toni Cade Bambara Note, October 5, 1994.

32. Louis Massiah, Interview by author, November 2012.

33. Louis Massiah, "How She Came by Her Name" in *Deep Sightings and Rescue Missions* (New York: Vintage Books, 1996), 241–42.

34. Ibid., 241.

35. Ibid.

36. Ibid., 240.

37. Pam Fraser Solomon, Letter to Toni Cade Bambara, November 21, 1994, Spelman Archives, Atlanta.

38. Ibid.

39. Toni Cade Bambara, Letter to Trina Robbins, January 28, 1995. Courtesy of Trina Robbins.

40. Aishah Shahidah-Simmons, Interview by author, May 2012.

41. Ibid.

42. Shahidah-Simmons, Interview by author, May 2012.

43. *100 Years of Black Film: Imaging African American Life, History & Culture* (Washington: Smithsonian Institute, February 1–4, 1995).

44. Toni Cade Bambara, Letter to Helen Brehon, March 9, 1995. Courtesy of Walter Cade III.

45. Dorothy Allison, e-mail message to author, August 20, 2001.

46. Dorothy Allison, "What It Means to Be Free," in *Tanner Lectures in Human Values* (Palo Alto: Stanford University, May 2001).

47. Ibid.

48. Toni Cade Bambara, "Song of the Can Opener." Reading version for Dartmouth College, May 5, 1995, Spelman Archives, Atlanta.

49. Ibid.

50. Ibid.

51. Toni Cade Bambara, Journal Entry, April 2, 1995.

52. Lisa J. Randall, Letter to Toni Cade Bambara, July 5, 1995, Spelman Archives, Atlanta.

53. Daryl Cumber Dance, Letter to Toni Cade Bambara, August 3, 1995.

54. Daryl Cumber Dance, *Honey, Hush! An Anthology of African American Women's Humor* (New York: W.W. Norton, 1998).

55. Sonia Sanchez, interview by author, May 2012.

56. Morrison, Interview by author, March 2012.

57. Toni Morrison, "Massacre of the Innocents: Toni Morrison on the Murders that Shamed America," *The Independent On Sunday*, March 25, 2000.

58. Ibid.

59. Morrison, Interview by author, March 2012.

60. Ibid.

61. Ibid.

62. Ibid.

Appendix: A Call to Action

In May 1985, the "Roots in Georgia" symposium sponsored by *The Georgia Review* at the University of Georgia attracted two dozen writers, including Toni Cade Bambara. On May 16, the opening day of the conference, Bambara introduced Macon-born novelist John Oliver Killens, colleague and friend. Invoking primacy and truth in writing and planting seeds for activism, the author began her speech with a stinging indictment of Philadelphia's city government–ordered military-style police assault and bombing of an African American row-house neighborhood to evict a black liberation commune. Less than a week after the city's decimation of a black neighborhood in Philadelphia, the city where Bambara now lived, the writer denounced the "official version of things" as reported in the news. Like a protagonist in her fiction, Bambara tackled racist stereotypes and applauded community organizing in her speech. In this breathtaking 11-minute introduction of Killens, the author also made personal references—her parents and conjuring grandmother—before closing with optimism and a look to the future. Speaking free of notes, only Bambara's worn copy of *And Then We Heard the Thunder* rested on the lectern.

The speech is an excerpt from the archival video footage of a 15-tape set of the "Literary Roots" symposium on 34-inch U-Matic video-cassettes held by the Georgia University Libraries' Walter J. Brown Media Archives & Peabody Awards Collection. The transcript is verbatim and unedited.

I am reading the dedication in John Oliver Killens' *And Then We Heard the Thunder:*

> To my mother and to Harriet Tubman, who stands head and shoulders above most Americans in my private Hall of Fame and to my buddies, fallen and standing, and to Chuck and Barbara and to all young people everywhere. May they never hear the manmade thunder, nor see the terrible lightning.

They dropped a bomb on the Black community in the City of Brotherly Love.

On Mother's Day, they delivered a specially requisitioned item of anti-personnel weaponry to the forces in Philadelphia who would declare war on people—on a neighborhood—that has been highly organized against red-dogging activities of real estate agents and a number of developers who would steal that turf—who want it badly, as badly as they wanted Hilton Head Island, as badly as they want Daufuskie Island, as badly as they want Johns Island, and Simons Island and in my hometown of Atlanta, Buttermilk Bottom and Magnolia Street.

They dropped a bomb on a building they were pretty sure was filled with dynamite and ammunition, were certainly sure was filled with people, predominantly children. And, when they dropped that bomb, what were they saying to that neighborhood—people who have been down to City Hall and to the Police Department for months and months asking for assistance in the development of their neighborhood?

And what were they thinking when they allowed those buildings to burn hour after hour—all those homes consumed, all those irreplaceable photo albums burned up, those family bibles, the graduation pictures, the plaques and awards for civic duty, all that cherished china, all that furniture bought and paid for by working season in and season out for the expressed purpose of trying to live in a dignified manner?

Were they telling that neighborhood, "We'll show you for coming down into City Hall and to the Police Department criticizing our behavior"?

And what were they saying when they unleashed mad dog hatred on an organization they said on television was militant to let you know they were black and radical to let you know they were hated and extremist to let you know they were prepared to unleash mad dog hatred fire power?

Were they saying to people who wear dreads, "Yes, you may have gotten under the fence and busted up the near monopoly of a multi-billion dollar drug trade that used to be in the hands of a private club. You may have the gangi trade and you may have reggae, but we have a bomb and we will drop it because we can"?

And what were they saying to the city of Philadelphia? We drop it because we can—because Rizzo lives—no matter who is in the Mayor's office.

And the mayor said to all those people dispossessed and dislocated, "My prayers are with you. I take full responsibility." But what exactly does that mean?

Does that mean a willingness to stand trial for murder? Does it mean a willingness to step down from office and declare a state of out of control madness? Does it mean a willingness to demand the resignations of people who behind closed doors ordered a custom tailored bomb to be dropped on Mother's Day?

In the city of Philadelphia now, the authorities are huddled together piecing together those little highly selective facts of disinformation that will comprise the official version of things. And we will not hear about the real estate developers who wanted that turf. We will not hear about acts of terror against MOVE people and Rastas. We will not hear about sealed envelopes being passed and circulated throughout police departments in the United States that have put a bull's eye on anybody wearing dreads. We will not hear about that highly organized neighborhood—its lawyers, its counselors, its community organizers who've been attempting to secure that neighborhood against the encroachment of real estate developers. We will hear instead the official version of things.

The elders in my community frequently say, "It is not how little we know that hurts so, but that so much of what we know ain't so."

And it's in that vein that I'm deeply honored to introduce John Oliver Killens because John Oliver Killens for many years has always stood for something in this world.

A man of great intelligence, of great courage and of great imagination for whom things matter such as the truth, such as the capacity to cut through the official versions of things and deliver up usable truths to people not only as a writer, and he's been a writer longer than some of us have been on the planet. There are numerous books and papers and lectures, anthologies, fiction, non-fiction, political, imaginative.

Not only as a developer of other writers and he has been engaged in that task for some years—conducting workshops, and for that matter, as a founder of the Harlem Writers Guild in the '40s which probably is the longest on going-writers' league in this country.

And not only as an educator, he has been in the classroom sharing, teaching, developing for years, but primarily as an intelligent thinking person for whom life is blessed and sacred.

It was my daddy who first gave me this copy of *And Then We Heard the Thunder*, the World War II classic. It was very important to people like my daddy and members of his generation that somebody validate their experience, their insights, what they went through in the U.S. armed forces in the '40s, what they experienced overseas, what they saw in the concentration camps—mainly thousands and thousands of Senegalese soldiers, thousands of Herero Germans, thousands of Afro-Americans who are never discussed when we talk about Bergen-Belsen or Auschwitz or the other death camps. The book has been extremely important for lots of people who know that the official version of that war as laid down in *Life Magazine* and in Pathe Newsreel and in *Readers Digest* is not all there is to say about what happened. And we are lucky for the book, *And Then They Heard the Thunder,* is out in print again and available.

It was my mother who gave me the first copy of *Youngblood* and said, "Here, try this on for size." When she realized there was a writer growing up in her house, she wanted to offer us the best. And that was good. And so John Oliver Killens has been very well known in my household—in the bookcase—to anybody walking through.

And I think at this moment rather than begin listing the publications, the awards, the honors, the travels, the insights, much of which you can find in your handy reference books, I think since I am wearing my grandmother's serious jewelry that I would ask you to join me in conjuring up a few things.

We would hope we could see that the manuscript John has been working on for some years about Pushkin, that it receive an immediate contract and be translated immediately into 25,000 languages.

That his anthology of Black southern voices which will be published by New American Library and out in '86 that that become a classroom college circuit best seller and a mass market best seller as well.

That the classic *And Then They Heard the Thunder,* which ought to be on the screen, be made into a motion picture immediately so that we might see that.

And that *Youngblood* which always seemed to me to be a two-part movie made for television series that perhaps could appear at American Playhouse and then appear on commercial television and then appear abroad. That that be adapted.

And that *Cotillion* that has been adapted, and in my mind was always an opera, that that appear on Broadway soon because that would give a lot of people who've wanted to say to John Oliver Killens, "Thank you," an opportunity to get elegant and to go to the Broadway theaters and sit in those very comfy seats and then glance up at him himself in his China blue cap and stand up for John Oliver Killens, the way he has stood up for us these very many years.

Thank you, John.
And, thank you.

Source: Printed with permission from University of Georgia Libraries.

Selected Bibliography

Allison, Dorothy. "What It Means to Be Free." Tanner Lectures in Human Values, Stanford University, Palo Alto, May 2001.

Anderson, Jack. "Etienne Decroux Is Dead at 92; Master of Modern French Mime." *The New York Times*, March 21, 1991.

Anderson, Jervin. "Standing Out There on the Issues." *The New Yorker*, April 28, 1996.

Andrews, Munya. *The Seven Sisters of the Pleiades: Stories from Around the World*. North Melbourne, Australia: Spinifex Press Pty Ltd., 2004.

Bambara, Toni Cade. "Black English." *The New York Times*, September 3, 1972.

Bambara, Toni Cade. "Black Theater." In *Black Expressions: Essays by and about Black Americans in the Creative Arts*, edited by Addison Gayle, Jr. New York: Weybright and Talley, 1969.

Bambara, Toni Cade. "The Children Who Got Cheated." *Redbook*, January 1970.

Bambara, Toni Cade. "Dedication of Nelson Stevens Mural, Centennial Address." *The Tuskegee Centennial*, Tuskegee University Press, 1981.

Bambara, Toni Cade. *Deep Sightings and Rescue Missions*. New York: Vintage Books, 1996.

Bambara, Toni Cade. "'For Colored Girls'—and White Girls Too." Ms 5, no. 3 (September 1976).

Bambara, Toni Cade. Foreword to *This Bridge Called My Back: Writings By Radical Women of Color*, edited by Cherríe Moraga and Gloria Anzaldua. New York: Kitchen Table: Women of Color Press, 1981.

Bambara, Toni Cade. "Geraldine Moore The Poet." In *Something Else*, Marvin L. Greene, consultant-compiler. Glenview: Scott, Foresman and Company, 1970.

Bambara, Toni Cade. "The Golden Bandit." In *Jump Up and Say*, edited by Linda Goss and Clay Goss. New York: Simon and Schuster, 1995.

Bambara, Toni Cade. *Gorilla, My Love*. New York: Random House, 1972.

Bambara, Toni Cade. "Introduction of John Oliver Killens., 'Literary Roots' symposium, May 16, 1985." Excerpt on 34 inch U-matic-video cassettes held by the Georgia University Libraries' Walter J. Brown Media Archives & Peabody Awards Collection.

Bambara, Toni Cade. Preface to *Daughters of the Dust*, by Julie Dash. New York: The New Press, 1992.

Bambara, Toni Cade. Preface to *Southern Black Utterances Today*. Atlanta: Southern Exposure Press, 1975.

Bambara, Toni Cade. "Programming with School Daze." In *Five for Five: The Films of Spike Lee*. New York: Stewart, Tabori and Chang, 1991.

Bambara, Toni Cade. "Realizing the Dream of a Black University." *Observation Post*, February 14, 1969.

Bambara, Toni Cade. "Report from Part One." *The New York* Times Book Review, January 7, 1973.

Bambara, Toni Cade. *The Salt Eaters*. New York: Random House, 1980.

Bambara, Toni Cade. "Salvation Is the Issue." In *Black Women Writers (1950–1980): A Critical Evaluation*, edited by Mari Evans. New York: Anchor Books, 1984.

Bambara, Toni Cade. *The Sea Birds Are Still Alive*. New York: Vintage Books, 1982.

Bambara, Toni Cade. "Some Forward Remarks." In *The Sanctified Church*, edited by Zora Neale Hurston. New York: Marlowe and Company, 1981.

Bambara, Toni Cade. "Something in the Wind." *The Paper*. City College of New York, April 25, 1968. Spelman Archives, Atlanta.

Bambara, Toni Cade. "There'll Come a Day." *The Clipper* (John Adams High School), June 1955.

Bambara, Toni Cade. "Thinking About My Mother." *Redbook*, September 1973.

Bambara, Toni Cade. *Those Bones Are Not My Child*. New York: Pantheon, 1999.

Bambara, Toni Cade. "Vietnam and Black Struggle: Two Revolutions in the Making." *Black-World-View*, June–July, 1976.

Bambara, Toni Cade. "What It Is I Think I'm Doing Anyhow." In *The Writer on Her Work*, edited by Janet Sternburg. New York: W.W. Norton & Company, 1980.

Bambara, Toni Cade. "Working at It in Four Parts." Spelman Archives, Atlanta.

Bambara, Toni Cade, and Leah Wise, eds. *Southern Black Utterances Today*. Atlanta: Southern Exposure Press, 1975.

Bambara, Toni Cade, ed. *The Black Woman: An Anthology*. New York: Washington Square Press, 1970.

Bambara, Toni Cade, ed. *Tales and Stories for Black Folks*. New York: Zenith Books, 1971.

Baraka, Amiri, and Larry Neal, eds. *Black Fire: An Anthology of Afro-American Writing*. Baltimore: Black Classic Press, 2007.

Bell, Roseann P., Bettye J. Parke, and Beverly Guy-Sheftall, eds. *Sturdy Black Bridges: Visions of Black Women in Literature*. New York: Doubleday, 1979.

Biondi, Martha. *The Black Revolution on Campus*. Berkeley and Los Angeles: University of California Press, 2012.

"Bishop Lived in and Loved Jersey City." *Jersey Journal*, September 15, 1966.

Black Heritage: A History of Afro-Americans, Three Black Writers, produced by Larry Neal, WCBS-TV, 1969. New York: The Schomburg Center for Research in Black Culture.

Boyd, Valery. "Osage Avenue Docu Shoots for Truths of Bombing in City of Brotherly Love." *The Atlanta Journal and Constitution*, March 24, 1989.

Braxton, Joanne M., and André Nicola McLaughlin, eds. *Wild Women in the Whirlwind: Afra-American Culture and the Contemporary Literary Renaissance*. New Brunswick, NJ: Rutgers University Press, 1990.

Bukhari, Safiya. *The War Before: The True Life Story of Becoming a Black Panther, Keeping the Faith in Prison, and Fighting for Those Left Behind*. New York: Feminist Press, 2010.

Chametzky, Jules, and Sidney Kaplan, eds. *Black and White in American Culture*. Amherst: University of Massachusetts Press, 1969.

Chevigny, Bell Gale. "Stories of Solidarity and Selfhood." *The Village Voice*, April 12, 1973.

"Clark Sponsors Writers' Meet." *Atlanta Daily World*, March 28, 1974.

Cleage, Pearl. "Beverly's Boots," In *Deals with the Devil and Other Reasons to Riot*. New York: Ballentine Books, 1993.

Connolly, Paul H, ed. *On Essays: A Reader for Writers*. New York: Harper & Row, 1981.

"Creative Arts Program Going Strong in Atlanta." *Atlanta Daily World*, October 9, 1977.

Curran, Mary Doyle. *The Parish and The Hill*. New York: The Feminist Press, 1986. Originally published Boston: Houghton-Mifflin, 1948.

Dance, Daryl Cumber. *Honey, Hush! An Anthology of African American Women's Humor*. New York: W.W. Norton, 1998.

Day, Dorothy. *Loaves and Fishes*. New York: Harper & Row, Publishers, 1963.

Dee, Ruby. "Review: The Sea Birds Are Still Alive." *Freedomways*, Summer 1977.

Diawara, Manthia. "Yeelen: Brightness." California Newsreel Catalogue, San Francisco, California.

Eisen-Bergman, Arlene. *Women of Viet Nam*. San Francisco: People's Press, 1974.

Federal Writers Project. *The WPA Guide to New York City*. New York: The New Press, 1939.

Frye, Charles A. *Towards A Philosophy of Black Studies*. San Francisco: R & E Research Associates, 1978.

Frye, Charles A., with Charlene Harper, Linda James Myers, and Eleanor W. Traylor. "A Symposium on Toni Cade Bambara's The Salt Eaters." *Contributions in Black Studies*. Vol. 6.

Gayle Jr., Addison, ed. *Black Expression: Essays by and About Black America in the Creative Arts*. New York: Weybright and Tally, 1969.

Giddings, Paula. "Toni Cade Bambara on Her First Novel: A Call to Wholeness from a gifted Storyteller." *Encore*, June 1980.

Gilliard, Deric. "Witchbird's Warning: To Thine Own Self Be True." *Atlanta Daily World*, April 28, 1981.

"Girl Orators Barred." *The New York Times*, April 4, 1914.

Greenberg, Cheryl Lynn. *Or Does It Explode? Black Harlem In The Great Depression*. New York: Oxford University Press, 1991.

Griaule, Marcel. *Conversations with Ogolemmeli: An Introduction to Dogon Religious Ideas*. London: Oxford University Press, 1965.

Hanrahan, Claire. "Alderson: Reclaiming the Vision." *Western North Carolina Woman*, Vol. 1. February/March 2003, http://www.seniorwomen.com/articles/articlesHanra hanAlderson.html.

"Harlem Women's Committee to Promote Anti-Discriminatory Legislation." *The New York Times,* March 26, 1939.

Hass, Jeffrey. *The Assassination of Fred Hampton: How the FBI and the Chicago Police Murdered a Black Panther*. Chicago: Lawrence Hill Books, 2011.

Holmes, Barbara A. "'Dem as Could Fly Home": Indigenous Women and Science." *Race and the Cosmos: An Invitation to View the World Differently*. Harrisburg: Trinity Press International, 2002.

Holmes, Linda Janet. "The Life of Lena Edwards." *New Jersey Medicine* 85, no. 5 (May 1988).

Holmes, Linda Janet, and Cheryl Wall, eds. *Savoring the Salt: The Legacy of Toni Cade Bambara*. Philadelphia: Temple University Press, 2008.

hooks, bell. *Remembered Rapture: The Writer at Work*. New York: Henry Holt and Co., 1999.

hooks, bell, and Cornel West. *Breaking Bread: Insurgent Black Intellectual Life*. Boston: South End Press, 1991.

Imperato, Pascal James. *African Folk Medicine: Practices and Beliefs of the Bambara and Other Peoples*. Baltimore: York Press, 1977.

"Interview with Toni Cade Bambara." *The Drum* 12, no. 1 (Spring 1982).

Jefferson, Margo. "Blue Notes." *Newsweek Magazine*, May 2, 1977.

"Key Women Participate in Workshop at JFK." *Atlanta Daily World*, December 15, 1977.

"Kres Mersky at the Codfish Ball." *Hollywood Review*. March 24, 1976. Spelman College Archives, Atlanta.

Leabhart, Thomas. *Etienne Decroux (Routledge Performance Practitioners)*. London: T & F Books UK, 2009.

Lewis, Thabiti, ed. *Conversations with Toni Cade Bambara*. Jackson: University Press of Mississippi, 2012.

Lovelace, Alice. "In Praise of Toni Cade Bambara." *In Motion Magazine*, February 20, 2000.

Mahone, Barbara. "A Handsome Family Quilt," *First World*, 1977.

"Mailman Leaves Art Exhibit on Route," *The Amsterdam News* (New York), April 2, 1966.

Medsger, Betty. *The Burglary: The Discovery of J Edgar Hoover's FBI*. New York: Knopf, 2014.

Midnight Ramble. Film. Directed by Peal Bowser. Boston, 1994.

"The Modern School Is 30 Years Old." *The Amsterdam News* (New York), September 12, 1964.

Moore, Jenny. *The People on Second Street*. New York: William, Morrow & Company, Inc., 1968.

Moraga, Cherríe L. *A Xicana Codex of Changing Consciousness: Writings, 2000–2010*. Durham: Duke University Press, 2011.

Morejón, Nancy. *Where the Island Sleeps Like A Wing: Selected Poetry by Nancy Morejón*. San Francisco: The Black Scholar Press 1985.

Morrison, Toni. "Massacre of the Innocents: Toni Morrison on the Murders That Shamed America." *The Independent on Sunday*, March 25, 2000.

"Neighborhood Arts Center Scheduled to Open in May." *Atlanta Daily World*, April 24, 1975.

"Neighborhood Cultural Festival Planned at Art Center, August 30." *Atlanta Daily World*, August, 22, 1975.

"Noted Writer, Educator, Addresses Education Forum." *Atlanta Daily World*, January 25, 1976.

"The Order is to Charge!" *The Amsterdam News* (New York), March 25, 1939.

Pomerantz, Gary M. *Where Peachtree Meets Sweet Auburn*. New York: Penguin Books, 1996.

"Railroad Workers Gave Impetus to Jersey City Growth." *The New Jersey Afro-American*, March 27, 1947.

Reed, Ishmael. *Airing Dirty Laundry*. Boston: Addison-Wesley, 1993.

Reed, Ishmael. *The Last Days of Louisiana Red*. Champaign: Dalkey Archives Press, 2000.

Reed, Ishmael. "Pee Wee's Wreath." *The New York Times*, December 16, 1976.

Rich, Adrienne. "Review: *The Salt Eaters*." *New Women's Times*, December 1980/ January 1981.

Robbins, Trina. "Savoring Toni Cade Bambara." *Bitch Magazine*, Summer 2008.

"Ryan's Removal Asked as Color Discrimination Against Teachers Is Charged." *The New York Times*, April 11, 1935.

Saba, Furaha. "Toni Cade Bambara Interprets the Health and Sexuality of Women." *Southern Rural Women's Network Newsletter*, January, 1983.

Salaam, Kalamu ya. "Searching for the Mother Tongue: An Interview with Toni Cade Bambara." *First World* 2, no. 4 (1980).

Sinclair, Abiola. "Remembering Adam Clayton Powell Jr." *The Amsterdam News* (New York), December 1992.

"Sojourner South Protest Apartheid." *Atlanta Voice*, September 15, 1979.

Soum, Corrine. "A Little History of a Great Transmission or Simplon's Tunnel." London: Theater de L'Ange Fou& International School of Corporeal Mime, 1999, http://www.angefou.co.uk/published-work/simplons-tunnel.html

Sparks, Peggy Matthewson. *Hope Farm/Greer School: Memories of Childhood*. Rutland, VT: Parchment Press, 2006.

"Spelman Plans Movies on Black Women in Literature." *Atlanta Daily World*, November 3, 1977.

"Spelman Protestors Granted 'Amnesty' By Trustees Board." *Atlanta Daily World*. August 20, 1976.

"Spelman Slates Symposium on the Black Aesthetic." *Atlanta Daily World*, February 5, 1981.

"Spelman Trustees Vow to Reconsider Decision to OK Dr. Stewart as Pres." *Atlanta Daily World*. April 29, 1976.

Tate, Claudia, ed. *Black Women Writers at Work*. New York: Continuum International Publishing Group, 1983.

Taylor-Guthrie, Danille, ed. *Conversations with Toni Morrison*. Jackson: University Press of Mississippi, 1994.

Traylor, Elenor W. "Music as Theme: The Jazz Mode in the Works of Toni Cade Bambara." In *Black Women Writers (1950-1980): A Critical Evaluation*, edited by Mari Evans. New York: Anchor/Doubleday, 1984.

Traylor, Elenor W. "*The Salt Eaters*: My Soul Looks Back in Wonder." *First World* 2, no. 4 (1980).

Trescott, Jacqueline. "Black Writers in the 70s." *The Washington Post*, May 6, 1977.

Vertreace, Martha M. "Toni Cade Bambara: The Dance of Character and Community." In *American Women Writing Fiction: Memory, Identity, Family, Space*, edited by Mickey Pearlman. Lexington: The University Press of Kentucky, 1989.

Watkins, Mel. "Hard Times for Black Writers." *New York Times*, February 22, 1981.

White, Shane, et al. *Playing the Numbers: Gambling in Harlem between The Wars*. Cambridge: Harvard University, 2010.

Wideman, John Edgar. "The Healing of Velma Victory." *The New York Times*, June 1, 1980.

Wilentz, Gay. "A Laying on of Hands: African American Healing Strategies in Toni Cade Bambara's *The Salt Eaters*. In *Healing Narratives: Women Writers Curing Cultural Dis-ease*. New Brunswick: Rutgers University Press, 2000.

Williams, Vernon J. *Rethinking Race: Franz Boas and His Contemporaries.* Lexington: The University Press of Kentucky, 1996.

Willis, Susan. "Problematizing the Individual: Toni Cade Bambara's Stories for the Revolution." In *Specifying: Black Women Writing the American Experience.* Madison: University of Wisconsin Press, 1987.

Index

Please note: page numbers in *italics* followed by a *p* indicate photographs. Works are by Bambara unless otherwise noted.

Adero, Malaika, 159, 199, 200

African Diaspora, xviii, xx, 67, 98, 112, 129, 134, 152, 176, 182, 189

African Folk Medicinal Practices and Beliefs of the Bambara and Other Peoples (Imperato), 102–3

Ain't Suppose to Die a Natural Death (film), 130

Airing Dirty Laundry (Reed, essay on Toni Cade Bambara in), 113–14, 125

Akomfrah, John, xx, 171, 189

Alderson Prison, 79; Bambara Award at, 62; writing workshops at, 62

Alexander, Lillian, 5

Algarin, Miguel, 57

Allison, Dorothy, 196–98

All Us Come Cross the Water (Clifton), 71

"The American Adolescent Apprentice Novel" (master's thesis), 104

American Book Award: *Beloved* (Morrison), 137; *The Salt Eaters* (Bambara), xix

And Then We Heard the Thunder (Killens), 205–8

Angelou, Maya, 108, 173

Anthologies: *Bitches and Sad Women*, 91, *See also* Works by Toni Cade Bambara

Anti-apartheid campaigns, 115; Advisory Board of Sisters in Support of Sisters in South Africa (SISA), 149; international activists and cultural workers, 149

Antologia de cuentosnorteamericanos (Rodriguez Feo, ed.), 158

"The Apprentice" (short story), 65

Ashes and Embers (Gerima), 176

Atlanta, xviii; academic community, 68–69; Bambara's promotion of as black arts capital of the South, 109, 135–36; black cultural background of (1970s), 58–59; historically black colleges, 57, 59; Jubilee Bronze Award (Bambara awarded), 99–100; missing and murdered in, 143; Neighborhood Arts Center (NAC), 62–63, *See also* Reverse migration South (move to Atlanta in the mid-70s); *Those Bones Are Not My Child* (Bambara)

Atlanta University, 61, 72–73, 79, 85, 150

"At the Still Center of a Dream" (Anne Tyler review of *The Salt Eaters*), 116

Audre Lorde panel speech on spirituality and healing (Black Arts Festival), *186p*

Baldwin, James, 9, 40, 47, 72, 138, 149, 151; death of, 173
Ballard, Allen B., 42–43
Bambara, Toni Cade: acknowledgements for her work, 201; background information/summary of, xvii–xxii; birth of (Miltona Mirken Cade, March 25, 1939), 5; Black Belt at the Federation of Southern Cooperatives Meeting (Eppes, AL), 122p, 124; "Black Women Walk on Water Achievement Awards" (Morrison and Bambara), 181–82; cancer diagnosis (November 1993), 190; with cousin Carole Brown, 20p; curriculum vitae, 69; death of (age 56, December 9, 1995), xx, 185, 199–200; documentaries and, xx; dream work/analysis/journaling, 97; on her writing, 77, 92; honorary doctorates from SUNY Albany and Denison University in Ohio, 178; illness/treatment, 185, 189, 190, 192–93, 197; letters to mother Helen, 104–5, 108, 153–54; letter to daughter Karma, 153; marriage and divorce to Anthony Batten, 39–40; memorials for, 199–200; multi-artistic interests/identities, 84, 139; 1990–1995 years, 185–201; origin of name change to Bambara (1970), 35–36, 47; places lived, xviii; pregnant with daughter Karma, 35, 48p; private life, 175; renaming herself Toni, 5; roles of, xviii; separation from father Walter Cade and, 21–22; short stories submitted for the Queen's College John Golden Award for fiction (1959), 37; speaking at the National Black Arts Festival, 144p; Spelman College students honoring her 50th birthday, 186p; testimonies to her influence, xxi–xxii, See also Film; Works by Toni Cade Bambara
Bambara people of Mali, 47, 182; African Folk Medicinal Practices and Beliefs of the Bambara and Other Peoples (Imperato), 102–3
Baraka, Amiri, xx, 138, 157, 173, 199; The Dutchman (play), 179
Baraka, Amiri and Larry Neal, eds., Black Fire, 42–43
Batten, Anthony (husband), 39, 173
Bearden, Romare, 49, 72, 84
Bell, Roseann P., 71
Bellamy, Faye, 122p; "Being Me Is a Gas" (poem), 71
Beloved (Morrison) winner of the American Book Award and the Pulitzer Prize, 121–22, 137, 175
Bibbs, Lavada, 110
Billops, Camille, 192
Bitches and Sad Women (feminist anthology), 91
Black Arts Movement, xvii–xviii, 42–43, 44, 46, 51, 57, 62, 99, 135–36
The Black Book (Morrison), 60
Black Enterprise (Petry, ed.), 110
Black Expression (Gayle, ed.), 44
Black Fire (Baraka and Neal, eds.), 42–43
The Black Heritage Corporation, 135
Black Panther Party, 89
Black Power Movement, 43, 57
Black Scholar Press, 157–58
"Black Theater" (essay), 44
Blackwell, Gloria, 103
The Black Woman (anthology, Bambara ed.), xix, 35, 45–47, 50, 60, 66, 158, 182, 195, 201; contributors to, 45–46; distribution in Cuba, 52; influence on filmmakers, 130; revolutionary call for liberation, 78
The Black World, 90, 108
Black World View, "Viet Nam and Black Struggle: Two Revolutions in the Making," 85
The Bluest Eye (Morrison), 49, 107, 121, 174
Boggs, Grace, 66–67
The Bombing of Osage Avenue (documentary narrated by Bambara), xx, 169–71, 180, 182

Bond, Julian, 106
"Book Concert" (Lewis), 50
"Books and Other Acts: Contemporary
    Women Writers and Social
    Change" Dartmouth conference,
    196–97
Bowser, Pearl, 190
Brooks, Gwendolyn, 110, 151, 158;
    Report From Part One, 52, 135
Brown, Carole (cousin), *20p*, 28, 31;
    contributor to *The Black Woman*,
    46; letters to, 117, 154–55
Brown, H. Rap, 81
Brown, Marie, 71
Brown v. Board of Education, 24–25, 35
Brown, Wesley, xx, 199
Burford, Walter, 69–70
Byrd, Rudolph, 173

Cade, Helen Brent Henderson (mother),
    61; birth of, 2; contributor to *The
    Black Woman*, 46; creative influence
    of, 16, 31; description of by Jenny
    Moore, 23; dissolution of marriage
    to Walter Cade, 13–16; education,
    2–4; influence on Bambara's short
    stories, 24; intolerance of racism,
    11–12, 23; involvement in Grace
    Episcopal Van Vorst, 24; "just
    do it" conversations, 64; marriage
    to Walter Cade, 4; militancy
    instilled in children by, 25; move to
    Atlanta, 107–8; music and, 8; as
    orphan, 2; son Walter Cade III on
    mother's resiliency, 14; as young
    suffragette, 3
Cade, Miltona Mirken (renamed herself
    Toni): birth of (March 25, 1939), 5,
    See also Bambara, Toni Cade; Works
    of Toni Cade Bambara
Cade, Selika (grandmother), 4
Cade, Walter (father): background,
    4; employment, 4–7; family
    problems and dissolution of
    marriage to Helen Cade, 13–16;
    marriage to Helen Brent Henderson,
    4; separation from Bambara,
    21–22
Cade, Walter (grandfather), 4

Cade III, Walter (brother), 5, 8, 44; on
    family problems, 13–14; police
    racism against in Jersey City, 22–23;
    relationship with, 6; visual artist
    and musician, 31
Callaloo, 134, 136
Carew, Jan, 57, 171
Carleton College, Writer in Residence,
    173–74
*Cecil B. Moore: Master Tactician of Direct
    Action* (film), 169
Charles, Pepsi, 57
Chevigny, Bell Gale, 37, 40–41, 50, 187–88
"The Children Who Got Cheated"
    (essay), 45, 135
Childress, Alice, 48–49, 178
Chisholm, Cheryl, 48–49, 63–64, 66,
    161–62, 188, 199
"Christmas Eve At Johnson's Drugs N
    Goods" (short story), 21–22
Cisse, Souleman, *Yeelen* (film),
    182
City College New York: faculty member
    at, 42; Master's Degree in Modern
    American Literature at (NY), 42;
    militant student protests at, 45; new
    "Harlem University" curriculum
    suggestions, 43; writers at, 42
Clark College, Atlanta, 61, 64, 73,
    100, 103, 150; "Fifth Annual
    Writer's Workshop/Conference"
    (Ford Foundation and the English
    Department at Clark College), 60;
    mother's attendance, 3; presentation
    of the Vietnam trip to the School of
    Social Work, 85; promised faculty
    appointment at, 68
Clarke, John Henrik, 1, 86
Cleage, Pearl, 68, 107, 110, 150, 180
Clifton, Lucille: *All Us Come Cross the
    Water*, 71; "Magic Mama," 126
Come As You Are (film project), 172
Cooper, Angelle, 103
Cortez, Jayne, 157
Costain, Pam, 79, *80p*
Cotillion (Killens), 208
Cotton, Dorothy, 78
Cousins. *See* Brown, Carole (cousin);
    Morton, Kenneth (cousin)

Cuba: "The Apprentice" and, 65; "The Lesson" and, 84
Cuban filmmakers, 159
Cuban travels, 52–53, 86, 157–59, 179–80
Cullen, Countee, 7, 12
Cultural workers, 58, 183, 201; anti-apartheid campaigns and, 149; defining, xviii
Curran, Mary Doyle, 36–37, 40; *The Parish and the Hill*, 37

Dandicat, Edwidge, 201
Dartmouth "Books and Other Acts: Contemporary Women Writers and Social Change" conference, 196–97
Dash, Julie, 130
"Daughters of the Dust" (film by Dash), 129, 176–77, 188
Daves, Joan (agent), 132–33
Davis, Angela, 123, 149, 174, 179–80
Davis, Ossie, 87, 127, 136
Davis, Thulani, xx, 199
Day, Dorothy, *The Christian Worker* (ed.), 24
Debussy, Claude, 8
Decroux, Etienne, 41
Deep Sightings and Rescue Missions (short stories), xx, 169
Dee, Ruby, 87, 89–90, 136; in one-woman show of "Medley" (Bambara), 136–37
Dent, Tom, 110
"The Desert Encroaching" (Onwueme), 178
De Veaux, Alexis, 157
Diawara, Manthia, 176, 182, 195, 199
Dobbs-Janzon, Mattiwilda, 59
Documentaries: Bambara and, xx, 182–83, 201, *See also* Film
Dodson, Howard, 63, 67, 151
Dodson, Jualynne, 63, 67, 72–73, 104
Dooley, Ebon, 85, 103
Douglass, Jan, 51–52, 57, 59, 61, 67, 72, 86, 101–2, 114, 151
Drama of Nommo (Harrison), 130
Dream analysis groups, 100–101, 115

Dream theme, in *The Salt Eaters*, 110–11, 115–16
Dream work/analysis/journaling, 97, 148
Du Bois, W.E.B., 7
Duke University Division of Afro-American Studies Visiting Professor, "Introduction to Third World Literature" course, 69–70
The Dutchman (Baraka), 179

Early years (Harlem), 1–18; Bernice Food Stores Baby Contest, 6; birth of Bambara (Miltona Mirken Cade, March 25, 1939), 5; "extended" family and, 9; mother's intolerance of racism, 11–12; mother's records of Bambara, 5–6; move to 151st Street, 8–9; move to Dunbar Co-Op apartments, 7–8; problems at home and the dissolution of parents' marriage, 13–16; relationship with brother, 6; relationship with father, 6–7; schooling, 10–13, *See also* Harlem
Edelman, Marian Wright, 100
Education: "The American Adolescent Apprentice Novel" (master's thesis), 104; early schooling, 10–13; high school, 28–31; honorary doctorates, 178; junior high school, 25–26; Master's Degree in Modern American Literature at City College New York, 42; Queens College attendance, 31, 35–40; State University of New York, Buffalo— pursuing doctorate in American Studies at, 177–78
"The Education of a Storyteller" (short story), 24
Edwards, Lena, 21
Edwards, Mel, 157
Eisen, Arlene, 78–79, 84; *Women of Viet Nam*, 78
Ellis, Thomas Sayers, 187
Ellison, Ralph, 40, 47, 196–97
Embryo (Troupe), 50
Essays: *Airing Dirty Laundry* (Reed), 113–14; on Pan-Africanism

(Long), 71, *See also* Works by Toni Cade Bambara

Etienne Decroux School of Mime (Manhattan), 41

Evans, Mari, 149, 151, 157

Fairy tales, rewriting, 60, 68, 148; *See also Tales and Stories for Black Folks*

Film: *100 Years of Black Film* (conference sponsored by the National Museum of American History), 195; *Ain't Suppose to Die a Natural Death*, 130; Bambara and, xx, 38–39, 100, 123, 129–30, 133–34, 152–53, 182–83, 189–91, 194; *Birth of a Nation*, 190; Birth of Black Cinema Project (SUNY Albany), 176; black filmmakers, 129–30; *The Bombing of Osage Avenue* (documentary narrated by Bambara), xx, 169–71, 180, 182; Chisholm and, 64; Cuban films, 179–80; "Daughters of the Dust" (film by Dash), 129, 176–77, 188; Image Weavers (women of color filmmakers), 195; *Midnight Ramble: The Story of the Black Film Industry* (documentary), 190; Nora Zeale Hurston screenwriting project and end of, 138–39; *The Salt Eaters* and, 129–32; Scribe Video Center (Philadelphia), xx, 169, 171–72, 182, 192, 194, 195, 201; *Seven Songs for Malcolm X* (film narrated by Bambara), xx, 171, 189; *Silence Broken* (Shahidah-Simmons), 195; silent film, 190; Third World cinema movement, 157; Washington DC film conference, 194–95; *Yeelen* (Cisse), 182

First World (Hoyt, ed.), 108–9, 114, 136, 150–51

"For Colored Girls—and White Girls Too" (review by Bambara), 91

For Colored Girls Who Have Considered Suicide/When the Rainbow Is Enuf (Shange), 91, 92, 130

Franklin, Shirley, 87

Freedomways magazine, 86–87, 89

"From Inside the First World" (Moraga in *A Xicana Codex of Changing Consciousness*), xx

Frye, Charles, 135

Fuller, Hoyt, 72, 108–10, 114; death of, 150–51, 152

Futterman, Donna, *80p*

Gayle, Addison, 42, 46, 60, 70–71, 110

Gayle, Addison, ed., *Black Expression*, 44

The Georgia Review "Roots in Georgia" symposium introduction speech of John Oliver Killens by Bambara, 205–8

Georgia Writers Hall of Fame, Bambara inductee, xxi

"Geraldine Moore the Poet" (short story), 44

Gerima, Haile, 64; Ashes and Embers (film), 176

Giovanni, Nikki, xvii, 57, 110, 130

"A Girl's Story" (short story), 66, 135

Glascoe, Myrtle, *122p*

Global disappearances: Bambara's activism concerning, 144–45, *See also Those Bones Are Not My Child*

Goddess Sightings (work-in-progress), 196

"Going Critical" (short story), 190–91

Goldberg, Art, 36, 42

"The Golden Bandit" (short story), 68

Goldoni, Carlo, 40

Gonzalez, Leila, 134

Gopaul, Lina, xx, 189

Gorilla, My Love (short stories), xix, 35, 41, 49–50, 60, 62, 77, 82, 90, 130, 191

Gossett, Hattie, 46, 49, 52, 57, 132

Grandfathers. *See* Henderson, James (grandfather); Cade, Walter (grandfather)

Grandmothers. *See* Henderson, Annie Austin (grandmother); Cade, Selika (grandmother)

Graves, Earl, 110

Great grandmother. *See* Williams, Maggie Cooper (great grandmother)

Great kitchen tradition of storytelling, 60

The Great MacDaddy (Harrison, play), 130

Great Migration to northern cities, 2

Greenlee, Sam, *The Spook Who Sat by the Door*, 60

Grosvenor, Verta Mae, 46, 157, 173; *Vibration Cooking*, 43

Guy-Sheftall, Beverly, 101, 105–6, 107, 180; interview of Bambara, 71–72

Guy-Sheftall, Beverly and Roseann P. Bell, "Images of Black Women," 71

Guy-Sheftall, Beverly, Roseann P. Bell and Bettye J. Parker, Sturdy Black Bridges: Visions of Black Women in Literature, 71

"Hammer Man" (short story), 44, 193

Hampton, Fred, 89

Harden, Lakota, 174–75

Harding, Rose Marie, 61, 63

Harding, Vincent, 46, 61, 63, 67

Harlem, xviii; black organizations in, 1; political and cultural icons, 1; protests in the 1930s, 5; Work Projects Administration (WPA) Writers Project Harlemites' stories, 4, *See also* Early years (Harlem)

Harlem Renaissance (1920s), 5, 7

Harlem's influence on Bambara's short stories, 1

Harlem's Speakers Corner, 31

Harlem Welfare Center, employment at, 40

Harlem Writer's Guild, 152, 207

Harper, Charlyn, 135

Harris, Estella (later, Akua Kamau-Harris), 62–63, 71, 79, 103, 178

Harrison, Paul Carter: *Drama of Nommo* (play), 130; *The Great MacDaddy* (play), 130; letter to Bambara on

translating *The Salt Eaters* into film, 130–32

Hatch, John, 192

Hatch-Billops series on artists, 192

Healing theme, in *The Salt Eaters*, 97–98, 110–16

"The Health and Sexuality of Women" (workshop), 124

"Hearing James Brown" (Long), 71

Henderson, Annie Austin (grandmother), 2

Henderson, James (grandfather), 2

Henderson, Mae, 127

High school: achievements in, 31; John Adams High School (Ozone Park, Queens), 28–31

Historically black colleges, 57, 59; art collections at, 78; first Women's Studies program at (Spelman), 71

Hobson, Charles, 63–64

Holland, Endesha, 178

Holmes, Linda Janet (biographer), first meeting Toni Cade Bambara, xv

Honorary doctorates, SUNY Albany and Denison University in Ohio, 178

Horowitz, Berny, 40

Howard University, 199; daughter Karma attending, 178

"How to Think Black: A Symposium in Toni Cade Bambara's *The Salt Eaters*" (Frye), 135

Hudson, Corrine, 73

Hughes, Langston, 1, 60, 157; "Good Morning, Revolution," 69

Hunter, Kristen, 114

Hurston, Zora Neale, xvii, 73, 108, 123; *I Love Myself When I Am Laughing* (Walker, ed.), 122; *The Sanctified Church* (Bambara's introduction to), 139; screen writing project, 133, 138–39, 143; *Their Eyes Were Watching God*, 174

"I AM BECAUSE WE ARE" mural (Tuskegee University) unveiling, 128

If Blessing Comes. See Those Bones Are Not My Child

I Love Myself When I Am Laughing (Hurston), 122
"Images of Black Women in Literature and Film" (Bambara's course at Spelman), 102–3, 105–6
Image Weavers (women of color filmmakers), 195
Imperato, Pascal James, *African Folk Medicinal Practices and Beliefs of the Bambara and Other Peoples*, 102–3
Independent black schools, 66
In Love and Trouble: Stories of Black Women (Walker), 122
Institute for Protection of Mothers (Vietnam), 82
Institute of the Black World (IBW), 46, 61, 63, 67, 80–81, 85
International Women's Playwright Conference (SUNY), 178
"Introduction to Third World Literature" course taught at Duke University, 69–70

Jackson, Irene Dobbs, 59
Jackson, Jr. Maynard, 59, 73, 99, 103, 107
Jefferson, Margo, 90
Jennings, William, 84, 136–37
John Adams High School (Ozone Park, Queens) attendance, 28–31
Johnson, James Weldon, 12
Johnson, Mildred, 12
"The Johnson Girls" (short story), 46, 50, 199
Jomandi Productions, staging of "Witchbird" short story, 150
Jones, Claudia, 1
Jordan, June, xvii, 139, 147, 151
Jordon, Millicent Dobbs, 100
Joseph, Gloria I., 148–49, 157–58
Jubilee Bronze Award (Bambara awarded), 99–100
Junior high school years, 25–26

Keyishian, Harry, 45
Kidd, David, 103
Killens, John Oliver, 60; *And Then We Heard the Thunder* (Killens), 205–8; *Cotillion*, 208; *Pushkin,*

The Great Black Russian, 152, 208; "Roots in Georgia"/"Literary Roots" symposium introduction speech of John Oliver Killens by Bambara, 205–8; *Youngblood,* 152, 208
King, Woody, 149
Kinney, Esi, 151
"Kres Mersky at the Codfish Ball" (one-woman show of Bambara short story), 91

Lafayette, Bernard, 78
Larsen, Nella, xvii
The Last Days of Louisiana Red, 113
Lee, Spike, 85
Leonard, John, review of *The Salt Eaters* in the *New York Times* book review, 98–99
"The Lesson" (short story), 84, 199
Levine, George, 50–51
Lewis, Gene (father of daughter Karma), 46, 50, 51–52
Lewis, Ida, 149
"Little Red Riding Hood" (Bambara revised), 148
Livingston College campus at Rutgers University: Bambara's Black Literature class, xvii; cluster of Third World writers, faculty, and administrators at, 57–58; creative teaching approaches at, 50–51; resignation of tenured professorship, 59; Speaker of the Faculty Chamber, 52; Third World and Black Studies courses cutbacks, 57
Lomax, Michael, 99, 107
Long, Richard A., 69, 72, 79, 110, 151; essay on Pan-Africanism, 71; "Hearing James Brown" (poem), 71
"The Long Night" (short story), 89
Lorde, Audre, 46, 149, 157
Lovelace, Alice, 84–85
Lower Jersey City family relocation, xviii, 19–26; black population and businesses in Jersey City, 21; compared to Harlem, 21; description of neighborhood, 19–21; Grace Episcopal Van Vorst

and, 23–24; junior high years,
   25–26
Lucia (Cuban film), 52, 158
Lynch, Acklyn, 149

Madhabuti, Haki, 110, 151
Maggie Magaba Trust (women's
   anti-apartheid self-help group),
   149
"Maggie of the Green Bottles" (short
   story), 14–15
"Magic Mama" (Clifton), 126
Malcolm X: murder of, 43; Pan-African
   spirit of, 189
"Mama Load" (short story), 125–27
Marceau, Marcel, 41
Marshall, Paule, xvii, 46, 122, 137
Masekela, Barbara, 57
Masekela, Hugh, 137
"Massacre of the Innocents" (essay on
   Those Bones Are Not My Child by
   Morrison), 200
Massiah, Louis, 169, 180, 190, 192, 199
Maynard, Valerie, 61
McDonald, Mary, 59, 60
Medgar Evers College, Black Storyteller's
   Conference, xxi, 177
"Medley" (short story), 136–37, 199
Memorials, for Bambara, 199–200
Meridian (Walker), 122
Mersky, Kres, 90–91
Micheaux, Oscar, 129
Middle Passage, xxi, 134
*Midnight Ramble: The Story of the Black
   Film Industry* (documentary), 190
Miller, E. Ethelbert, 102
Mime studies, 40–41
Mirken, Milton, Bambara's namesake, 5
"Mississippi Ham Rider" (short story),
   38–39
Moore, Honor, 23, 26
Moore, Jennie, 23–24, 26; *The People on
   Second Street*, 23
Moore, Paul, 23–24, 26–27, 78
Moraga, Cherríe L., 196; "From Inside
   the First World" (in *A Xicana Codex
   of Changing Consciousness*), xx
Morejon, Nancy, 158–59
"*Mujer Negra*" (poems), 158

Morrison, Toni, xvii, xviii, 121–23,
   130, 137, 173, 199; on Bambara's
   genius, 200–201; *Beloved* winner of
   the American Book Award and the
   Pulitzer Prize, 121–22, 137, 175;
   The Black Book, 60; "Black Women
   Walk on Water Achievement
   Awards" (Morrison and Bambara),
   181–82; *The Bluest Eye*, 49, 107,
   121, 174; commencement speaker
   at Spelman College, 106–7; editor
   of *Deep Sightings and Rescue
   Missions* (Bambara), xx; editor
   of *Gorilla, My Love* (Bambara),
   49; editor of *Those Bones are Not
   My Child* (Bambara), xx, 200;
   as editor on Bambara's writing,
   49–50, 132–33; on first novel
   The Salt Eaters (Bambara), 138;
   friendship with Bambara, 175–76;
   named distinguished writer by
   the American Academy of Arts
   and Letters, 106; posthumously
   published *Those Bones Are Not My
   Child* (Bambara), 181; Princeton
   University Atelier workshop
   program, xxii; *Song of Solomon*,
   106–7, 121; *Sula*, 107, 121; *Tar
   Baby* screenplay (screenplay by
   Bambara), 143, 155–56
Morton, Kenneth (cousin), 8, 15, 21, 31
Mother. *See* Cade Henderson, Helen
   Brent (mother)
MOVE, 169
"*Mujernegra*" (Morejon), 158
Murray, Albert, 60
Myers, Kim, 23–24
Myers, Linda James, 135
"My Man Bovanne" (Mersky's stage
   performance of Bambara short
   story), 91
"My Man Bovanne" (short story), 91,
   199

NAACP, 1, 12, 21
National Black Arts Festival, Bambara
   speaking at, *144p*
National Book Critics Circle Award, *Song
   of Solomon* (Morrison), 107, 121

National Endowment for the Arts,
    Hatch-Billops series on artists, 192
National Endowment for the Arts
    grant, 154
National Endowment for the
    Humanities, 79
Native Son (Wright), 107
Neal, Larry, 42, 46
Negro Digest (Hoyt, ed.), 44, 108, 126,
    150
Negroes with Guns (William), 82
Neighborhood Arts Center (Atlanta),
    62–63, 78, 99, 110, 136, 137, 146;
    co-workers, 84–85; first writer-in-
    residence (Bambara), 84; reading
    and book signing of *The
    Salt Eaters*, 127; resignation from,
    87
Neo-Black Arts Movement in the South,
    135–36
New Orleans Afri Kan Film and Arts
    Festival, Toni Cade Bambara Award
    for Cultural Leadership, xxi
New York Council of the Arts, Hatch-
    Billops series on artists, 192
New York Times, 90; Bambara's review
    Report From Part One (Brooks),
    135; on black exceptional writers
    (Bambara, Morrison, Walker, and
    Marshall), 122
Novels. *See* Works by Toni Cade
    Bambara

100 Years of Black Film (conference
    sponsored by the National Museum
    of American History), 195
Oakland, CA, memorial for Bambara,
    200
Obayani, Kambon, 133–34
O'Neal, Sondra, 135, 151
"On the Issue of Roles" (Bambara essay
    in *The Black Woman*), 46
Onwueme, Tess, 178–79; "The Desert
    Encroaching", 178
"The Organizer's Wife" (short story),
    86–89, 89
"Our Language Patterns, and What, If
    Anything, To Do About Them?"
    (flyer), 103

Paley, Grace, 90
Pan-Africanism essay (Long), 71
Pan-African movement, 151
Pan-African spirit, of Malcolm, X,
    189
Pan-religiosity, xxii
Papp, Joseph, 137
The Parish and the Hill (Curran), 37
Parker, Bettye J., 71
The People on Second Street (J. Moore),
    23
Petry, Phil, 110
Philadelphia, xviii, xx; *The Bombing
    of Osage Avenue* (documentary
    narrated by Bambara), xx, 169–71,
    180, 182; move to/work in, 167–88;
    preparing to leave Atlanta for
    Philadelphia, 159–62; Scribe Video
    Center, xx, 169, 171–72, 182, 192,
    194, 195, 201, *See also* Film
Poet Laureate (2012) Natasha
    Tretheway, 187
Poets: beat poets, 37; black women, xvii
Poets and Writers Series, Simpson
    College, 185
Poindexter, Jane, 168, 199
Potlikker, 103
Powell, Jr., Adam Clayton, 5
Pushkin, The Great Black Russian
    (Killens), 152, 208

Queens College attendance, 31,
    35–40; age at acceptance (16), 36;
    employment after, 40; multiple arts
    forms involved in, 36; social circle
    at, 36; writing skill recognition at,
    36
Queens, New York family relocation, xviii,
    26–31; attendance at John Adams
    High School in Ozone Park, 28–31;
    music giants in Queens, 28

Randall, Dudley, 151
Randolph, Phillip, 7
Rawls, Melanie, 114
"Raymond's Run" (short story), 9–10,
    60, 126, 199
Reagan, Bernice, 123
Redbook, 45, 67, 90, 125–27

Reed, Ishmael, 46, 136, 137, 199; *Airing Dirty Laundry* (Essay on Bambara in), 113–14, 125
Report From Part One (Brooks), 52, 135
Reverse migration South (move to Atlanta in the mid-70s), 57–76, 91–92; academic roadblocks, 68, 91; Atlanta University and, 72–73; beginning the novel *The Salt Eaters*, 97–99; Beverly Guy-Sheftall's interview of Bambara, 71–72; daughter Karma's attendance at Martin Luther King School, 67; guest editor of *Southern Black Utterances Today* (*Southern Exposure*), 70–71; letters to daughter Karma, 61; new home/neighborhood, 61–63; pondering/preparing for move, 59–62; preparing to leave Atlanta for Philadelphia, 159–62; promoting alternative educational institutions, 66–68; reasons for move, 57–59; promised Clark College faculty appointment, 68; revitalizing burned out activists/community organization, 64–66
Rich, Adrienne, 149; review of *The Salt Eaters*, 116
Riddle, John, 137
Robbins, Trina, 29–30; letter to, 193–94
Robeson, Paul, 1, 7
Robinson, Emile Birchett, 25
Rodriguez Feo, José, 158
"Role Alternatives for Black Women: Where to From Here in the Black Freedom Struggle" (keynote address by Bambara), 103–4
"Roots in Georgia"/"Literary Roots" symposium introduction speech of John Oliver Killens by Bambara, 205–8
Ross, Edyth, 72
Ross, Herbert, 69, 72, *168p*
Ross, Loretta, 149
Ross, Susan, 61, 72, 167–68, 180
Ross, Suzanne, 52
Rushing, Andrea Benton, 29, 151–52, 160–61

Russell, Charles, 46
Rutgers University Livingston, Assistant Professor at, 69, *See also* Livingston College campus at Rutgers University

Salaam, Kalamu ya, 133, 151
The Salt Eaters (novel), xix–xx, 49, 124, 146, 177, 185, 191, 198, 200–201; Adrienne Rich's review, 116; "At the Still Center of A Dream" (review in *Washington Post* by Anne Tyler), 116; color in, 112; critical attention, 121; dance and music in, 112–13; dream themes, 110–11, 115–16; drop-off in sales, 138; Eleanor Traylor's review, 115; film possibilities, 129–32; healing theme, 97–98, 110–16; "How to Think Black: A Symposium in Toni Cade Bambara's *The Salt Eaters*" (Frye), 135; Ishmael Reed's criticism of, 113–14; John Edgar Wideman's review of, 115–16; John Leonard's *New York Times* book review, 98–99; New and Noteworthy Paperbacks (*New York Times*), 137; process of writing, 111; promotion of, 127–28; published (1980), 121; Seven Sisters in, 98, 114, 115–16, 125, 198; synopsis/themes of, 97–98, 111–17
Sanchez, Sonia, xvii, 57, 62, 110, 136, 151, 179, 181, 200; *We Be Word Sorcerers*, 114–15
The Sanctified Church (Hurston, Bambara's introduction to), 139
Sankofa ("go back and fetch it" concept), 198
The Sankofa Projects, xxi
Saran, Ama, 67, 71
Schomburg Research Center in Black Culture (NY), memorial for Bambara, 200
Scribe Video Center (Philadelphia), xx, 169, 171–72, 182, 192, 194, 195, 201

The Sea Birds Are Still Alive
(short stories), xix, 77–79; abuse
of women in, 82; liberation
struggles in, 87–88; reviews of,
89–91; Tran Van Dinh on, 101;
Vietnam trip and, 86
"The Sea Birds Are Still Alive" (short
story), 87–88
SEEK (Search for Education,
Empowerment, and Knowledge
(City College NY), 42, 50
Sellers, Lenore, 12–13
Sembene, Ousmane, 176
Seven Sisters, xviii, 98, 114, 115–16,
125, 198, *See also The Salt Eaters*
Seven Songs for Malcolm X (film narrated
by Bambara), xx, 171, 189
Shabazz, Betty, 149
Shade, Stella, 123–24
Shahidah-Simmons, Aishah, 194–95
Shakur, Assata, 179
Shange, Ntzoke, *For Colored Girls
Who Have Considered Suicide/When
the Rainbow is Enuf*, 91, 92,
130
Short stories. *See* Works by Toni Cade
Bambara
Silence Broken (Shahidah-Simmons),
195
Sisters in Support of Sisters in South
Africa (SISA), 149, 150
Slave ship *Henrietta Marie*, 190
Smith, Barbara, 42
Smith, Karma (daughter): attending
Howard University, 178; attending
Martin Luther King School
(Atlanta), 67; Bambara pregnant
with, 35, *48p*; birth of to Bambara
and Gene Lewis (April 1, 1970),
46; letters from Bambara, 61,
153; move to Atlanta and, 58;
participating in adult activities,
68; trip with Bambara to St. Croix,
148–49
Smith, Tracy K., 187
Solas, Huberto, 52
Song of Solomon (Morrison), 106–7;
National Book Critics Circle Award,
107, 121

Southern Black Utterances Today guest
editor with Leah Wise (*Southern
Exposure*), 70–71, 74, 191
Southern black women, xix–xx
Southern black writing, definition of by
Bambara and Wise, 70
Southern Coalition of African American
Writers (SCAAW, Atlanta), 99,
109–10, 114, 135, *144p*
Southern Rural Women's Network,
122p, 124–25
Spelman, A.B., 57
Spelman College, Atlanta, 61, 71;
Bambara and, 100–107; Bambara
suggested for honorary degree,
107; "The Black Aesthetic and
the Writer" symposium, 147;
Coordinating Council of Literary
Magazines conference at, 109; end
of teaching at, 105; "Images of Black
Woman in Literature and Film"
course (Bambara), 102–3, 105–6;
jazz program, 136, 137; students
honoring Bambara's 50th
birthday, *186p*
Spencer, Taronda, 106
Spicer, Osker, 114
The Spook Who Sat by the Door
(Greenlee), 60
Stevens, Nelson, 127, 128–29
Stewart, Donald, 100–102, 107
Stone, Donald, 106, 114
"Story" (short story), 134–35
"Storytellers Conference" talk (Medgar
Evers College), xxi
Student Workers Alliance (Laos), 83
*Sturdy Black Bridges: Visions of Black
Women in Literature* (Guy-Sheftall,
Bell, and Parker, eds.), 71
Sula (Morrison), 107, 121
Sundiata, Sekou, 61
SUNY Albany, 175–76; honorary
doctorate, 178
SUNY Buffalo, pursuing doctorate in
American Studies at, 177–78
"The Survivor" (short story), 41,
160
Swans, Sandra L., 87
"Sweet Town" (short story), 38

Tales and Stories for Black Folks
(Bambara, ed.), xix, 35, 47–49,
59–60, 68
Tar Baby screenplay (screenplay by
Bambara), 143, 155–56
Tate, Claudia, interview with Bambara
about truth-telling, 117
Taylor, Clyde, 190, 195, 199
Theater, 36; "Black Theater" (Bambara)
essay on, 44; studies of in Europe,
41
Their Eyes Were Watching God
(Hurston), 174
"There'll Come a Day" (poem), 30
The Third Life of Grange Copeland
(Walker), 122
Third World cinema movement, 157
*This Little Light of Mine: A Dramatization
of the Life of Fannie Lou Hamer*
(Young, one-woman show), 125
Thomas, Joyce Carol, 200
Those Bones Are Not My Child (Bambara,
Morrison, ed. previously *If
Blessing Comes*), xx, 197; delay
in publishing, 181; development
into a novel, 145; epilogue, 162;
"Massacre of the Innocents" (essay
on by Morrison), 200; murders
of black people in Atlanta and,
143–51; posthumously, 181;
prologue, 143–44; published, 200;
reason for book, 144–45; story syn-
opsis, 146–47; writing block and,
195–96
Toni Cade Bambara Award for Cultural
Leadership (New Orleans Afri Kan
Film and Arts Festival), xxi
Torture, of Vietnamese women, 82–83, 89
Tran Thanh Tuyen, 81
Travels: Brazil vacation, 133–34;
Cuba, 52–53, 157–59, 179–80;
European, 40–42; international
travel goals, 86; Laos, 83; London,
189; promoting *The Salt Eaters*,
127; Sicily, 188; St. Croix, 148–49;
Vietnam, 78–86, *80p, See also*
Vietnam Mission on Reconciliation
Trescott, Jacqueline (*The Washington
Post*) interview with Bambara,
100–101

Tretheway, Natasha, U.S. Poet Laureate
(2012), 187
Troupe, Quincy, *Embryo*, 50
"True Story of Chicken Licken" (short
story), 60
Tubman, Harriet, 89, 129, 133
Turner, James, 151
Tyler, Anne, review of *The Salt
Eaters*, 116

University of Alabama in Tuscaloosa
conferences, 123–24
University of Ibadan in Nigeria
writer-in-residence (offer to
Bambara), 151–52
University of Medicine and Dentistry
of New Jersey (UMDNJ), birth
room opening and speech,
127–28
"Unlearning Racism" workshop,
174–75
"Using Astrology as a Tool for Self-
Understanding" (workshop),
110
"Using Dreams to Unlock and Unblock
the Creative Self" (workshop),
110

Valerio, Anthony, 188–89
Van Dinh, Tran, 101
Vibration Cooking (Grosvenor), 43
"Viet Nam and Black Struggle: Two
Revolutions in the Making"
(in *Black World View*), 85
Vietnam Mission on Reconciliation:
arrival, 81; Bambara's notes on trip,
81–83, 85–86; counterrevolutionary
interrogation and torture of
Vietnamese women, 82–83;
delegation, 79, *80p*; Hanoi's
Reunification (Thong Nhat) Park,
80p; Laos stopover on return
trip, 83; medicinal supplies and
antiwar materials, 80–81; meetings
with Vietnamese women, 82;
negotiations with customs officials,
81; parallels in the struggles of
blacks in U.S. with Vietnamese, 86,
89; presentation of trip at Clark
College, 85

Vietnam Women's Union, 78, 79, *80p*, 81, 83, 85
Vietnam Workers' Party, 83
Voigt, Daisy, 46
Volpe, Edmond, 42

Walke, Chadra Pittman, xxi
Walker, Alice, xvii, 46, 60, 121–23; editor of *I Love Myself When I Am Laughing* (Hurston), 122; *In Love and Trouble: Stories of Black Women*, 122; *Meridian*, 122; *The Third Life of Grange Copeland*, 122
Walker, C.J., 7
Walker, Geraldine, 22
Walker, Mildred Pitts, 157
Walker, Monica, 123
"Wall of Respect" (street mural), 108, 128
"The War of the Wall" (short story), 129
Washington, Mary Helen, 147, 187
Waters, Sylvia, 28
Weathermen/Underground, 78, 83
Webb, Barbara, 52
W.E.B. Du Bois: A Biography in Four Voices (documentary with Bambara's involvement), xx, *168p*, 169, 199
We Be Word Sorcerers (Sanchez), 114–15
West, Dorothy, *The Wedding for the Philadelphia Enquirer*, 195
Whitehorn, Laura, 78–79, *80p*, 81, 83–84
White supremacist groups, reemergence in the South, 67
Wicke, Anne (translator for Bambara's work into French), xxi
Wideman, John Edgar, *The Salt Eaters* review, 115–16
Wilk, Mel, 185
William, Robert Franklin, *Negroes with Guns*, 82
Williams, Maggie Cooper (great grandmother), 2, 6, 8, 14
Williams, Wayne, 145, 147
Winters, Joyce, 114, 151
Wise, Leah, 67, 70–71, 108, 191–92; article on the Cultural Revolution (China), 71; *Southern*

Black Utterances Today guest editor with Bambara (*Southern Exposure*), 70–71, 74
"Witchbird" (short story), 87; staging of by Jomandi Productions, 150
"Witchbird's Warning: To Thine Own Self Be True" (*Atlanta Daily News* review), 150
Wolf, Deborah Cannon Partridge, 36
Women of Viet Nam (Eisen), 78
Women's Studies program, Spelman College, 71
Works by Toni Cade Bambara: "The Apprentice" (short story), 65; "Black Theater" (essay), 44; *The Black Woman* (anthology, ed.), xix, xxi, 35, 45–50, 52, 60, 66, 78, 130, 158, 182, 195, 201; "The Children Who Got Cheated" (essay), 45, 135; "Christmas Eve At Johnson's Drugs N Goods" (short story), 21–22; *Deep Sightings and Rescue Missions* (essays and short stories, ed. by Toni Morrison), xx; "Dumb Show" (short story), 53; "The Education of a Storyteller" (short story), 24; "Geraldine Moore the Poet" (short story), 44; "A Girl's Story" (short story), 66, 135; *Goddess Sightings* (work-in-progress), 196; "Going Critical" (short story), 190–91; "The Golden Bandit" (short story), 68; *Gorilla, My Love* (short stories), xix, 35, 41, 49–50, 60, 62, 77, 82, 90, 130, 191; "Hammer Man" (short story), 44, 193; "The Johnson Girls" (short story), 46, 50, 199; "The Lesson" (short story), 84, 199; "The Long Night" (short story), 89; "Maggie of the Green Bottles" (short story), 14–15; "Mama Load" (short story), 125–27; "Medley" (short story), 136–37, 199; "Mississippi Ham Rider" (short story), 38–39; "My Man Bovanne" (short story), 91, 199; "On the Issue of Roles" (essay in *The Black Woman*), 46; "The Organizer's Wife" (short story), 86–89; "Raymond's Run" (short

story), 9–10, 60, 126, 199; *The Salt Eaters* (novel), xix–xx, 49, 124, 129–35, 137–39, 146, 177, 185, 191, 198, 200–201; scripted for television, 123; *The Sea Birds Are Still Alive* (short stories), xix, 77–79, 82, 86–92, 101; "The Sea Birds Are Still Alive" (short story), 87–88; *Southern Black Utterances Today* guest editor (*Southern Exposure*), 70–71; "Story" (short story), 134–35; "The Survivor" (short story), 41, 160; "Sweet Town" (short story), 38; *Tales and Stories for Black Folks* (short stories, ed.), xix, 35, 47–49, 59–60, 68; "There'll Come a Day" (poem), 30; *Those Bones Are Not My Child* (novel, previously *If Blessing Comes*), xx, 143–48, 150, 195–96; "The War of the Wall" (short story),

129; "Witchbird" (short story), 87, 150

Wright, Richard, 47; *Native Son*, 107

Yeelen (film by Cisse), 182
Yoruba traditions/culture, 51, 134, 152, 158
Young, Andrew, 136
Young, Billie Jean, 122p; *This Little Light of Mine: A Dramatization of the Life of Fannie Lou Hamer* (one-woman show), 125
Young, Kevin, 187
Youngblood (Killens), 152, 208

Zamani Soweto Sisters (women's anti-apartheid self-help group), 149
Zembezi's International Night Club (Atlanta viewing of *The Bombing of Osage Avenue* by the African Film Society), 180

About the Author

LINDA JANET HOLMES is a writer, independent scholar, and long-time women's health activist. She was coeditor with Cheryl Wall of the anthology *Savoring the Salt: The Legacy of Toni Cade Bambara,* and her short story, "The True Story of Chicken Licken," was included in Bambara's *Tales and Stories for Black Folks.* An oral historian, Holmes has published extensively on the practices of African American midwives in the South. She received a National Endowment for the Humanities Fellowship and was the guest curator of "Reclaiming Midwives," a multimedia exhibition funded by the Ford Foundation at the Smithsonian Institution Anacostia Museum in Washington, D.C. The writer also previously managed a million-dollar grant fund to address health disparities in the state of New Jersey.